PRAISE FOR

AFTER THE FACT

"Don't read this book alone. Make sure there's someone seated next to you at all times, because you're going to want to stop every three or four minutes and say, 'No way! Did you know . . . ?' This book is filled with surprises—and also with meticulous research, crisp writing, and biting humor. *After the Fact* reminds us that history can and should be fun. It's so good you'll have to share it."

—Jonathan Eig, *New York Times* bestselling author
of *Get Capone, Opening Day*, and *Luckiest Man*

"Christopher Columbus in chains? Pocahontas in London? Who knew? Owen Hurd brings history to life in this wonderfully readable book that will engage everybody who cares about this country's history. You'll laugh when you read that Jackie Robinson took a job at Chock Full o' Nuts, you'll cry when you find out what happened to freedom fighter Harriet Tubman, and you'll never look at history the same again."

—Richard Cahan, author of *Vivian Maier: Out of the Shadows*
and *The Lost Panoramas*

AFTER THE FACT

The Surprising Fates of American History's Heroes, Villains, and Supporting Characters

OWEN J. HURD

A PERIGEE BOOK

A PERIGEE BOOK
Published by the Penguin Group
Penguin Group (USA) Inc.
375 Hudson Street, New York, New York 10014, USA

Penguin Group (Canada), 90 Eglinton Avenue East, Suite 700, Toronto, Ontario M4P 2Y3, Canada (a division of Pearson Penguin Canada Inc.) • Penguin Books Ltd., 80 Strand, London WC2R 0RL, England • Penguin Group Ireland, 25 St. Stephen's Green, Dublin 2, Ireland (a division of Penguin Books Ltd.) • Penguin Group (Australia), 250 Camberwell Road, Camberwell, Victoria 3124, Australia (a division of Pearson Australia Group Pty. Ltd.) • Penguin Books India Pvt. Ltd., 11 Community Centre, Panchsheel Park, New Delhi—110 017, India • Penguin Group (NZ), 67 Apollo Drive, Rosedale, Auckland 0632, New Zealand (a division of Pearson New Zealand Ltd.) • Penguin Books (South Africa) (Pty.) Ltd., 24 Sturdee Avenue, Rosebank, Johannesburg 2196, South Africa

Penguin Books Ltd., Registered Offices: 80 Strand, London WC2R 0RL, England

While the author has made every effort to provide accurate telephone numbers, Internet addresses, and other contact information at the time of publication, neither the publisher nor the author assumes any responsibility for errors, or for changes that occur after publication. Further, the publisher does not have any control over and does not assume any responsibility for author or third-party websites or their content.

First edition: August 2012

Library of Congress Cataloging-in-Publication Data

Hurd, Owen.
After the fact : the surprising fates of American history's heroes, villains, and supporting characters / Owen J. Hurd.
p. cm.
Includes index.
ISBN: 978-0-399-53753-0
1. United States—History—Anecdotes. 2. United States—Biography—Anecdotes. I. Title.
E178.6.H88   2012
973—dc23   2012009639

PRINTED IN THE UNITED STATES OF AMERICA

10 9 8 7 6 5 4 3 2

Most Perigee books are available at special quantity discounts for bulk purchases for sales promotions, premiums, fund-raising, or educational use. Special books, or book excerpts, can also be created to fit specific needs. For details, write: Special Markets, Penguin Group (USA) Inc., 375 Hudson Street, New York, New York 10014.

To Geralyn,
Who walks in beauty, like the night
Of cloudless climes and starry skies

Contents

Acknowledgments

Many people lent their ears and opinions in the early stages of this book's genesis, especially my sibling editorial team of Clare Abbene, Cheri Carpenter, and Bill Hurd. I also routinely drew on the love and support of my other brother, John, and sister, Ellen, as well as my mother, Mary Lee Hurd.

My clear-eyed and levelheaded agent, David Fugate, took a chance on what he instinctively knew was a good idea and helped shape it into a viable book proposal. Perigee senior editor Meg Leder was a big fan from the start and helped make the final product immeasurably better.

Fellow Chicago author Jonathan Eig was kind enough to review a portion of the manuscript. Dave Leitch read every page of the manuscript, providing useful and encouraging feedback all the way. He unfailingly responded to each chapter before the next one was delivered to him. My attempts to keep pace with him kept me on schedule.

Finally, I would be unable to write any book-length work without the love and support of my family, including my incredibly understanding wife, Geralyn, whose keen editorial instincts helped shape the book in its earliest stages, and my son, Patrick, who surprises and delights me almost every day on his way to becoming a very impressive young man. I love you both so very much.

Introduction

We're all familiar with the momentous events in our nation's history: Columbus's journey to the Americas, the signing of the Declaration of Independence, Abraham Lincoln's assassination, the Japanese attack on Pearl Harbor. But what about the lives lived after the fact?

What happened, for example, to Paul Revere after his famous midnight ride? A better messenger than soldier, Revere was later kicked out of the militia for his role in the Penobscot Expedition, the most disastrous naval blunder of the Revolutionary War.

What became of Lewis and Clark in the years after their exploration of the American interior? Meriwether Lewis suffered a precipitous downfall, committing suicide just three years after the duo's triumphant return from the wilderness. William Clark, on the other hand, lived a successful and fulfilling life, marred only by his government's shameful treatment of the American Indians he had befriended.

What became of the men who dropped the bombs on Hiroshima and Nagasaki? Or the scientists who developed the bomb? Or the survivors of those horrific attacks? And why did it take sixty years to publish the first eyewitness account written by a Western reporter to enter Nagasaki?

Instead of rehashing the well-known events in American history, this book picks up where traditional histories leave off, kind of like History 101 meets Where Are They Now? See what became of our nation's heroes and villains as well as the supporting characters who played key roles in major historical events. After all, famous people don't stop living after they've achieved their greatest triumphs or committed their most notorious crimes.

Some of the stories provide tales of scandal and degradation— of people who once breathed rarefied air, only to lose their status, their wealth, or their sanity long after the nation's attention veered elsewhere—like Mary Lincoln, who spent the rest of her life in grief and poverty (sometimes actual, other times perceived), suffering bouts of despair and madness.

Other stories show how the human spirit can overcome seemingly insurmountable challenges and crushing grief. Elizabeth Custer, for example, after her husband's foolhardy last stand, became a successful author and champion of her late husband's legacy.

The signing of the Declaration of Independence provides examples that cut across the spectrum of triumph and tragedy. Most people think of the event as a symbolic act that began and ended on July 4, 1776. Not so for the flesh and blood men who actually signed this slap in England's face. For them, it was an act of defiance with real consequences. Nine of the signers would die during the American War of Independence. Several were wounded in battle, while others languished in British prisons. One of Georgia's signers, Button Gwinnett, was killed in a duel stemming from a dispute over a botched military expedition.

Just about every one of the signers suffered vast financial losses, as the British forces targeted the homes and business interests (not to mention families) of those who dared challenge King George's authority. Some of the signers—Benjamin Franklin, John Adams, and Thomas Jefferson—of course went on to serve their country with distinction and to enjoy the benefits of their hard-earned freedoms. A few others met with strange ends, like George Wythe, who was murdered by an inheritance-seeking grandnephew. And many of the signers slipped into obscurity. Ever heard of William Floyd, Stephen Hopkins, or George Taylor? Didn't think so.

These are the types of stories found in the pages of *After the Fact*—stories that surprise and confound, that illuminate the events themselves by providing a context seldom considered.

People often ask me where I came up with the idea for *After the Fact*. A couple years ago I was reading *Manhunt: The 12-Day Chase for Lincoln's Killer*, a thoroughly informative and entertaining account of the immediate aftermath of the assassination. In more than three hundred pages, the author, James Swanson, meticulously and dramatically relates the events of April 14–26, 1865, in which John Wilkes Booth assassinated President Abraham Lincoln in Ford's Theatre and then met his own end, trapped in a burning tobacco barn in northern Virginia. In the seventeen-page epilogue that closed the book, Swanson ran down the list of actors who played roles in one of the nation's most intriguing dramas, explaining what became of them in the years that followed. As fascinating as I found the main body of the book, this section provided a treasure trove of intriguing information, compelling me to embark on my own research into what happened after the fact.

What became of Booth's brothers and sisters? What about his coconspirators? Which of the conspirators were hanged? What became of those who received lesser sentences? And which ones got away scot-free?

What became of the man who shot Booth in the burning tobacco barn in Virginia? Who, if anyone, claimed the cash rewards offered for the capture of Booth and the others?

What was the fate of the surviving Lincolns?

Most people have heard stories about Mary's depression and battered psyche, but what about her skirmishes with Congress, the press, and her son Robert, not to mention her turncoat seamstress and ingrate daughter-in-law? And what about Robert? How was it that he became a kind of presidential bad-luck charm, figuring in the next two presidential assassinations?

What happened to Colonel Henry Rathbone and his fiancée, Clara Harris, the only other people sitting in the president's balcony at Ford's Theatre when Booth sneaked in and shot Lincoln? (In short, they married, he went crazy and killed her.)

The logic of *After the Fact* is that some of the most offbeat and illuminating stories occur in the denouement that follows the climax. We begin with the earliest explorers to the so-called New World, before moving on to cover landmark events throughout American history all the way up to the Watergate scandal of Richard Nixon's administration. I decided not to include any more recent events, because the characters in those dramas may yet add more chapters to their biographies.

True history buffs will surely be familiar with at least a couple of the stories presented here, but they will just as certainly be surprised by new facts and insights.

CHAPTER ONE

AGE OF DISCOVERY

S OME explorers just don't know when to quit. But isn't that what makes a good explorer? The will to fly in the face of danger has certainly made many a reputation. However, it's also led to a fair share of ill-fated demises.

Vasco Núñez de Balboa is best known for his discovery in 1513 of the Pacific Ocean—or at least for being the first European to realize that another huge ocean stood just opposite the isthmus of Panama. His thanks? He was later arrested for treason and shipped back to Spain, where an ax-wielding executioner required two hacks to separate Balboa's head from his neck.

On a 1524 voyage, Giovanni da Verrazzano was the first explorer, after Leif Eriksson, to explore and map much of the Atlantic Coast from Newfoundland to South Carolina. His name is mostly forgotten now, but it does grace three United States bridges, the Verrazano-Narrows Bridge in New York, the Verrazano Bridge in Maryland, and the Jamestown Verrazzano Bridge in Rhode Island, which gets extra points for spelling his name correctly (regardless of what spell-check says). But the Italian explorer pushed his luck on a subsequent voyage to the Americas. Wading ashore a Caribbean island to greet some friendly seeming natives, Verrazzano was immediately set upon by what turned out to be ravenous cannibals. His brother watched in horror from a nearby boat as Verrazzano was unceremoniously disassembled and eaten.

Not all explorers met such grisly ends, but as we'll see, the glory of discovery is often followed by suffering and disgrace.

Columbus in Chains

There are many fanciful stories about the events leading up to Columbus's epic sea voyage to the Americas—how he labored to persuade ignorant monarchs that the world was round, how Queen Isabella sold Spain's royal jewels to finance the expedition, and how Columbus was forced to recruit a crew of convicts because proper sailors were too fearful of the journey. (All untrue.) Our story begins after Columbus made his pivotal voyage to the Americas, landing in 1492 on the island he named Hispaniola, shared in modern times by Haiti and the Dominican Republic.

On January 16, 1493, Christopher Columbus weighed anchor off the shores of Hispaniola and sailed back toward Spain. This time he sailed aboard the *Niña*. His flagship, *Santa Maria*, the vessel Columbus commanded on his unwitting way to the Americas, had been lost on Christmas 1492—a victim to the shallows off Hispaniola.

Over the course of the two-month journey back to Europe, Columbus would have ample time to reflect on his discoveries—on the route taken toward what he still claimed to be the East Indies, on the peoples he encountered, and on the economic opportunities to be exploited. No doubt relying on the daily journals he religiously kept throughout his voyage, he composed a letter to his sponsors, King Ferdinand II and Queen Isabella I.

It was a delicate task. Columbus had promised a shorter, less-expensive trade route to Japan, China, and India. But instead of ancient, sophisticated kingdoms, eager to engage in trade, Columbus encountered a relatively small, primitive civilization. In his letter, Columbus shifted his focus to colonization and to harvesting natural resources.

Unfortunately, Columbus found little in the way of that most coveted resource, gold. The indigenous peoples, called Tainos, had certainly talked a lot about the abundance of gold on the island, and some of them even wore small golden trinkets. At least one local chief exhibited an intricate ceremonial mask bearing gold leaf features. The Indians repeatedly promised to show Columbus where more gold was to be found, but never did.

Apparently, the Europeans' obsession with gold did not trigger the locals' suspicions. Why would it? Columbus found them to be an "artless and generous" people, freely sharing all that they had. In the letter, he writes, "If it be asked for, they never say no, but do rather invite the person to accept it, and show as much lovingness as though they would give their hearts." And it didn't matter what they got in return, no matter how worthless.

Columbus caught his men trading "fragments of broken platters and pieces of broken glass, and strap buckles" with the natives. In exchange, these "senseless brutes" would readily fork over "gold to the weight of two and a half castellanos," about half an ounce. Columbus forbade his men from exploiting the ignorance of the locals, who were apt to treat the most worthless item as if it were "the best jewel in the world."

And yet, despite all the talk of gold, Columbus was returning to Spain relatively empty-handed, unless you count the birds, plants, and Indians he commandeered, most of which died on the return journey. How was he to compensate for this seemingly paltry tribute?

Columbus offered to provide his sponsors with spices, cotton, and aloe wood, "as much as their Highnesses will order to be shipped."

Failing that, Columbus would provide Spain with Christian souls. Those who refused to convert—or were simply denied the opportunity—Columbus would gladly enslave, once again promising his sponsors "as many [slaves] as they shall order to be shipped."

Columbus did not fail to note that the islanders were fairly defenseless. "They have no other weapons than the stems of reeds in their seeding state, on the end of which they fix little sharpened stakes." Besides, they seemed so naturally good-natured and averse to conflict that they would easily be tamed. In his journals, Columbus noted ominously, "I could conquer the whole of them with fifty men, and govern them as I pleased."

Ignorant of Columbus's designs, the Indians were quick to indulge the Spaniards at every turn. When the *Santa Maria* ran aground, it was the local Indians who leaped into action, paddling canoes out to the boat and transporting every single item of value to shore. The local chieftain, Guanacagarí, even turned some of his subjects out of their homes to provide Columbus with adequate storage space.

Turning lemons into lemonade, Columbus dismantled the shipwrecked *Santa Maria*, using the salvaged wood and nails to build a small fort on Hispaniola, where he left several dozen men with a sufficient amount of guns, ammunition, and provisions to last them a year. Even though these first American settlers were vastly outnumbered by the hundreds of thousands of indigenous peoples, Columbus was confident in their safety. He had cultivated a "great friendship with the king of that land, to such a degree that he prided himself on calling and holding me as his brother." Besides, the Indians he met were "the most timorous creatures there are in the world."

Of course, things happen and the relationship could take a turn for the worse, especially in Columbus's absence. Even so, he was confident that "the men who remain there are alone sufficient to destroy all that land."

Turns out he was wrong. When Columbus returned to Hispaniola the following year, he found the fort in ashes, alongside the bones of his slaughtered countrymen. Whether they too persistently pressed for information about where to find gold or took liberties with Taino women, they must have worn out their welcome one way or another.

Columbus made four journeys to the Americas in all, eventually reaching the South American continent on his third journey and Central America on his fourth. But the first time he returned—this time with seventeen ships and about a thousand soldiers—he put his colonial plans into action. Finding the locals "all of a good size and stature," as well as "ingenious," especially for the ease with which they picked up the Spanish language, Columbus concluded, "they ought to make good and skilled servants."

They did and they didn't. As governor of the islands claimed for the Spanish Crown, Columbus imposed a brutal system of tribute in which islanders were forced to mine gold for their Spanish taskmasters. Coming up short could mean horrific penalties, like torture and mutilation. The Tainos rebelled, but their primitive weapons were no match for the Spaniards' "crossbows and small cannon, lances, and swords." A Spanish observer, Bartolomé de Las Casas, also pointed out the advantage of domesticated animals. On horseback, Columbus's army had a distinct advantage over the Tainos. "A still more terrible weapon against the Indians," according to Las Casas, were the "twenty hunting dogs, who were turned loose and immediately tore the Indians apart."

European domestication of animals presented yet another threat to the Tainos, one that was less obvious but far more lethal. Having long interacted with farm animals like pigs, sheep, cows, and poultry, Europeans built up immunities to diseases like smallpox and the plague. With absolutely no previous exposure to these diseases, indigenous Americans had no immunities whatsoever. The results were devastating.

Between the wars, the slave trade, and disease, the native population on Hispaniola plummeted from a million in 1496 to 200 in 1542. An entire civilization was virtually wiped out in a mere fifty years.

Columbus and his brothers—whom he put in charge of various operations and lands—also showed little restraint when dealing with the Spanish subjects who colonized these new lands, doling out punishments just as brutal and draconian as those imposed on the Tainos. Complaints made their way back to Spain, and Columbus was arrested in the Caribbean and shipped back to Spain in chains.

Columbus was eventually exonerated and released from jail. Still stripped of his governorship, the ailing and aging sailor embarked on one last journey of discovery to the Americas. This time his ship wrecked on the shores of Jamaica, where Columbus and his crew lived on the hospitality of the native islanders for over a year. Finally rescued in June 1504, Columbus returned to Spain, where he spent the remainder of his days, profiting from his discoveries up to the time of his death on May 20, 1506.

Columbus's reputation has of course suffered in recent years, as more people become familiar with the less savory aspects of his history. It doesn't help that Columbus did not discover America. The honor for that goes of course to the indigenous peoples who had been living in the "New World" for tens of thousands of years. Columbus was also beaten to the punch by Erik the Red and his son Leif, who settled the shores of Greenland and Newfoundland about five hundred years earlier. However, in terms of setting in motion a world-altering migration and settlement of a previously unknown landmass, Columbus deserves the credit—or blame, depending on your perspective.

So, why are our two continents named after Amerigo Vespucci, a comparatively minor explorer? Why do we not live in the United States of Columbia?

Partly because of Columbus's post-discovery decline and partly because of luck. It's not clear that Columbus ever knew that he had discovered a new continent. But Vespucci did. In a series of letters written to Italian nobles, but obviously intended for a public audience, Vespucci outlined his theory, that the lands being explored by Columbus, Vespucci, and others were not the westernmost part of the Indies— which is what Europeans called lands now known as China and Japan—but a completely distinct landmass, a "Mundus Novus" (New World), bordered on each side by different oceans.

These letters made their way to Germany, where a mapmaker by the name of Martin Waldseemüller was planning a new world map. This was the first map to depict the new lands as a separate continent and to identify them as "America," using a traditionally feminine form of a Latin spelling of Vespucci's first name. Otherwise, we might be living in the United States of Vespuccia.

Although a thousand copies of the four-and-a-half-by-eight-foot wall map were printed in 1507, only one survives intact today. It was discovered in 1901 at the Wolfegg Castle in Württemberg, Germany. The Library of Congress purchased the map in 2003 for $10 million.

Loose Ends

- Columbus spent his last few years entreating the king of Spain to reinstate his titles, along with the corresponding monetary privileges. These legal cases outlived Columbus and were taken up by his heirs, especially his firstborn son, Diego, who succeeded in regaining the governorship of the Indies. He was later named viceroy of the Indies.

- Little is known about the *Pinta*, but the *Niña* became Columbus's preferred sailing vessel. Included among Columbus's flotilla on his second journey to the New World, the *Niña* was the flagship for Columbus's side expedition to Cuba. The *Niña* made her final journey to the Americas in 1498.

- Vicente Yáñez Pinzón, who was captain of the *Niña* on Columbus's first voyage, later discovered the Amazon River in 1500. His older brother, Martín Alonzo Pinzón, who had commanded the *Pinta* on the first voyage, died shortly after the return voyage to Spain.

- While on a subsequent journey to the Americas, Columbus's first mate on the *Santa Maria*, Juan de la Cosa, was killed by natives living in present-day Columbia.

Henry Hudson, Adrift

In the early 1600s English explorer Henry Hudson made four journeys in search of more advantageous trade routes with East Asia. The last two, in 1609 and 1610, brought him to North America, where he sought the fabled Northwest Passage, an all-water shipping lane through North America to the Pacific Ocean. In the process, Hudson mapped portions of the New England coast, including Cape Cod, before venturing up the Hudson River. In July 1610, Hudson steered his aptly named ship, *Discovery*, into what would later be called Hudson Bay. He spent the next few months exploring the unknown waters, trying to figure out if it did indeed offer passage to the South Seas.

Yet, when the *Discovery* sailed back into its English port in October 1611, it returned without Hudson, the first mate, and many others, including the captain's teenage son, John. Only eight members of the original twenty-four-man crew were aboard. Emaciated and desperate looking, some too weak to stand, they were set upon by family members—as well as the voyage's financiers—who had anticipated the *Discovery*'s return for more than six months.

The ship bore ominous signs, including top decks stained with blood as well as the bloodstained clothing of several missing crew members. The possessions of other missing sailors had been divvied up among the remaining crew. A search of the navigator's desk turned up a note that hinted at a potential mutiny.

The survivors had a miraculous story to tell—and a lot of questions to answer.

To hear the survivors tell it, there had been a mutiny all right, but none of them had taken part in it. As temperatures dropped and icebergs multiplied, they said, Captain Henry Hudson put a vote to his men: Should they head to the southernmost portion of the bay, spend the winter there, before resuming their voyage in the spring? Or should they return to England before ice choked off the straits, trapping them in the northern section of the bay?

Those who wished to return were outvoted by Hudson and a clique of loyal sailors who decided to stay put, assuming the weather there would not be too much worse than an English winter. That was their second mistake. The first mistake was putting it to a vote. Hudson may have believed that the crew would be more likely to accept the outcome if they had a say in it. Instead, it broadened existing divisions between two camps, hardening the resolve of those who were determined to overthrow the captain.

It was at about this time that *Discovery*'s mathematician penned his secret note, hidden in the navigator's desk, detailing a challenge to the captain's authority by captain's mate Robert Juet. Juet allegedly made drunken accusations and suggested that bloodshed was imminent. Hudson demoted Juet, replacing him with Robert Bylot.

Things continued to get worse, thanks to the cold. The crew had also underestimated the amount of food required to make it through winter, and one of the men died, probably due to a combination of exposure and starvation. However, a crew member's journals suggested that maybe there was more to the death: "God pardon the Master's uncharitable dealing with this man," it said, providing no further details. Whatever the case, all the survivors agreed that Hudson was inconsistent and deceptive in the manner he doled out rations, favoring superior officers as well as those who voted with him to winter in Hudson Bay.

It all became too much for crew member Henry Greene, who along with Juet and three other crew members staged a mutiny. As soon as the summer's rays released the *Discovery* from its icy grip, the mutineers overpowered Captain Hudson and his loyal crew members. They then attempted to recruit as many of the neutral crew members to join them. One of them, Abacuk Prickett, later claimed that he attempted to talk the mutineers out of it, but Greene insisted that "he would rather be hanged at home than starved abroad."

Hudson and eight others, including his son and the ship's carpenter, were placed in a small canoe-shaped boat and cast adrift as the *Discovery* sailed back toward England. They were never seen or heard from again. Several of the holdouts, including Bylot and Prickett, were permitted to remain on the ship, despite their alleged refusal to formally join the mutiny.

Still starving and having little luck at fishing, the remaining sailors aboard the *Discovery* decided to take their chances on land, despite the threats posed by polar bears and the inscrutable Inuit Indians. On shore, they were ambushed by Inuits, who slashed the Englishmen with knives and shot them with arrows. Several English died on the beach, while others succumbed on the decks of the *Discovery*—hence the bloodstains.

Robert Juet died of starvation on the voyage back to England, the last of the alleged mutineers to get his comeuppance.

The authorities back in England were suspicious enough of the survivors' version of events that they tried four of them for mutiny and Hudson's murder. The survivors themselves must have realized how far-fetched their tale seemed—that none of the perpetrators survived to face justice. Yet, lacking any physical evidence or eyewitness testimony, the court was obliged to find all suspects not guilty.

It's surprising that Prickett and Bylot, fresh off the disastrous journey, reenlisted on the *Discovery*, which returned to Hudson Bay in 1612, once again spending the winter there. They found no traces of Hudson or the Northwest Passage and returned to England in 1613, but not before losing five men in yet another struggle with the Inuit.

After two subsequent expeditions aboard the *Discovery* (captained no less by Robert Bylot), English explorer William Baffin finally determined in 1616 that if there was a Northwest Passage it would not be found in Hudson Bay.

Weary of sea adventures, Abacuk Prickett became a London haberdasher.

James Cook, Cooked

In terms of American history, Captain James Cook is best known for his discovery of the Sandwich Islands, which we now call the Hawaiian Islands, our fiftieth state. Cook first landed there in January 1778, visiting Kauai briefly before heading northeast toward the Pacific Northwest. Throughout the spring and summer Cook and his crew mapped the coastal territory north from Vancouver Island to Alaska and the Bering Strait. Yet, with winter approaching, Cook decided to steer his ships, *Discovery* and *Resolution*, south back toward the islands that had provided his men with so many tropical comforts the year before.

Nothing in their previous visit to Kauai could have prepared them for the welcome they received on the Big Island of Hawaii. Canoes with thousands of natives swarmed Cook's ships, with some of the more eager greeters climbing aboard the British vessels. Cook quickly realized that it would be fruitless to enforce his standard policy forbidding sexual relations with the local women.

"No women I ever met with were more ready to bestow their favors," he wrote in his journal. The native men were also willing to ingratiate themselves to their new guests. Having identified Cook as the man in charge of the expedition, local chiefs escorted him on shore, bestowing gifts, bowing to him, and calling him "Lono."

The islanders then performed a series of mysterious ceremonies, all seeming to celebrate the arrival of Lono. There was a feast of pork and liquors. And more sexual favors. The islanders established a beach camp for the British visitors and treated them with great deference. Cook's reception at the Big Island, which "seemed to approach adoration," vastly exceeded anything the English explorers had experienced at Tahiti or Bora Bora. Rather than question the reasons for this royal treatment, Cook and his men eagerly indulged in it.

But just as quickly, the mood changed. The natives suddenly "became inquisitive as to the time of our departing & seemed well pleased that it was to be soon." Taking the hint, Cook made arrangements to resupply his ships with food, water, and firewood, quitting the islands to great fanfare on February 4. As their sails filled with a fresh wind, one member of the crew recorded his impressions of the Hawaiian people in his journal. "No quarrels," he predicted, "could possibly arise in our intercourse with them." He had no idea how quickly his assessment would be put to the test.

Cook had intended to explore some of the other islands in the Hawaiian archipelago, but a bad storm intervened, damaging a mast. To make the necessary repairs, Cook sent his able mate, William Bligh, in search of an appropriate harbor. Finding only rough surf, they resolved to return to the Big Island to make the repairs within friendly environs.

This time, their reception could not have been chillier. Greeted a month earlier by a hysterical celebration, they now found deserted beaches. Cook sent a small boat into the harbor with several marines. His men were confronted by a somber delegation of priests, inquiring about the reason for their return. Cook and his men did their best to make their repairs quickly and be on their way, but their work was repeatedly interrupted by the now-quarrelsome islanders. Instead of graciously bestowing gifts, they struck hard bargains, usually preferring iron daggers in exchange for food and other essential items sought by the sailors. Other islanders took to stealing British property. On one occasion, the islanders stole one of the explorers' boats, a crime that Cook was determined to punish.

Angrily stumbling ashore on the uneven lava beach, Cook demanded to see the local chief. A crowd formed, hurling jeers and then stones at Cook and his men. Cook had planned to take the chief hostage in order to get the boat back, but the chief sat down on the beach and refused to budge. A native warrior then approached Cook, jabbing a spear in his direction. Shots were fired and a melee broke out.

"Take to the boats!" Cook implored, but it was too late. A swarm of natives descended on Captain Cook, bashing his head with rocks and stabbing him repeatedly. He and four of his men were killed, as the rest of the British made their escape. Safely aboard the *Discovery* and *Resolution*, the remaining sailors struggled to come to grips with these events—and wondered in vain what caused such a reversal in attitude toward them. It took years of study by cultural anthropologists before theories began to emerge about what went wrong.

It seems as though Cook was the victim of bad timing. His original arrival on the shores of Hawaii coincided with the island's Makahiki Festival, in which they celebrate the ascendancy of Lono, the god of fertility and peace. To this day academics are arguing about whether or not the Hawaiians actually perceived Cook as the personification of Lono. Regardless, by returning during the ascendancy of Kū, the god of war, Cook was unwittingly pushing his luck. His haughty and dictatorial attitude toward the natives sealed his fate.

The islanders cooked the captain's dead body in an underground barbecue pit, pulling his limbs apart and removing the flesh from his bones. By some accounts, they ate his heart and buried some of his bones in various caves on the island. Several days later a canoe paddled out to the British ships. Permitted to climb aboard the natives returned a portion of Cook's remains—his arms, legs, skull, and hands. The crew committed Cook's remains to the ocean in a ceremonial burial, before resolving to continue his mission, to find the Northwest Passage. First, they exacted a measure of revenge on the Hawaiians, burning their homes and killing as many as a hundred villagers.

Unfortunately the ice floes and other deprivations made it impossible for the new captain, Charles Clerke, to get any farther than Cook had in the previous year, and they turned back toward England via the Indian Ocean and the Cape of Good Hope.

LOOSE ENDS

- John Montagu, the fourth Earl of Sandwich, sponsored many of Cook's voyages as the first lord of the admiralty. The would-be namesake for the Sandwich Islands was later replaced in favor of a derivation of the native name for the Hawaiian Islands. His moniker is more famously attached to the less dignified but ubiquitous luncheon staple, the sandwich.

- First mate William Bligh would get his first chance to command his own naval exploration on the *Bounty*. Cast adrift in the middle of the Pacific Ocean by Fletcher Christian and his band of mutineers, Bligh miraculously steered the small lifeboat nearly four thousand miles in forty-seven days, landing at Timor with all hands but one alive and well. He was later named governor of New South Wales in Australia, where he once again displayed his "unfortunate capacity for breeding rebellion," leading to yet another mutiny, this one land based. Bligh was imprisoned in Sydney for more than a year. After his release he returned to England where he died in 1817.

- An American sailor who accompanied Cook on his last Pacific voyage was John Ledyard. While living in Paris in 1786, the peripatetic Yank made the acquaintance of America's ambassador to France, Thomas Jefferson, with whom he shared a scheme for traversing the American frontier. With Jefferson's support, Ledyard received funding to explore lands from Moscow to the Bering Strait, through Alaska and finally all the way to the eastern

American seaboard—a reverse Louis and Clark journey and then some. However, Ledyard was arrested and deported from Russia and the rest of the trip was put on hold. Preparing for an overland journey to the interior of Africa, Ledyard died in 1789 at the age of thirty-seven. But the idea for the Corps of Discovery lived on in Jefferson's imagination, until taken up fifteen years later by Meriwether Lewis and William Clark.

- One of the natives who greeted Cook's ships and later drove the British from the island, Kamehameha, would later become the first king of the unified islands of Hawaii in 1819.

CHAPTER TWO

EARLY SETTLERS AND PILGRIMS

THE Age of Discovery was of course followed by a wave of settlement throughout the New World. The first long-term European settlements ended in disaster, including the French at St. Augustine, Florida (wiped out by the Spanish), and the Lost Colony of Roanoke (succumbed to unknown forces—maybe starvation, maybe marauding Indians).

The English fared better the next few times around, with Jamestown in Virginia and Plymouth in New England. Here we take a look at what happened after three of the most influential events in America's early settlement history: Captain John's salvation from death courtesy of Pocahontas, the first Thanksgiving, and the Salem witch trials. The aftermaths show that not all interactions between the settlers and the Native Americans were violent. On the other hand, one of our nation's most celebrated occasions of good faith and cooperation turned out to be a short-lived co-alignment of self-interests.

John Smith, Pocahontas, and John Rolfe

On December 30, 1607, the story goes, Captain John Smith, a British colonist living in Virginia's Jamestown settlement, was sentenced to death by Chief Powhatan, a powerful tribal leader whose kingdom covered much of the Chesapeake Bay region. Smith was forced to his knees, head positioned on a large stone. Several warriors closed in, clubs aloft, ready to "beat out his brains." Just then Powhatan's youngest and favorite daughter, Matoaka, sprung to Smith's side, placing her own head upon Smith's. Touched by this humanitarian gesture, Powhatan spared the life of the Englishman. Of course, most people know Matoaka by her nickname, Pocahontas, which means "playful, mischievous one."

Scholars have argued for years about how much truth there is to the story. After all, the only eyewitness to write about the event was Smith himself—and his account came seventeen years later.

Whether Smith was truly the object of Pocahontas's benevolence or not, we do know he was captured by local Indians. Whenever the outspoken Smith became a nuisance to the other members of the Jamestown leadership, it seems, they would send him on a lengthy excursion into unknown lands, ostensibly to map the region and trade with the Indians, but they may have also hoped that hostile natives would dispatch the gadfly captain. It was during one such excursion that Smith was captured by members of the Pamunkey tribe, led by Powhatan's younger brother Opechancanough. Three others in his scouting party were killed in the raid, but Smith's quick-thinking Indian guide told the ambushers that Smith was a *werowance*, or chief. Following custom, they were obliged to spare Smith's life. They took him prisoner and eventually let him go after Pocahontas's act of benevolence.

Having escaped one attack and one execution at the hands of the American Indians, Smith returned to the fort at Jamestown, where he was once again sentenced to death, this time by his English compatriots. Upon his return, a newly elected council promptly had put Smith on trial for the deaths of the men he lost on the trading expedition. Found guilty, the punishment was death by hanging. But last-minute fortune smiled on Smith yet again, as an English supply ship appeared on the horizon, bringing with it a Captain Christopher Newport who immediately assumed control over the colony and commuted Smith's sentence.

This was not only the second time Smith faced the executioner in one week, but the third time altogether since arriving on American shores. On the journey over, Smith was imprisoned for some vaguely mutinous activity. An execution was planned, then delayed. When the ships arrived in Virginia and the official charter was unsealed, the colonists learned to their surprise that the Virginia Company had designated Captain John Smith as one of seven inaugural council members. It certainly wouldn't do to dispose of a fellow councilman, so Smith got his first reprieve.

Smith had long been an outspoken critic of the colony's leadership, composed mostly of what he considered genteel loafers. A lowborn son of modest ancestry, Smith had little patience for the leisure class, especially when the survival of the group would require the sweat of every individual. Droughts, spoilage, and unfamiliar hunting grounds made for scarce food supplies, and Smith did not hide his disgust with those who lived off the efforts of others.

For the next couple of years, the Jamestown settlement existed on the edge of survival, a survival that relied greatly on food provided by the Indians as well as on provisions shipped from England. Smith did what he could to help the settlement become more self-sufficient. Not only did he keep the inhabitants of the fort safe from attack but he was also a shrewd negotiator, striking bargains with the natives that none of his contemporaries could match. His new bond with Powhatan and his increasing fluency in the Algonquin language helped. Yet, his efforts were routinely frustrated by a revolving door of foolish and mendacious council presidents.

Ultimately, Smith would get his chance to lead the colony starting in September 1608. Under his direction, the colony flourished. Smith supervised infrastructural improvements, including a new freshwater well and the construction of wooden houses. Smith's egalitarian rule was guided by the fundamental principle, "He that will not work shall not eat."

Pocahontas remained Smith's friend throughout his remaining days in Virginia. She often visited Jamestown, sometimes to bring food to the English or to check on how they were doing. She once even warned Smith of an ambush her father had planned, saving Smith's life a second time. Pocahontas showed obvious kindness to the English, and Smith spoke of her in restrained but affectionate terms, calling her the "nonpareil" of her people. But the two most likely never shared anything close to a romantic relationship. In 1609 Smith was severely injured in an explosives accident and shipped back to his homeland. The remaining Jamestown settlers told Pocahontas that he was dead.

With Smith out of the picture, relations between the English and Chesapeake natives deteriorated, and the settlement fell on hard times, thanks also to a drought that resulted in what the settlers referred to as the Starving Time. Jamestown settlers resorted to eating their horses and dogs, even rats. When those sources of nutrition ran out they turned to pieces of leather, starched collars—and worse.

So great was our famine that a Savage we slew and buried, the
poorer sort took him up again and [ate] him. . . . And one amongst
the rest did kill his wife, [salted] her, and had eaten part of her before it was known; for which he was executed, as he well deserved.

During this time of profound suffering, the previously charitable
Pocahontas was nowhere to be found. The next time the English
encountered Pocahontas, in the spring of 1613, they kidnapped
her, holding her hostage for the return of several English prisoners.
Powhatan called their bluff, refusing to negotiate his daughter's release. The spurned Indian princess eventually decided to live among
the English. A recently arrived gentleman named John Rolfe fell in
love with Pocahontas; they married in April 1614, and had a baby,
Thomas, in 1615. The following year the Rolfe family traveled to England on a sort of public relations junket promoting the English colony in America.

Pocahontas, now going by her Christian name, Rebecca Rolfe, was
a big hit in London, gaining introductions to King James and Queen
Anne, and "was publicly treated as a prince's daughter; she was carried
to many plays, balls, and other public entertainments, and very re-
spectfully received by all the ladies about the Court." She was even
reunited with Captain John Smith, an awkward meeting in which the
Pamunkey princess admonished the captain for not coming to see her
sooner. He had recently returned from an exploration of New England, he explained, and was busily making arrangements for another.

Pocahontas was greatly impressed with London. The metropolis
with a quarter million inhabitants dwarfed the villages she was ac-
customed to, and architectural wonders like London Bridge and St.
Paul's Cathedral obviously would have inspired awe in the Indian

princess. If Pocahontas had her way, the Rolfes would have stayed in England, but her husband was keen to revolutionize the tobacco farming industry back in Virginia. Pocahontas relented but would never return to her homeland. As they made preparations to return to America, Pocahontas became ill. She died in March 1617 at Gravesend on the Thames. Rolfe left his son with relatives and returned to Virginia.

Smith spent the rest of his life writing about his adventures and trying to drum up support for further explorations of the region. He never did make it back. On his last attempt, the ship he was commanding was twice attacked by pirates. They fought off the first attackers, and Smith negotiated his way out of the second attack. But while on board the enemy ship, his crew decided against following Smith to America. They ditched him and sailed back to England.

Imprisoned on the French ship *Don de Dieu* for four months, Smith wrote the bulk of his book *A Description of New England* (thereby coining the term still used to describe the region). During a particularly bad storm, Smith saw his chance to make an escape. As the crew scrambled for cover, Smith slipped off in a lifeboat. Battered by waves, wind, and rain, he eventually made it to shore, along with his manuscript. The *Don de Dieu* was not so lucky; it sank in the storm, taking its crew of sixteen to their deaths.

Smith's published works brought him notoriety, but little else. A copy of his *Description of New England* wound up in the hands of a group of Puritans, who would eventually make their way to Plymouth. (They declined Smith's offer to come along as a guide.) A lifelong bachelor, Smith died poor and alone in London on June 21, 1631.

LOOSE ENDS

- John Rolfe would never see his son, Thomas, again. He returned to Virginia, where his innovations in growing a sweeter strain of tobacco resulted in skyrocketing tobacco exports to the Old World. The twice-widowed Rolfe remarried Jane Pierce in Virginia. They had a daughter who died before reaching adulthood. John Rolfe died in 1622.

- Thomas Rolfe moved back to Virginia in 1635, taking up the family business. He married Jane Poythress, with whom he had a daughter. Thomas Rolfe died in 1675.

- Powhatan and his people lived in relative peace with the English from the time of Pocahontas's marriage to John Rolfe in 1614 to the time of his death, about five years later. His younger brother Opechancanough, however, took a more confrontational approach to the growing English presence, engineering attacks on outlying settlements that killed five hundred colonists in 1622 and again a similar tally in 1644. Opechancanough was captured after this second battle and killed.

- In 1607 the original Jamestown settlers traveled from England to Virginia aboard three ships, the *Susan Constant*, the *Godspeed*, and the *Discovery*. Little is known about the fates of the first two ships, but the *Discovery* would eventually be the same ship that Henry Hudson steered into Hudson Bay in 1610, and the same ship that was commandeered from him by mutineers.

After the First Thanksgiving

In the fall of 1621, the residents of what would eventually come to be known as Plymouth, Massachusetts, decided to celebrate their first successful harvest season. The crops were in, and an especially bountiful hunting expedition provided enough meat to feed the colony for weeks. Considering the hardships endured up until then—half of the one hundred colonists had died since their arrival the previous year—it would have been almost profane to let this newfound abundance go unacknowledged.

With preparations for a feast under way, ninety Pokanoket Indians arrived at the colony. Unexpected and uninvited, they were welcomed just the same. Indian hunters contributed five deer to supplement the stews of raccoon, bear, ducks, geese, and maybe turkeys.

The first Thanksgiving might not have included the now-traditional roast turkey, stuffing, and cranberry sauce, but every year we still honor the essential principles of gratitude, goodwill, and friendship that were in such healthy supply that fall in 1621. However, those feelings wouldn't last.

As the three-day feast came to an end, Tisquantum, the last remaining Patuxet Indian, could gaze over his former village, now occupied by the English Separatists commonly referred to today as the Pilgrims. A few years earlier, it was a thriving Native American settlement, part of the Pokanoket confederacy ruled by Massasoit. Between 1614 and 1619, approximately 90 percent of the Patuxet had been wiped out by European diseases introduced by previous visitors to the New England region. The few surviving Patuxet Indians abandoned the village, unable to keep up with the ever-increasing number of corpses.

How did Tisquantum, or Squanto, as he was also known, avoid

this fate? Captured in 1614 by English sailors, he was sold into slavery in Spain. Making his escape, he found his way to England and later finagled passage on a ship bound for New England. He returned to find his village deserted and bereft of life.

Squanto played a major role in the success of the Pilgrim colony. Without his agricultural advice, the Pilgrims may not have been in any position to celebrate a Thanksgiving in the first place. (His fellow tribesmen had already done their part, dying off just in time to provide the Pilgrims with an uninhabited clearing to settle.) Fluent in English and Algonquin tongues, Squanto served as interpreter and diplomat between the Pokanokets and the Pilgrims. Plymouth governor William Bradford considered Squanto a loyal adviser, but neither Massasoit nor Miles Standish, Plymouth's military specialist, ever trusted him entirely.

With good reason. Squanto apparently harbored profound misgivings about the fate of his tribe and the ascendancy of the English in his homeland. It wasn't long before he was conspiring with other minor tribes in an attempt to foment ill will between the Pilgrims and Massasoit. The plot was uncovered, and Squanto died shortly thereafter of what appeared to be an infectious disease, but others suspected poisoning.

Then Massasoit himself fell gravely ill with symptoms resembling typhoid fever. Plymouth elder Edward Winslow was sent to nurse the Pokanoket chief back to health, which he did. Massasoit showed his gratitude by warning the English that a combined force of Narragansett and Massachusett Indians was poised to attack Plymouth. Miles Standish mounted a preemptive attack, killing a half dozen prominent warriors in a surprise attack that not only derailed the planned offensive but threw their enemies into a profound disarray.

According to Winslow, the terrified Indians "forsook their houses, running to and fro like men distracted, living in swamps and other desert places, and so brought manifold diseases amongst themselves, whereof many are dead."

A little terror, it seems, goes a long way. With these common enemies neutralized, the Pilgrims and Pokanokets lived peaceably alongside each other for many years.

The tradition of an annual Thanksgiving, however, did not take hold right away. In fact, it was another hundred and fifty years before the tradition became anything more than a regional celebration, observed occasionally.

General George Washington called for a thanksgiving of sorts in 1778, on the occasion of France's alliance with the American rebels. Eleven years later, as president, Washington urged all Americans to observe Thursday, November 26, "as a day of public thanksgiving and prayer" to acknowledge "the many and signal favors of Almighty God." But it remained an intermittent holiday, often celebrated differently depending on regional customs.

The virtues of the Thanksgiving holiday as observed in New England were promoted by a number of prominent women in the 1800s, including Harriet Beecher Stowe, author of *Uncle Tom's Cabin*; Margaret Fuller; and Lydia Maria Child.

The woman who raised the campaign to a cause célèbre, however, was New England editor and journalist, Sarah Josepha Hale, who contended, "Thanksgiving like the Fourth of July should be considered a national festival and observed by all our people." She made this argument in published articles and editorials, as well as private letters to elected officials, including five presidents. Finally, Abraham Lincoln saw the value in the enterprise, especially during a time of civil war. He issued a proclamation on October 3, 1863, saying in part:

I do therefore invite my fellow citizens in every part of the United States, and also those who are at sea and those who are sojourning in foreign lands, to set apart and observe the last Thursday of November next, as a day of Thanksgiving and Praise to our beneficent Father who dwelleth in the Heavens.

The only other official change to the holiday came in 1941, when Congress moved the observance day from the last Thursday in November to the fourth Thursday in November, thereby lengthening the Christmas shopping season.

Loose Ends

- As governor, William Bradford subsequently managed the relations with Indians and oversaw the financial, military, and legal management of the settlement. He wrote a detailed account of his life and times called *Of Plymouth Plantation*.

- As one of the leaders in the Plymouth community, Edward Winslow held various offices, including governor. Winslow returned to England on several occasions to represent the colony's interests. Later in life, on an expedition to the West Indies, he died of some unknown disease and was buried at sea.

- Miles Standish continued to provide his military services to the colony. He later led a military expedition to Penobscot, but failed to reclaim a trading post from the French.

- John Billington was one of Plymouth's more persistent trouble-makers, often siding with the colony's disaffected rabble-rousers. He later killed a man in a dispute over hunting rights and was executed by order of Governor Bradford.

- Though not one of the religious Separatists, John Alden was one of the sailors aboard the *Mayflower* who decided to stay on at Plymouth colony. He was also one of the signatories of the May-flower Compact. Alden's son, also named John, would later be accused in the Salem witch trials. Awaiting trial, he escaped from jail and fled; he returned after the fervor died down and was acquitted.

Salem Witch Trials

The Salem witch trials stand as one of our nation's most dramatic ex-amples of the power of fear and paranoia. The witch hunt, started in January 1692 by two adolescent girls, Abigail Williams and Elizabeth Parris, swiftly turned neighbors and friends against each other. Before the year was over, nineteen men and women were hung at the public gallows. Another man, Giles Corey, was pressed to death under a pile of heavy rocks, a procedure intended to elicit a plea.

Finally, growing doubts about the quality of the evidence against the defendants caused authorities to cancel future executions and ultimately free all remaining prisoners. Over the following five years, many involved in the proceedings began to entertain serious misgiv-ings about what had taken place. One particularly guilt-stricken indi-vidual was Samuel Sewall, one of the magistrates who served on the special court presiding over the witch trials. Clearly susceptible to the influence of portents and omens, Sewall and his family suffered a number of personal tragedies in the years after the trials. Two of his young children died—one after suffering "fits" eerily reminiscent of the ones experienced by the young accusers. A third child was deliv-ered stillborn. Sewall's house caught fire on one occasion and was bom-barded by a violent hailstorm another.

The wife of Cotton Mather, a minister whose writings had stoked witchcraft paranoia, gave birth to a baby mysteriously unendowed with an anus. The deformed child died within days. A former colleague on the witch trial court dropped dead one afternoon for no apparent reason. An outbreak of contagious disease claimed thousands of lives. Indians massacred ninety people in New Hampshire.

If the Puritans were beginning to suspect that God might be punishing them for the witch trials, the clincher came in the form of a plague of locusts, or some sort of insect infestation that devastated the season's pea crop.

Clearly something had to be done. The general court of Massachusetts issued an order for a day of fasting on January 14, 1697. Citizens were implored to reflect on "the late tragedy raised amongst us by Satan and his instruments, through the awful judgment of God." Sewall, judging himself acutely responsible for the tragedy, issued the following public apology, read aloud at his church:

> Samuel Sewall, sensible of the reiterated strokes of God upon himself and family; and being sensible, that as to the guilt contracted, upon the opening of the late Commission of Oyer & Terminer at Salem . . . he is, upon many accounts, more concerned than any that he knows of, desires to take the blame & shame of it, asking pardon of men, and especially desiring prayers that God who has an unlimited authority, would pardon that sin, and all other his sins.

It was an astoundingly bold act of contrition. Unlike others who begged forgiveness for their roles in the tragedy, Sewall did not offer any excuses or seek to assign blame to supernatural forces. A statement signed by members of the jury, by contrast, suggested that it wasn't all their fault.

"We fear we have been instrumental," they said, "with others, though ignorantly and unwittingly, to bring upon ourselves and this people of the Lord the guilt of innocent blood." In other words, the devil made me do it. In light of this exculpatory evidence, they went on, "we also pray that we may be considered candidly and aright by the living sufferers, as being then under a strong and general delusion, utterly unacquainted with, and not experienced in, matters of that nature."

Abigail Williams, one of the original child accusers, finally came clean nine years after the trials. Her apology suggested that her guilt should be mitigated by her youth, which made it easier to make her "an instrument for the accusing of several persons of a grievous crime, whereby their lives were taken away from them, whom now I have just grounds and good reason to believe they were innocent persons."

Perhaps Sewall's forthrightness and honesty foreshadowed his future acts of courage. From this point on, Sewall never shrunk from his pursuit of justice, no matter how unpopular the cause. His commitment to justice is best illustrated by his support of two downtrodden peoples: the Indians and blacks.

Despite all that had transpired regarding the witch trials, Sewall foresaw an exalted future for America, and he was convinced that the quality of that future depended on how the colonists treated the Native Americans. Stealing their land and exterminating them would merely invite God's wrath. Sewall sought to Christianize and educate the Indians (donating land and money to build schools and pay for their education), but he also wanted to help them preserve their unique culture on their own lands. He was instrumental in establishing an Indian settlement on Martha's Vineyard.

Sewall was also very sympathetic to black slaves living in New England, far in advance of any organized abolitionist movement. He published a pamphlet arguing for the outlawing of slavery, even if he believed that "they can never embody with us, and grow up into orderly families, to the peopling of the land." Sewall criticized the act of "taking Negros out of Africa, and selling of them here," thereby separating "men from their country, husbands from their wives, parents from their children."

Sewall once persuaded two reluctant slave owners to permit a marriage between their respective slaves, negotiating the terms and presiding over the ceremony. In a separate court dispute, Sewall granted another slave his freedom from a master who had promised to liberate him after an agreed-upon term of servitude but later reneged on the deal. The farsighted Puritan judge even opposed a law prohibiting miscegenation and submitted an amicus brief in support of a slave murdered by his master, arguing:

> The poorest boys and girls within this province, such as are of the lowest condition; whether they be English, or Indians, or Ethiopians, they have the same right to religion and life, that the richest heirs have. And they who go about attempting to deprive them of this right, they attempt the bombarding of HEAVEN: and the shells they throw, will fall down upon their own heads.

Not all of Sewall's moral crusades were as dignified. He once lobbied to replace the names of the days of the week—because of their "pagan" origins—with numbers. He also never missed an opportunity to speak out against the wearing of periwigs, presumably because they were a sign of vanity.

One of the judges who flatly refused to admit error or apologize for his role in the Salem witch trials was John Hathorne. As chief justice of the court in charge of these trials, Hathorne took on the role of chief judge and prosecutor, berating defendants and passing harsh sentences despite flimsy evidence. His grandson Nathaniel Hawthorne (some say he added the *W* to distinguish himself from his repulsive ancestor) of course wrote several short stories and a novel, *The Scarlet Letter*, denigrating the puritanical excesses of earlier generations.

Ironically, one of the real-life sources for the story of Hester Prynne may have come from a court case heard by Samuel Sewall in 1721. A woman named Jemima Colefix apparently committed adultery. Found guilty, Colefix was sentenced to a public display of shame, followed by a whipping. Finally, she was obligated to "forever hereafter wear a capital A of two inches long and proportional bigness cut out in cloth of contrary color to her clothes and sewed upon her upper garment on her back in open view."

CHAPTER THREE

THE AMERICAN REVOLUTION

O UR nation's most significant historical figures often seem to
hang suspended in time, especially when their fame is so closely
associated with a single event. Paul Revere is one such figure, known
almost exclusively for his famous midnight ride. Some may know that
he was also a noted silversmith, but few are aware of his role in the
Boston Tea Party (before his ride) or about his subsequently disappointing military career. The same goes for many of the signers of the
Declaration of Independence—other than the marquee names, like
Benjamin Franklin, Thomas Jefferson, and John Adams. It turns out
that this bold act of defiance had real and sometimes tragic consequences for many of the signers.

Paul Revere, After the Midnight Ride

Everybody knows the story of Paul Revere and his famous midnight ride: the lanterns in the church steeple (one if by land, two if by sea), Revere dashing horseback across the New England countryside shout ing, "The British are coming!" Never mind that much of this story is the product of folklore and poetic license. More about that later.

But what happened to Paul Revere after the midnight ride?

Did he distinguish himself on the battlefield during the American Revolution? Did he sign the Declaration of Independence or help write the Constitution? Not exactly, no, and no.

It was three o'clock in the morning on April 19, 1775, and Paul Revere had been up all night—a harrowing night in which he had rid-den from Charlestown, just across the river from Boston, to Lexington, where he warned John Hancock and Sam Adams that British soldiers were on their way to arrest them. Dodging British patrols he also made it halfway to Concord, where he was supposed to deliver the message that Redcoats were on their way to seize hidden caches of arms and ammunition. Unfortunately, he and two other riders, William Dawes and Dr. Samuel Prescott, were captured by patrols on the road to Con-cord. Dawes and Prescott made a daring escape, leaving Revere behind with his captors. Prescott made it to Concord, fulfilling Revere's mis-sion for him. Stranded in the countryside by the Brits—who also took his horse—Revere walked back to Lexington.

Several hours later, when the shot heard round the world rang out in Lexington, Revere was nowhere to be found. Instead, he was oc-cupied with hiding a trunk containing John Hancock's personal pa-pers and correspondence. As the Redcoats arrived in town, Revere was helping Hancock's secretary drag the cumbersome trunk into the sur-rounding woods. Upon his return to Lexington Common, he would have found eight of his comrades mortally wounded. There's no record that Revere participated in any of the revolution's initial battles. Maybe he finally gave in to exhaustion and slept through it all.

Although many of Revere's Boston patriots participated in the Battle of Bunker Hill two months later, there's no indication that Revere fought alongside them. As the siege of Boston wore on for the better part of a year, Revere jockeyed for a military commission in the Continental Army, but he was passed over time and again. Instead he was relegated to a series of noncombat duties. He was hired to print currency to help finance the Revolution. Next Revere was recruited to design and oversee the construction of a gunpowder mill in Acton, Massachusetts. After the British ultimately evacuated Boston on March 17, 1776, General George Washington prevailed upon Revere to repair cannons disabled by the retreating British and to salvage cannons from an enemy ship wrecked off the coast of Cape Cod.

Revere's first military commission finally came in April, but he was given the relatively lowly rank of major, in the Massachusetts militia—a notch down from the Continental Army. Revere was later promoted to lieutenant colonel and placed in command of Fort William on nearby Castle Island. Without any threat of British attack, he had only a few occasions to fire his cannons, usually in salute to allied ships passing in or out of Boston Harbor or to mark annual Fourth of July celebrations. The only ships he ever fired his cannons at belonged to the American Navy—in an effort to retrieve deserters who were attempting to escape on privateers.

Then, on June 26, 1779, Revere got the chance he'd been waiting for. British ships had recently deposited seven hundred soldiers on a peninsula in Penobscot Bay (modern-day Castine, Maine). A month later, the Americans countered with about one thousand ground troops, including an artillery regiment under Revere's command. Nothing really happened for several weeks as American Navy Commodore Dudley Saltonstall and Army General Solomon Lovell bickered over which military branch should lead the attack.

Meanwhile, a reinforcement of British warships arrived in Penobscot Bay and chased Saltonstall's flotilla up the Penobscot River, where several American ships ran aground and were besieged by the enemy or set afire by retreating American forces. In the confusion, Revere's men scrambled onto different boats heading upstream or sought safety in the nearby woods. By the time Revere tracked down the majority of his men four days later, the entire naval fleet was lost and the American forces were captured, killed, or scattered. The Americans lost nearly five hundred soldiers—the British only seventy.

Revere's behavior during the hectic retreat was oddly unheroic. At one point Brigadier General Peleg Wadsworth had attempted to commandeer a small boat from Lieutenant Colonel Revere in order to evacuate the crew of an imperiled ship. Despite being outranked, Revere refused to turn over the vessel, as it contained "all his private baggage."

Next, Revere ignored Lovell's orders to retrieve several cannons from a nearby island. The way he saw it, the Penobscot expedition was essentially over, so Revere no longer considered himself under Lovell's command.

Saltonstall absorbed most of the blame for the fiasco, but Revere also found himself in hot water. Wadsworth formally charged Revere with disobeying the orders of a superior officer. Revere was also accused of "unsoldier-like behavior tending to cowardice." In February 1782, several months after Cornwallis had surrendered to Washington at Yorktown, a military court acquitted Revere of all charges, deeming that he stood "with equal honor as the other officers in the same expedition"—a backhanded compliment if ever there was one.

As Boston returned to postwar normalcy, Paul Revere resumed his silversmith business, specializing in tableware, bowls, tankards, serving trays, and pitchers. To this day many private collectors and public institutions covet silverworks bearing the Revere touchmark—some valued at upward of $750,000.

Eventually, Revere branched into other metals. By the 1790s he was New England's most sought-after manufacturer of iron and copper church bells. Revere's foundry provided bells to more than three hundred customers and also produced sheets of copper used to clad military ships, such as the *Constitution*, also known as "Old Ironsides."

Reaching the age of eighty-three, Revere outlived two wives and eleven of his sixteen children. He also outlasted the other two riders who joined him on the midnight ride. William Dawes, who fought at Bunker Hill and worked as a commissary in the Continental Army, died in 1799 at the age of fifty-three. Dr. Samuel Prescott fared worse. A sailor in the American Revolution, he was captured by the British and died a wretched prisoner of war in 1777.

Curiously, when Paul Revere died, on May 10, 1818, none of his obituaries even mentioned the midnight ride. So why does nearly every American remember it now? And why is much of what we remember about it wrong? Forty-three years after Revere's death and eighty-five years after the famous ride, Paul Revere was immortalized by Henry Wadsworth Longfellow—incidentally, a grandson of Revere's nemesis, General Peleg Wadsworth.

Longfellow's poem, "Paul Revere's Ride," first published in the *Atlantic* in January 1861, famously begins:

Listen my children and you shall hear
Of the midnight ride of Paul Revere

A Northern poet sympathetic to the Union cause, Longfellow had sought a subject with which he could draw parallels between the country's Founding Fathers and the cause of preserving the Union. He found it in Colonel Revere, who provided Longfellow with a symbol of courage and action. Another factor in Revere's favor: unlike other more prominent revolutionaries, he had never owned slaves.

Longfellow's imaginative account of these events may have provided the Union cause with a rousing call to arms. But it also succeeded in coating the Boston patriot in a mythical patina that, to this day, obscures Revere's true historical significance. Scholars have thoroughly debunked many of the inaccuracies over the years, pointing out that Revere was not the solitary rider, that the lanterns in the Old North Church steeple were signals not *to* him but *from* him to other messengers, and that Revere failed to carry the alarm all the way from Boston to Lexington to Concord.

It didn't matter to Longfellow that he got so many details wrong. Faced with the urgent and real threat of secession, the poet blithely sacrificed historical accuracy on the altar of national preservation.

After the Declaration of Independence

Based on some of the stories that have been passed down through the generations, it's not difficult to imagine the signing of the Declaration of Independence as a jovial, backslapping affair, complete with good-natured jibes at the expense of King George III. Too bad the most commonly repeated anecdotes are most likely apocryphal. John Hancock probably didn't pen an especially large signature so that King George could read it without his spectacles, and Ben Franklin probably didn't remark, "We must indeed all hang together, or most assuredly we shall all hang separately."

This second quote, though it has since taken on an air of jaunty defiance, hints at the underlying anxiety that must have been weighing on the minds of the men who signed their names to this printed attack on English authority. Another signer, William Williams of Connecticut, did in fact predict—if less poetically—that if the Americans lost the War of Independence all the signers would most likely be executed.

Despite the potential dangers, the initial public reactions to the signing were joyous and raucous. Two hundred copies of the declaration were printed and distributed throughout the colonies. John Hancock delivered one copy to General Washington in New York, where he read it aloud to his troops, inciting a riotous celebration. The unruly colonists upended a gilded, lead statue of George III, cutting off its head and placing it on a wooden pike. A mere month later, however, the realities of warfare quickly squelched any rejoicing. The British attacked with a force of thirty-two thousand Redcoats, trouncing Washington at the Battle of Long Island.

Many of the signers continued their service to the country as members of the Continental Congress, but several of them also actively participated in the war effort. The grandiose John Hancock thought he—not George Washington—should be in charge of the Continental Army. In recognition of Hancock's lack of military experience, Congress overruled him, and Hancock instead served as president of Congress through 1777.

Connecticut signer Oliver Wolcott led several militias in the Battle of Saratoga, a pivotal victory for the Americans. His troops were well supplied with ammunition, as Wolcott brought with him some of the forty thousand bullets his enterprising family had fashioned from the remains of King George's fallen statue.

Three signers from South Carolina, Edward Rutledge, Thomas

Heyward Jr., and Arthur Middleton, were captured by British troops advancing into Charleston. They spent a year imprisoned at Fort St. Marks in St. Augustine, Florida, before being released as part of a prisoner swap in July 1781.

George Walton, a signer from Georgia, fought in several battles as a colonel in the militia. During the siege of Savannah, a gunshot felled him from his horse, and he was captured. The British eventually exchanged him for a naval captain held prisoner by the Americans.

The military career of Walton's colleague from Georgia, Button Gwinnett, was disastrous by comparison. It was bad enough that he was passed over for the position of general in charge of the Continental Army's Georgia brigades. Even worse, the honor went to his longstanding political rival, Lachlan McIntosh. From that point on, Gwinnett did everything in his power to undermine McIntosh's authority. Later, as governor of Georgia, which also carried with it the title of commander in chief of Georgia, Gwinnett performed an end-around on McIntosh and organized his own invasion of British strongholds in Florida. The poorly planned expedition self-destructed, leading to formal charges, but Gwinnett was found not guilty of any wrongdoing.

His problems were not over, however. McIntosh publicly insulted Gwinnett for the fiasco, calling him a "scoundrel and a lying rascal." Following the antiquated customs of the day, Gwinnett challenged McIntosh to a duel: pistols at twelve feet. The two pistols fired almost simultaneously, each man sustaining a wound to the leg. McIntosh would recover, but three days later Gwinnett died of gangrene, on May 19, 1777.

At least one signer enjoyed an illustrious military career. Thomas Nelson Jr. of Virginia led troops in several battles, most notably at

Yorktown where British general Charles Cornwallis finally surrendered to the American forces.

Not all of the signers were itching to get into the thick of the battle, but danger still found some of them. Two future presidents, John Adams and his son John Quincy, were sailing for France in 1778, when their ship was attacked by the British navy. Fortunately for them—and the nation—father and son both managed to dodge the cannonballs lobbed their way.

New Jersey signer John Stockton was home helping his family escape approaching British regiments when he was captured and imprisoned. He was released, allegedly after signing a declaration of allegiance to the king, and returned home, where he died of cancer in 1781. Stockton's colleague from New Jersey, John Hart, was also hounded by the advancing British forces. On the lam for about a month, the sixty-five-year-old recent widower sought shelter in caves, other times spending winter nights in open fields.

Many of the signers also suffered crippling financial losses. Hancock came out of the war relatively unscathed, but other wealthy signers lost their fortunes. One of the most generous benefactors to the revolutionary cause was Robert Morris from Pennsylvania. He donated an estimated $1 million to the fledgling American government and worked hard to drum up donations from wealthy friends and business associates. It paid off for the nation, but not for Morris. The government never paid him back. In fact, years later, when Morris's land speculation went bust, he was thrown in debtors' prison.

Virginia signer and mentor to Thomas Jefferson, George Wythe survived the Revolutionary War but would later fall victim to a devious plot. The aged lawyer was living in Virginia, along with two former slaves that he had not only freed but also designated as heirs to his estate. He later added his nineteen-year-old grandnephew George Wythe Sweeney to his list of heirs and stipulated that Sweeney would stand to inherit the entire estate should he survive the two former slaves. Shortly thereafter, Wythe and his two housemates fell simultaneously ill. One of Wythe's former slaves died, the other recovered and claimed she saw Sweeney tampering with the household coffeepot on the morning everyone became ill. Wythe lived just long enough to change his last will and testament, stripping Sweeney of any inheritance. Sweeney went free, however, because the law at that time prohibited the testimony of a black witness against a white defendant. As a principal author of Virginia's constitution, Wythe ironically wrote the laws that liberated his own murderer.

In the years after the war, many of the signers went on to serve as governors or as representatives in house and federal legislatures. Several also played leading roles in developing the Articles of Confederation and the U.S. Constitution. Roger Sherman of Connecticut is the only one to also sign the Articles of Association, Articles of Confederation, and the U.S. Constitution.

The three signers who served their countries in the most significant ways were of course Benjamin Franklin, John Adams, and Thomas Jefferson. Franklin's contribution to the war effort may have been equal to even George Washington's in that without him the French may have never sided with the Americans, providing much needed money, arms, and troops.

Adams and Jefferson, who had cooperated so gracefully in the process of drafting and revising the Declaration of Independence, later became bitter political rivals. The two signers faced off in the first presidential election after George Washington's two terms. Adams won, making Jefferson, the runner-up, vice president. (This was before the modern system of political parties and presidential tickets.) The two differed drastically in their notions of governmental powers—Adams the Federalist believing in a stronger federal government and Jefferson the Republican in favor of states' rights.

By 1800 the election rules had changed, and Adams ran alongside his vice presidential candidate, Charles Cotesworth Pinckney. The Federalists lost to Jefferson and his running mate, Aaron Burr. Adams skipped the inauguration, and the two signers fell out of contact for years, until a détente was brokered in 1812 by fellow signer Benjamin Rush (Pennsylvania). For the next fourteen years, Adams and Jefferson conducted a warm and collegial correspondence. Avoiding politics for the most part, they discussed religion, government, and philosophy. One of the last letters Jefferson wrote Adams was to congratulate him for the election of John Quincy Adams as the sixth president of the United States of America.

Jefferson died on July 4, 1826, fifty years to the day after the Continental Congress voted to affirm a revised Declaration of Independence. Adams died several hours later on the same day. Ignorant of Jefferson's death, his last words were, "Thomas Jefferson survives."

LOOSE ENDS

- One of President Thomas Jefferson's most significant post-Declaration accomplishments was his stewardship of the Louisiana Purchase and the subsequent voyage of discovery led by Lewis and Clark. To prepare his former secretary Meriwether Lewis for his exploratory expedition of the newly acquired western lands and beyond, Jefferson sent him to a number of experts in botany, cartography, and stellar navigation. Dr. Benjamin Rush, a signer from Pennsylvania, was called on to train Lewis in medical matters, providing advice on how to treat common ailments and injuries. Rush also supplied Lewis with thousands of his patented constipation relief pills, sometimes called Dr. Rush's Thunderbolts for the speed and strength of their effectiveness.

CHAPTER FOUR

THE WESTERN FRONTIER

THE story of America's western frontier is studded with adventure and peril, with riches found and lost. But the lives lived after the well-known exploits were sometimes more treacherous—at least for several members of Lewis and Clark's Corps of Discovery and for those contemporaries of George Armstrong Custer who managed to avoid the fate of his last stand.

Lewis and Clark Adjust to Domestic Life

Meriwether Lewis and William Clark are revered for their exploration of North America's western regions. As well they should be, for it was in many ways a miraculous accomplishment, a nearly eight-thousand-mile journey from St. Louis, then civilization's westernmost outpost, through uncharted lands and across astoundingly rugged mountain terrain, to the Pacific Ocean. Though they failed to achieve their primary mission—to find that ever-elusive all-water route to the Pacific—

it was of course through no fault of their own. The existence of a fabled Northwest Passage was finally debunked, at least as far as the North American interior was concerned.

They did, however, manage to establish relations with Native Americans, mostly friendly, setting the stage for a burgeoning fur trade. They discovered and recorded many unknown animal and plant species. They also succeeded in coming back alive and well. Only one man died during the expedition, and the cause of death was a burst appendix, a condition that would have killed Charles Floyd even with the best medical care available in 1804. Almost to a man, the members of the Corps of Discovery acted bravely and nobly, enduring harsh conditions, hunger, and uncertainty.

The mission's success can largely be attributed to the leadership provided by the captain duo of Lewis and Clark, who ably maintained discipline, navigated dangers, and negotiated safe passage through different Indian lands. But soon after Lewis and Clark landed their pirogues back on the riverbanks of St. Louis, things took a turn for the worse. On the surface, everything seemed fine, as the members of the expedition were feted by enthusiastic well-wishers on each stop of their trip back to Washington. They celebrated late into the night, sometimes tipping some twenty toasts—a novelty for men whose lips had not entertained intoxicating spirits for many months. Clark headed to Virginia to court his fiancée, Julia Hancock, while Lewis rode a wave of adulation to Philadelphia and finally Monticello, where he and Jefferson got down on the floor, like a couple of kids with a new toy, to examine the expedition's new maps of the West.

Now that the mission was over, it was time for the men of the Corps of Discovery to move on to the next phases of their lives. Lewis's primary objective at this point was to see to the publication of the journals he and Clark kept while on the trail—thousands of pages containing their observations on the country's geography, fauna, flora, native peoples, and commercial opportunities—not to mention a stirring tale of adventure. But Lewis early on showed signs of erratic, defeatist behavior. He stayed out too late and drank too much. He showed little interest in working on the journals.

Lewis's indifference toward the journals dates back to the tail end of the expedition. He recorded his final entry on August 12, 1806. Earlier that day, the buckskin-clad Lewis had been mistaken for a deer by a nearsighted hunter in his party, who accidentally shot him in the buttocks. Lewis recovered, but from this point the journal writing duties were handled exclusively by Clark. Although Lewis eventually met with a printer and made arrangements for engravings to be made of maps and illustrations, he completely neglected the text of the journals. Toted from city to city, they went unread and unedited.

Writer's block was just one indication of a deeper problem—a perverse tendency toward self-sabotage. In the months after the successful completion of the expedition, Lewis descended into a shapeless, aimless existence in which he accomplished little and seemed uncertain of what to do next. As he had years earlier, Jefferson tried to provide his former secretary with a sense of purpose, naming him governor of Louisiana. This was of course a great honor to Lewis, but perhaps also an overly daunting challenge. It turned out that Lewis was poorly equipped for the job, dragging his feet on important initiatives and other times making questionable policy decisions.

For one thing, Governor Lewis exercised his powers in ways that created conflicts of interest. During the expedition, an Indian chief named Sheheke had accepted Lewis and Clark's offer to travel with them to Washington to meet the "great father," President Thomas Jefferson. In 1809 Lewis hired a group of men to escort Sheheke back to his Mandan Indian village in present-day North Dakota. It's not surprising that many of the backwoodsmen hired were associates of Lewis as well as Clark (who had recently been appointed an agent in charge of Indian affairs in the Louisiana territory). Some had even been members of the Corps of Discovery. However, in this latest enterprise they would also be acting as representatives of the St. Louis Missouri River Fur Company, to which Lewis had granted an exclusive license to trade furs in the Louisiana territory. Once they returned Sheheke, they were authorized to engage in a trading expedition. Because Lewis and Clark each had a financial stake in the company, and because Lewis, as governor, requisitioned supplies needed for the round-trip journey, it amounted to a government-funded commercial boondoggle. At least that's the way many of Lewis's detractors saw it, including the new administration under James Madison.

Meanwhile, Lewis's personal life and finances were also on the rocks. Lewis had engaged in risky land speculation and generally spent more than he earned. It wasn't long before his debts greatly exceeded his assets. On top of it all, he failed time and again in his attempts to court a wife. And then there were the journals—those damn journals. Paradoxically, not a lick of work had been done on them, even though their publication would likely provide a solution to many of Lewis's problems, as they were sure to bring him a substantial income and buttress his rapidly degrading reputation.

His depression grew along with his list of problems. Lewis was drinking more than ever and had even acquired an opium habit. The last straw came in July 1809, when Lewis received a letter from the secretary of war, informing him that it would not honor the charges Lewis authorized for many of the supplies acquired for the Sheheke expedition. If Lewis were to be held personally responsible for the outlays, it would ruin him financially. Gathering up his papers, Lewis headed to Washington to explain himself. He never made it. After making two unsuccessful attempts at suicide, Lewis succeeded on the third, shooting himself twice—in the head and in the chest—at a small inn near Nashville.

The news staggered Clark but did not surprise him. He and others had often noticed Lewis's melancholy nature, especially when his comrade was not fully engaged in an all-consuming activity, like the expedition.

One of the first things Clark did was find someone to edit and publish the journals, which finally hit the shelves in 1814. He then returned to St. Louis, where he continued to help shape American Indian policies and pursue his interests in land speculation and fur trading. Clark was appointed governor of the newly named Missouri territory in 1813. Where Lewis had floundered in the role, Clark excelled. His military skills and familiarity with "the Indian character" came in handy in negotiating numerous treaties, opening up more land for trade and settlement.

Clark's post-expedition relationship with his slave York highlights a less savory aspect of Clark's character. It was of course not unusual for a son of pre–Civil War Virginia to grow up owning slaves. Clark, however, had seen firsthand how the character and mettle of a black man could equal that of any white. During the expedition, York had been an integral member of the Corps of Discovery, performing many of the same duties and enjoying some of the same rights as the others. On at least one occasion, he was permitted to cast a vote on an appropriate wintering spot. However, as Clark's chattel, York received no pay for his services, and upon their return to St. Louis, he found his status as a common slave unchanged.

Clark, who was capable of great sympathy for Native Americans, showed a puzzling disregard for York's humanity. In 1809, Clark wrote to his brother about a "severe trouncing" he delivered to York for being "insolent and sulky." York had been pleading for his freedom, or at least to be hired out to another master closer to his wife in Louisville. Clark eventually gave in, mostly because the disgruntled York was growing increasingly useless to him. Out of spite, he hired York for a time to a "severe master."

The master who owned York's wife soon moved, and York was returned to Clark's service, presumably never to see his wife again. Years later, Clark eventually did grant York his freedom and helped establish him in a delivery business. The business failed, and York decided to return to serve his master, but on his way he contracted cholera and died.

When Missouri achieved statehood in 1820, Clark lost the election for governor but was appointed superintendent of Indian Affairs. In this role, his attitude toward the native populations was inconsistent. He showed great sympathy to the Indians expelled by President Andrew Jackson, requisitioning supplies to relieve their suffering on the Trail of Tears. Yet he could also adopt a ruthless stance, as he did during the Black Hawk War, during which he pursued a war of extermination.

In 1834, Clark found himself in a financial predicament similar to Lewis's: defending $30,000 in expenses that the government initially refused to honor. Things worked out better for Clark, and he returned to St. Louis to resume his duties. He died on September 1, 1838.

Loose Ends

- The Shoshone Indian woman Sacagawea provided crucial assistance to the expedition, acting as a guide and interpreter. The wife—more like property—of Toussaint Charbonneau, Sacagawea had been acquired from Hidatsa warriors who had earlier captured her in a raiding party. Lewis and Clark met the couple at the Mandan village and hired them on for the rest of the expedition. Sacagawea gave birth to a son, Jean Baptiste, at the camp. He was just two months old when the Corps of Discovery resumed its westward journey in April 1805. It seems that Clark had formed a bond with Sacagawea, whom he nicknamed "Janey," and her son, whom he liked to call "Pompey" or "Pomp." On several occasions Clark offered to adopt and raise Pomp, an offer that Sacagawea and Charbonneau took him up on in 1809. Sacagawea later gave birth to a daughter named Lisette. Sacagawea died of some kind of fever in 1812 or thereabouts. By the following year, her daughter had also been entrusted to Clark's care. Little is known about Lisette, but Jean Baptiste studied in St. Louis and as a young man traveled through Europe. He eventually returned to the American West where he worked as a mountain man and guide to the likes of explorer John C. Frémont. In 1848 he moved to California, taking part in the California Gold Rush.

- Corps of Discovery member George Shannon was shot in the leg by Arikara Indians during the expedition to return Chief Sheheke to his tribe. Gangrene developed, so the leg had to be amputated. But Shannon survived and later became a lawyer, congressman, and district attorney.

- After the expedition, several of the adventurous members of the corps returned to the wilds to seek their fortunes in the fur trade, including the team of John Potts and John Colter. The two were ambushed by Blackfoot Indians, who killed Potts but had other plans for Colter. Instead of killing him outright, they decided to make a sport of it. The Indians stripped him naked and gave him a running head start. Colter outsprinted all but one warrior, whom he disarmed and killed. He didn't stop running again for eleven days, when he showed up at an American fort and trading post, exhausted, famished, and covered in wounds.

- Expert hunter and trapper George Drouillard ran into trouble of a different sort. He killed a man during a fur trapping dispute and was brought back to St. Louis, where he was tried for murder. Fellow corps member George Shannon was on the jury, which may explain why he was acquitted of the crime. During a later trapping expedition, Drouillard was killed by Blackfoot Indians.

- Sheheke provides one of the most pitiful stories related to the Lewis and Clark expedition. In the two years spent in St. Louis before returning to his people, the Mandan chief's wife and son both died. By the time he finally returned to his people they had turned against him. Disgraced and disillusioned for the rest of his life, he was killed by hostile Sioux Indians in 1832.

- In 1870, Patrick Gass, the last remaining member of the Corps of Discovery, died at the age of ninety-eight.

After the Last Stand

On June 27, 1876, Lieutenant Edward Godfrey led a scouting party toward the edge of the Little Bighorn River. He was looking for Lieutenant Colonel George Armstrong Custer and the 210 soldiers under his command—part of a three-pronged ambush on a Sioux Indian village. The battle had not gone well for the U.S. Army. The first wave of attack commanded by Major Marcus Reno was rebuffed by a larger than expected force of Sioux warriors. At the same moment Custer was launching his assault from the opposite side of the village, Reno was already in the midst of a panicked retreat to a hillside timber. Soon, Reno was reinforced by troops under the command of Major Frederick Benteen. The plan had called for Benteen to follow Custer's charge, but he instead came to Reno's aid—a decision that would earn Benteen short-term scorn and long-term praise. Benteen was no fan of Custer's, it's true, but his orders in the battle were vague, and he justifiably responded to an immediate and present need. If it hadn't been for Benteen, Reno would have certainly lost many more than the 50-odd of his men who fell to the Sioux on June 25.

Custer, we all know, was not so lucky. As Godfrey approached the banks of the Little Bighorn, he found Custer and his men, the "marble-white bodies," stripped and scalped, like inert figurines bleached by the glaring midday sun.

"The naked mutilated bodies, with their bloody fatal wounds," Godfrey said, "were nearly all unrecognizable and presented a scene of sickening, ghastly horror!" The unmistakable visage of George Armstrong Custer, however, laid undisturbed, scalp intact. If not for the bullet holes—one in the head, the other through the ribs—the faint, unlikely smile lingering on Custer's lips might have tricked Godfrey into believing that the legendary Indian fighter was yet living.

In all, the U.S. Army would lose 263 soldiers on that day, including all 210 of Custer's men. It took another week to carry the news back to Fort Abraham Lincoln, located in the Dakota Territory, where twenty-four wives learned that they were now widows. Chief among them was Elizabeth Bacon Custer.

Now, without husband, children, or any other close relatives yet surviving, the thirty-four-year-old Libbie, as she was known, would spend the next fifty-seven years of widowhood, unwaveringly devoted to her late husband's memory, shaping his reputation in the contemporary consciousness and building a legacy that she hoped would outlive her and her husband.

It wasn't an easy task. The perception among many military men was that Custer had led his men to slaughter. According to the *New York Times*, "It is the opinion of Army officers . . . including Gens. Sherman and Sheridan, that Gen. Custer was rashly imprudent to attack such a large number of Indians, Sitting Bull's force being 4,000 strong."

President Ulysses S. Grant agreed, telling reporters, "I regard Custer's massacre as a sacrifice of troops, brought on by Custer himself, that was wholly unnecessary—wholly unnecessary."

The negative assessments were countered by more sentimental portrayals of the events penned by poets and sympathetic biographers. Custer's most influential hagiographer was Frederick Whittaker. In his book, *The Complete Life of General George A. Custer*, published less than a year after the Battle of the Little Bighorn, Whittaker placed the blame squarely on the shoulders of Reno and Benteen. Libbie agreed, at least in terms of Reno, who she considered a coward. The theory was that Reno had beaten a too-hasty retreat in the face of Indian resistance. (It didn't help that he was at the head of the retreat instead of bringing up the rear.) A court of inquiry later exonerated Reno of any wrongdoing in the battle, but his troubles weren't over. Having a penchant for drink, Reno was implicated for several instances of drunken, boorish behavior. He got into barroom fistfights, made unwanted advances to a fellow officer's wife, and was even caught peeping into the bedroom window of his commanding officer's daughter. Reno was finally kicked out of the army in 1880.

Benteen's post–Little Bighorn career was marred by alcohol, too. A military inspector sent to check on reports of Benteen's "excessive use of intoxicating liquors" found the major "obstinate and unreasonable, and so abusive to those about him as to make it impossible to transact any business with him." Found guilty in a court-martial, Benteen's military career was over. It didn't stop him from criticizing his deceased rival Custer. Benteen countered Whittaker's biography with charges of Custer's vanity, ineptitude, and even marital infidelity with a Cheyenne woman captured in a previous battle.

Many other would-be critics held their tongues, ostensibly out of respect for Custer's widow, Libbie. Perhaps her most effective weapon in the public relations battle, then, was her longevity. Libbie lived to the age of ninety. Over those years, she also became a noted author and lecturer. She wrote three books glorifying her husband's career in the American West, including *Boots and Saddles* (1885) and the most highly praised *Tenting on the Plains* (1893). In addition to lionizing her husband, these books also showed how challenging life on a western outpost was for extended military families. Her books included adventurous tales of prairie fires, storms, and Indian attacks. At one point she describes how she and her servant saved three drowning men from a rain-swollen river.

The Sioux Indians may have won the Battle of the Little Bighorn, but it would be the last victory in their struggle to maintain their precious and vanishing way of life. Fearing retribution, the Sioux splintered into smaller groups and scattered throughout the plains regions of the Dakota and Montana territories. Crazy Horse held out for six months before surrendering to the U.S. Army. He was taken to Camp Robinson in Nebraska, where he was killed in a scuffle with soldiers.

Chased by reinforced army regiments, Sitting Bull led a contingent of Sioux warriors and their families north into Canada, where they sought refuge for the next five years. Finally, facing starvation, Sitting Bull and about two hundred Sioux Indians surrendered at Fort Buford in North Dakota. Placed under house arrest, Sitting Bull was treated with a surprising level of hospitality. At various times, Sitting Bull was granted his freedom, long enough to make highly publicized visits to the white man's metropolis. On trips to Bismarck, St. Paul, New York City, and Philadelphia the Sioux chief viewed his first locomotive (he refused to get on board), rode his first elevator, and tasted ice cream for the first time. He especially enjoyed Manhattan's dancing girls.

In 1885 Sitting Bull was given leave to join Buffalo Bill's Wild West show, parading about on horseback to the delight of large audiences and selling autographed portraits for two dollars apiece. During his theatrical tour, Sitting Bull developed a close friendship with William "Buffalo Bill" Cody and especially Annie Oakley, whom he liked to call "Little Sure Shot."

Libbie Custer was present at the first show featuring Sitting Bull and became a major supporter of the show's "Custer's Last Rally" segment. She wrote to thank Cody "for all that you have done to keep my husband's memory green." It appears Custer's widow held surprisingly little contempt for the Indians who killed her husband at Little Bighorn.

After his stint in show biz, Sitting Bull led the quiet life of a reservation farmer, but he still managed to court controversy. He refused to sign treaties handing over Sioux lands to the United States. Things came to a head in December 1890, when government-allied Indian agents were instructed to arrest Sitting Bull. Rousing the naked chief from an early morning slumber, the agents caused a stir that attracted a crowd of Sitting Bull's supporters. A scrum ensued followed by gunshots, and Sitting Bull was killed, along with his son and six supporters. Six Indian policemen also died in the fracas.

Sioux Indians loyal to Sitting Bull fled and were encamped at Wounded Knee, where troops in the Seventh Cavalry regiment attempted to broker a final surrender. But misunderstandings led once again to a disturbance, and ultimately violence. In the end, Custer's old regiment wiped out between two to three hundred Sioux, exacting a brutal revenge and closing the final shameful chapter in the Great Sioux War.

When Libbie Custer died in 1933 at the age of ninety, she left behind an estate valued at $110,000—which was $120,000 more than her husband had left her back in 1876. But she had managed to work her way out of debt, earning the respect of her public in the process, at a time when it was far more difficult for a woman to earn her own living. She traveled the world, including trips to Europe, India, and the Middle East. It was a fulfilling, if lonely, life.

"I have two regrets," she reflected, late in life, "my husband's death and the fact that I had no son to bear his honored name."

Buffalo Bill's Wild West show fell out of favor in the early 1900s, in part due to the nation's increasingly skeptical perspective on the value of expansionism. As Manifest Destiny gave way to foreign imperialism, Cody actually incorporated scenes of foreign wars into his western tableaux. In re-creations of the Battle on San Juan Hill and the Battle of Tianjin (Boxer Rebellion), Cody inserted dark-skinned Indian actors to fill roles as Spanish and Chinese soldiers. The dubious authenticity of these performances—on several levels—spelled the show's demise. William Cody himself suffered a slow, steady decline. Questionable—and wildly diverse—investments, from coffee suppliers to newspapers to gold mines to theatrical productions, drained his wealth. Cody's most audacious enterprise turned out to be his most disastrous: the town of Cody, Wyoming. Situated in the Big Horn River Basin, alongside the unfortunately named—especially because it was accurate—Stinking Water River, the development project eventually cost Cody much of his wealth. Legal battles with his wife would account for much of the rest.

CHAPTER FIVE

LITERARY LEGACIES

THE mid-nineteenth century was an especially fertile period in American literature, but some of the most prominent authors of this era had a hard time making a living off of their masterpieces. Although authors like Harriet Beecher Stowe and Louisa May Alcott were very successful, the same cannot be said for Nathaniel Hawthorne or Herman Melville. Despite writing works that would be heralded by future generations, both Hawthorne and Melville were forced to work regular jobs in order to support their families.

Poet and short story writer Edgar Allan Poe enjoyed a degree of critical success but he too made very little money. Instead of resorting to a mind-numbing career in the civil service, he simply lived poor—and frequently borrowed money from wealthier associates.

Edgar Allan Poe: Ludwig's Revenge

On October 3, 1849, a semiconscious man was found lying in a Baltimore street gutter. The man, dressed in ill-fitting, disheveled clothes—not his, it turned out—was highly distressed and mumbling incoherently. A Good Samaritan transported the man to a local hospital, where he was identified as Edgar Allan Poe. The renowned poet, critic, and writer of macabre stories was placed in the hospital's mental ward. Four days later, he died of unknown causes.

Was Poe drugged, beaten, and robbed? Or had he gone on one too many monumental benders? Because he was found on election day, some suggested that Poe had been the victim of "cooping," an obsolete electoral custom in which an individual was kidnapped, drugged, and forced to cast multiple votes for a political candidate. Cooping victims were often kept in a holding cell, akin to a chicken coop, and sometimes forced to swap clothes to fool election officials. That would explain Poe's strange wardrobe, but this theory has never been proven. All records related to Poe's hospital stay and death have been lost or destroyed, so it's likely the cause of death will never be known.

Two days after Poe's death, the *New York Tribune* published an obituary under the pseudonym, "Ludwig." It began:

> Edgar Allan Poe is dead. He died in Baltimore the day before yesterday. This announcement will startle many, but few will be grieved by it. The poet was well known personally or by reputation, in all this country. He had readers in England and in several states of Continental Europe. But he had few or no friends. The regrets for his death will be suggested principally by the consideration that in him literary art lost one of its most brilliant, but erratic stars.

Who was this mysterious Ludwig, and how did Poe get on his bad side? It could have been any number of people. Poe had a notoriously poisonous pen, which tended to make him more enemies than friends. As a literary critic he savaged the talents of contemporary writers, made spurious accusations of plagiarism, and even lobbed almost childish insults. Whoever it was showed a familiarity with—even a grudging respect for—Poe's literary prowess.

"As a writer of tales it will be admitted generally, that he was scarcely surpassed in ingenuity of construction or effective painting," the anonymous obituary writer conceded. Even so, this Ludwig could not resist taking shots at Poe's "naturally unamiable character," his "irascible, envious" nature, and his "cold repellant cynicism." Most unbecoming, though, Poe "had, to a morbid excess, that desire to rise which is vulgarly called ambition, but no wish for the esteem or the love of his species, only the hard wish to succeed, not shine, not serve, but succeed, that he might have the right to despise a world which galled his self-conceit."

An odd mix of praise and opprobrium, this obituary must have been written by a person intensely aggrieved by Poe, perhaps the victim of a stinging rebuke, delivered publicly, or a more private insult.

The list of individuals who likely felt justified in slandering the dead writer would have included fellow writer Charles Briggs, of whom Poe wrote, "Mr. Briggs has never composed in his life three consecutive sentences of grammatical English." Of editor Thomas Dunn English, Poe said, "No spectacle can be more pitiable than that of a man without the commonest school education busying himself in attempts to instruct mankind on topics of polite literature." English struck back in print, accusing Poe of forgery. Poe sued English for libel and won.

As Poe's supporters sought to identify and expose the culprit, Poe's mother-in-law (and aunt) Mrs. Maria Clemm, was already in negotiations with an editor named Rufus Griswold who was planning the definitive edition of Poe's works. Mrs. Clemm, whom Poe had loved as a mother, hoped that the work would secure her famous son-in-law's reputation as a literary genius. If the book also earned her a little cash, so much the better.

Clemm signed a contract authorizing Griswold to act as Poe's sole literary executor. In doing so, she unwittingly set in motion the literary world's most notorious instance of character assassination—for Rufus Griswold was, in fact, "Ludwig."

An editor, literary critic, and minor contemporary poet, Griswold had an ax to grind with Edgar Allan Poe. In 1842 Griswold had included a few of Poe's works in an anthology called *The Poets and Poetry of America*. Griswold also paid Poe, in advance, to write a review of the work. In it, Poe praises Griswold's "judgment, . . . dignity and candor," and describes him as "a man of taste, talent, and tact." Having said that, Poe proceeded to quibble with Griswold's judgment, taste, talent, and tact:

> We disagree then, with Mr. Griswold in *many* of his critical estimates. . . . He has omitted from the body of his book, some one or two whom we should have been tempted to introduce. On the other hand, he has scarcely made us amends by introducing some one or two dozen whom we should have treated with contempt.

Compared to the venomous attacks Poe was capable of, these criticisms seem fairly mild, especially since Poe concluded on an upswing. "Having said thus much in the way of fault-finding, . . . the book should be regarded as *the most important addition which our literature has for many years received.* It fills a void which should have been long ago supplied."

Still, Griswold was perturbed. Perhaps he had hoped to get more for his money. Or maybe he was adept at reading between the lines, because privately Poe called the book "a most outrageous humbug" and then lambasted it and Griswold in a series of public lectures. Publicly Griswold took the high road—at least for the time being. And why not? His book had been a commercial success, regardless of Poe's tepid review.

Several years later Griswold decided to include Poe in his latest anthology, *The Prose Writers of America.* "Although I have some cause of personal quarrel with you," Griswold wrote Poe, "I do not under any circumstances permit, as you have repeatedly charged, my private griefs to influence my judgment as a critic, or its expressions. I retain, therefore, the early formed and well founded favorable opinions of your works."

This literary spat may have amounted to little, if not for the introduction of a woman's attentions. Apparently, it was common in the mid-nineteenth century for poets to conduct literary romances with other poets, publishing poems with veiled references and cryptic expressions of ardor, whose meanings would be clear to a small circle of literati. So it was, in the mid-1840s, that Poe and Griswold, both married men, found themselves competing for the literary affections of poet Frances Osgood, herself married to painter Samuel Osgood. Poe eventually backed off, but Osgood's enduring admiration for Poe may have deepened Griswold's hatred of his rival.

"I was not his friend," Griswold later declared, "nor was he mine." Having secured the rights to publish Poe's works, Griswold embarked on his plan to defame Poe's character, saving his most vitriolic slanders for a biographical introduction he appended to *The Works of the*

Late Edgar Allan Poe. In these pages, many of the enduring falsehoods about Edgar Allan Poe's life and character were first invented—that "he was known as the wildest and most reckless student of his class" at the University of Virginia, that "his gambling, intemperance, and other vices, induced his expulsion from the university," and that he was kicked out of West Point and later deserted from the army. While it was true that Poe had a falling out with his adoptive father, John Allan, Griswold, unjustified by any facts, implied it was because Poe had made untoward advances upon Mr. Allan's second wife. It is impossible to deny Poe's struggles with intoxicants, but Griswold gleefully recounted and exaggerated many instances of depravity in his introduction.

Griswold reprinted numerous samples of Poe's correspondence (obtained from Mrs. Clemm). Griswold also forged other letters, making it seem as if Poe were apt to insult his friends behind their backs. Unfortunately, Griswold's perfidy had the desired effect. Even though some of Poe's friends defended him, others were stung by the forged letters. And much of Griswold's fictional biography of Poe was accepted as true and repeated often enough to impugn Poe's reputation for many generations.

LOOSE ENDS

- Maria Clemm lived to regret her decision to entrust Poe's copyrights to his literary adversary—in more ways than one. The contract with Griswold stipulated that Clemm was to be the sole recipient of profits from the sale of the book. Griswold gave her a half dozen copies of the book to do with as she pleased, but she never received a single penny in royalties.

- Rufus Griswold continued his career as a literary critic and anthologist, but his personal life was dogged by misfortune. He divorced his second wife—who, due to a physical deformity, was incapable of sexual intercourse—and remarried, but his third marriage would be turbulent and short-lived. A female poet with whom Griswold had a falling out encouraged the second wife to challenge the validity of the divorce, which she did, leading to an ugly scene in divorce court. Griswold's third wife left him in the wake of the publicity. His house was also destroyed in a gas explosion; Griswold suffered burns and lost seven of his fingernails. Later, informed that his daughter was killed in a train wreck, Griswold arrived on the scene to learn that she had survived, though she suffered severe injuries. Griswold died of tuberculosis in 1857.

Nathaniel Hawthorne, Diplomat, Vagabond, Copperhead

Maybe it's because his most famous works are set in early colonial times, but it's easy to forget that Nathaniel Hawthorne was not a seventeenth-century Puritan but a man of the nineteenth century. Born on July 4, 1804, he was a contemporary of New England's thrice-named literati: Ralph Waldo Emerson, Henry David Thoreau, Harriet Beecher Stowe, Edgar Allan Poe, Henry Wadsworth Longfellow— as well as the nominally deficient Herman Melville. Hawthorne lived through the War of 1812, the construction of the Erie Canal and the transcontinental railroad, the Mexican-American War, the California Gold Rush, and most of the Civil War.

By 1852, Hawthorne's most enduring works were already in print and garnering respectable reviews. But as many writers of serious fiction have learned, good reviews don't pay the bills. As hundreds of thousands of copies of *Uncle Tom's Cabin* were snatched up throughout the United States and other countries, *The Scarlet Letter* (published in 1850) sold only about ten thousand copies in its first decade in print. Sales of *The House of the Seven Gables* (1851) were lackluster, and *The Blithedale Romance* (1852) was a complete bust.

Hawthorne had a family to feed, so he fell back on the tried-and-true strategy employed by many a nineteenth-century novelist of limited means and transferable skills: He angled for a political appointment. Lucky for him, he happened to be an old school chum of Franklin Pierce, who was at the time running for president of the United States on the Democratic ticket. In 1852 Hawthorne wrote a campaign biography for his Bowdoin College buddy, in the hopes that once elected Pierce would reward the hard-up writer with an ambassadorship or some similar position. Pierce won the election and appointed Hawthorne the foreign consul to England in 1853.

At first Hawthorne was enthralled with the opportunity to return to his ancestral homeland. A few months of workaday realities in dismal, damp Liverpool quickly spoiled any illusions. Hawthorne's consular duties included helping Americans abroad who found themselves in legal and financial straits, which often brought him into contact with less savory members of society: sadistic ship captains, ignorant and degenerate sailors, prostitutes, insane persons, and so on.

However dreary and depressing, these four years represented the most profitable period of Hawthorne's life. In addition to a salary, Hawthorne was entitled to a payment of two dollars each time he signed off on a shipment of commodities destined for American shores.

"The autograph of a living author," Hawthorne reflected in his notebook, "has seldom been so much in request at so respectable a price."

The Hawthornes left Liverpool with savings of about $30,000—equal to about $900,000 in current values. From there it was off to

Italy. The peripatetic Hawthornes moved from Rome to Florence, then back to Rome, occupying numerous residences in each city. He had high hopes for each place before he got there, but each time the appeal quickly evaporated. Hawthorne managed to write a novel, *The Marble Faun* (1860), during the family's gypsy-like existence in Europe. Though little read today, this book turned out to be Hawthorne's best-selling book during his lifetime.

Returning to the United States in 1860, Hawthorne and his family settled into their newly renovated and expanded lodgings at Wayside in Concord. Hawthorne, however, felt increasingly isolated by his politics. A loyal Democrat, he was opposed to the abolitionist cause. At a time when Emerson, Thoreau, Longfellow, and the like were casting antislavery militant John Brown as a martyr to the cause of abolition, Hawthorne showed Brown little sympathy, saying, "Nobody was ever more justly hanged."

These views were completely out of sync with Hawthorne's Transcendentalist neighbors and most of his relatives. One of Hawthorne's sisters-in-law, Mary Peabody, had hidden a Brown conspirator in her attic. Elizabeth Peabody attempted to win the release of another conspirator. Hawthorne's neighbors, the Alcott family, actually welcomed John Brown's daughters and, later, a fugitive slave, into their home.

Hawthorne opposed the war because he felt it was a violation of states' rights for the North to impose the abolition of slavery on the South. Once the war broke out, Hawthorne showed no interest in preserving the Union.

"For my part I don't hope, nor indeed wish, to see the Union restored as it was. Amputation seems to me much the better plan, and all we ought to fight for is the liberty of selecting the point where our diseased members shall be lopped off." For Hawthorne it was a matter of cultural and economic dissonance. "We never were one people, and never really had a country since the Constitution was formed."

During the war years Hawthorne traveled to Washington, DC, and even met Abraham Lincoln in person at the White House. Hawthorne seemed bemused by Lincoln's contradictory presence. His "physiognomy is as coarse a one as you would meet anywhere in the length and breadth of the States," Hawthorne observed, but his appearance was redeemed by "a kindly though serious look out of his eyes, and an expression of homely sagacity, that seems weighted with rich results of village experience." Mustering scant praise, Hawthorne concluded, "On the whole, I like this sallow, queer, sagacious visage, with the homely human sympathies that warmed it; and, for my small share in the matter, would as [gladly] have Uncle Abe for a ruler as any man whom it would have been practicable to put in his place."

Further complicating Hawthorne's reputation was his enduring loyalty to the vastly unpopular Franklin Pierce, who persisted in speaking out against the war. The former president was even found to be corresponding with Confederate president Jefferson Davis, to whom he made seditious comments. Despite all this, Hawthorne inexplicably insisted on dedicating his most recent book—a memoir of his days in England—to his friend Pierce. Exasperated fellow New Englander Franklin Sanborn wrote, "Hawthorne has behaved badly and is a Copperhead of the worst kind."

Hawthorne's enigmatic behavior further constricted an already small circle of friends. Sickly, reviled by the abolitionists, and underappreciated as a writer, Hawthorne was depressed and unable to write. His wife suggested a trip to lift his spirits, so Hawthorne and his best friend Pierce began a journey through the New England countryside. They didn't get far. Stopping at a hotel, the feeble Hawthorne died in his sleep on May 19, 1864, Franklin Pierce at his side.

LOOSE ENDS

- Hawthorne's wife, Sophia, moved with her children to several locations in Europe, before she died in 1871. She was buried in Kensal Green Cemetery in London.

- When Franklin Pierce died in 1869, his will included a bequest for the children of Nathaniel Hawthorne.

- Hawthorne's son Julian also became a novelist. Though virtually unknown to modern readers, his works were more popular and enjoyed better sales than his father's. That didn't stop him from seeking additional ways to augment his income. Julian became a principal investor in a silver mine. He and other corporate officers were later found guilty of scheming to sell worthless shares in what turned out to be a fictitious operation. He served a prison sentence for fraud.

- Hawthorne's oldest daughter Una was engaged to be married, but when her fiancé died at sea she became a nun. Una died in 1877 at the age of thirty-three and was buried alongside her mother in London.

- Hawthorne's youngest daughter Rose Hawthorne married and had one son, who died in childhood. After becoming estranged from her husband, Rose also joined a convent, establishing the Dominican Sisters of Hawthorne in 1900. She died in 1926.

- In 2006 the remains of Sophia and Una Hawthorne were reinterred alongside the grave of Nathaniel Hawthorne at Sleepy Hollow Cemetery in Concord, Massachusetts.

Herman Melville's Descent into Obscurity

When *Moby-Dick* was first published in 1851, Herman Melville secretly hoped that the book would launch him into the literary stratosphere, making him the preeminent author of his time. He wrote impassioned letters to his mentor, the more famous Nathaniel Hawthorne, expressing his aspirations—and doubts—about *Moby-Dick*'s prospects.

"Though I wrote the Gospels in this century," Melville bragged to Hawthorne, "I should die in the gutter."

As predicted, instead of cementing his reputation, the publication of Melville's magnum opus marked the beginning of his slow, steady slide into critical and popular oblivion. The novel got a few respectable reviews, but most critics were either confused or downright offended by the book. The first published review called *Moby-Dick* "so much trash belonging to the worst school of Bedlam literature." Another critic deemed the book "a monstrous bore." Sizing up Melville's most recent output, a third critic thought he discerned a trend toward "increasingly exaggerated and increasingly dull" works.

"The truth is," the anonymous reviewer continued, "Mr. Melville has survived his reputation. If he had been contented with writing one or two books, he might have been famous, but his vanity has destroyed all chances for immortality, or even a good name with his own generation."

Melville may have counted on more sympathetic treatment in *The Literary World*, especially since the review was composed by his friend, editor Evert Duyckinck. But even one of Melville's allies had difficulty figuring out if *Moby-Dick* was "fact, fiction, or essay." The best Duyckinck could say was that the book was "a most remarkable sea-dish—an intellectual chowder of romance, philosophy, and natural history." Duyckinck was less impressed with the character of Captain Ahab, who, he complained, was "too long drawn out." Adding, "If we had as much of Hamlet or Macbeth as Mr. Melville gives us of Ahab, we should be tired even of their sublime company."

It's no surprise that sales were anemic from the start. It took five years to sell the first printing of twenty-five hundred copies, and about twenty years to sell out the second printing of just fewer than three thousand copies. By comparison, *Uncle Tom's Cabin*, written by Melville contemporary Harriet Beecher Stowe, sold three hundred thousand copies in its first year. It wasn't always this way for Melville. His first book, *Typee* (1846), a semiautobiographical account of adventures on the high seas and among Polynesian cannibals, was written for a broader, less discerning audience. It garnered enthusiastic reviews and enjoyed brisk sales. When the sequel, *Omoo*, appeared in the following year, four thousand copies sold in its first week on the market. The downward sales trend began with *Mardi*, *Redburn* (both 1849), and *White-Jacket* (1850) and continued with *Moby-Dick* and his next few novels—each one more artistically ambitious than the last, delving into metaphysical depths unsounded by average readers, and each one greeted with increasing levels of befuddlement and disdain.

There were times when reviewers completely threw up their hands, admitting that they did not understand a word of Melville's books. Critics saved their most splenetic commentary for Melville's next novel, *Pierre, Or the Ambiguities*, calling it "chaotic," "puzzling," "wild, inflated, repulsive," "immoral," and "a prolonged succession of spasms."

"That many readers will not" read this book, one reviewer cuttingly remarked, "is in our apprehension not amongst the 'ambiguities' of the age."

Not even Duyckinck could find anything nice to say about *Pierre*. Finding the book maddeningly inscrutable, he longed for the days when Melville played "the jovial and hearty narrator of the traveller's tale of incident and adventure." In other words, why couldn't he go back to writing harmlessly entertaining picaresques like *Typee*?

The consecutive failures embittered Melville, leading him to wonder if he'd ever find a large audience capable of appreciating his genius. On a more practical level, it also meant that he would probably have to get a real job. For a while, he tried lecturing and writing short stories for publication in magazines. Neither one of these pursuits proved terribly successful or profitable. Melville grew depressed, turning inward and increasingly to drink. There were rumors that he beat his wife, Lizzie, and once threw her down a flight of stairs. To protect his daughter from her drunken, abusive husband, Lizzie's father offered Melville a thousand dollars to go on vacation—solo. The struggling writer readily swallowed his pride and took to the sea for an extended trip to Europe and the Holy Land.

And then the Civil War began. Like Hawthorne, Melville abhorred the violence of war, but Melville lacked the partisanship that got his mentor into so much hot water. He began writing poems about the war—personal, heartfelt expressions of sorrow, despair, the horrors of modern warfare, and the muted joys found in victories. No longer motivated by the marketplace, Melville crafted dozens of poems on the war's pivotal events such as the hanging of John Brown; the battles of Shiloh, Antietam, and Gettysburg; and Sherman's March. By the end of the conflict Melville had an impressive collection of verse, which he arranged to have published in book form. *Battle-Pieces and Aspects of the War* was relatively well received by critics, but the book was once again a commercial failure.

Melville turned his back on his audience, such as it was, and took a page from Hawthorne's playbook, landing a job in the New York City customs house. His annual salary of $1,200 was equal to his lifetime earnings from *Moby-Dick*. It wasn't stimulating work, but it wasn't overly taxing either. The biggest problem Melville faced was how to preserve his integrity in a notoriously corrupt atmosphere. Melville quietly and resolutely fulfilled his duties, unfailingly refusing all bribes offered. Earning a steady living now, and no longer writing for publication, Melville fell into a comfortable routine. His marriage and family life seemed to improve, and his drinking diminished.

Each morning Melville and his eighteen-year-old son, Malcolm, would trudge off to their respective jobs. On one occasion, though, "Mackie" slept in after a late night out on the town. His mother called repeatedly through the locked door, but Mackie refused to come down for breakfast. Melville told his wife to let the boy sleep in and face the consequences at work. When Melville returned home that night Mackie's bedroom was still locked. Melville kicked in the door to find his son reclined on his bed, a pistol near his hand, a bullet wound through the temple. His death was initially reported as a suicide, but the local newspapers revised their theory weeks later. Noting that the young Melville was in the habit of keeping a loaded pistol beneath his pillow, they characterized his death as a tragic accident. Regardless, the tragedy devastated the Melvilles, making Herman a more sullen and distant father to his remaining children.

The last work Herman Melville published, in 1876, was a two-volume, eighteen-thousand-line epic poem, *Clarel*, about his trip to the Holy Land. Melville actually gave away more copies than were sold. Years later, the remaining unwanted copies were destroyed.

The deaths of several relatives had improved the Melville family's financial situation, permitting Melville to retire in 1886 after almost twenty years as a customs inspector. He was sixty-seven. At about this same time, several of Melville's British fans made pilgrimages to New York, in search of the once-famous author. "I sought everywhere for this Triton, who is still living somewhere in New York," remarked Scottish poet Robert Buchanan. "No one seemed to know anything of the one great imaginative writer fit to stand shoulder to shoulder with Whitman on the continent."

When Melville's obituary appeared in New York newspapers in 1891, many were surprised to find out that the author of *Typee* had not died years earlier. It speaks volumes that another notice erroneously called him "Hiram Melville." Another obituary even misspelled the title of what would become his most famous book (calling it *"Mobie Dick"*).

Lizzie stored Herman's unfinished work, including an unfinished manuscript about a young ingénue, the "handsome sailor." "Billy Budd," published in 1924, coincided with Melville's critical revival. Unappreciated for seventy years, Melville's work was suddenly rediscovered by a new generation of critics who placed *Moby-Dick* among "the greatest sea romances in the whole literature of the world" and declared it "undisputedly . . . the greatest whaling novel."

In his critical biography published in 1929, Lewis Mumford laments, "For three-quarters of a century *Moby-Dick* has suffered at the hands of the superficial critics," but now it can be agreed, *"Moby-Dick* stands by itself as complete as *The Divine Comedy* or *The Odyssey* stands by itself." Herman Melville—and *Moby-Dick*—had finally reached the iconic status that had proved so elusive during the author's lifetime.

Loose Ends

- Shortly after *Moby-Dick* was published in 1851, Herman Melville traveled to Nantucket Island, where he met George Pollard, the captain of the *Essex*, a whaling ship whose real-life encounter with a vengeful white whale was the inspiration for Melville's *Moby-Dick*. Pollard had little in common with the monomaniacal Ahab. For one thing, he didn't have a wooden peg leg. Unlike Ahab, Pollard obviously survived his ordeal, spending three months in a lifeboat with several other survivors, all of whom resorted to cannibalism. Pollard's nephew was one of those consumed. This horrific experience did not stop Pollard from commanding another whaling vessel, the *Two Brothers*. Unfortunately this ship sank too after running aground on rocks six hundred miles northwest of the Sandwich Islands. Rescued again, Pollard gave up the whaling game for good and became a night watchman back on Nantucket. His sister never forgave him for eating her son.

CHAPTER SIX

THE CIVIL WAR

JUDGING from the immense number of books published on it each year, the War between the States continues to be one of our country's most compelling dramas. Maybe that's because the list of dramatis personae is long and colorful. Yet, the stories of what happened to some of that drama's main characters remain obscure.

In this chapter we examine what happened to Harriet Tubman, who freed numerous slaves through the Underground Railroad, and John Brown, whose act of domestic terrorism incited moral outrage north and south of the Mason-Dixon Line. Finally, we'll see what happened to the perpetrators and victims of, as well as witnesses to one of the most shocking crimes in U.S. history, the assassination of Abraham Lincoln.

Harriet Tubman, at the End of the Line

In 1849 Harriet Tubman escaped from a Maryland plantation, ending twenty-two years of enslavement, during which she routinely suffered beatings and other abuses. Over the next ten years, Tubman sneaked back into the South on multiple occasions, risking her freedom and life to liberate numerous other slaves—between fifty and three hundred, depending on the source. It would be nice to be able to say that after her days on the Underground Railroad, Harriet Tubman enjoyed the freedoms she had struggled so hard to win and that her efforts were recognized and even honored. Or, failing that, that she was at least compensated for services rendered to the nation during the Civil War. It would be nice, indeed, but it would be far from accurate.

Harriet Tubman's career as a conductor on the Underground Railroad came to an end with the Civil War, but she remained a valuable weapon in the fight for black emancipation. Just after the war began, she reported for duty at a Union military camp in South Carolina. At first she was relegated to menial tasks, like cooking for officers and nursing sick and injured soldiers. Later, Tubman performed valuable espionage work, applying the knowledge and skills gained on the Underground Railroad to spy on the enemy, reporting on Confederate troop strength and movements. Teaming up with Colonel James Montgomery, a veteran of the Bleeding Kansas battles, Tubman even led a brigade of armed Union soldiers into battle.

According to a reporter on the scene:

> Col. Montgomery and his gallant band of 300 black soldiers, under
> the guidance of [Tubman], dashed into the enemies' country, struck

a bold and effective blow, destroying millions of dollars worth of commissary stores, cotton, and lordly dwellings, and striking terror to the heart of rebellion, brought off near 800 slaves and thousands of dollars worth of property, without losing a man or receiving a scratch!

Her country expressed its gratitude by not paying her for any of the work she did on behalf of the Union Army. On several occasions, military officials or elected politicians made halfhearted efforts to win her some form of compensation, but to no avail.

On her way home after the war, Tubman was taking a train from Philadelphia to New York. A white conductor told her to go into the smoking car. Not one to suffer indignities lightly, Tubman refused. The conductor resorted to force, but Tubman grabbed hold of a handrail. It took three men to break her grip. She was shoved to the smoking car and tossed in like a sack of potatoes. Tubman suffered a broken arm in the scuffle. Friends encouraged Tubman to sue the train company, but she never followed through.

Tubman lived the rest of her life in poverty, dependent on the charity of abolitionist benefactors. She had many generous supporters, including Franklin Sanborn, Gerrit Smith, and William Lloyd Garrison. Back in 1859 New York Senator William Seward sold Tubman a house near Auburn, New York. With a barn and farmland, the property was offered at a price well below its market value and on very generous terms. On top of that, the mere act of entering into a contract with a female fugitive slave was notable, for the Dred Scott case had just declared that blacks did not enjoy any rights as citizens. After the war, Tubman managed to scratch out a mean subsistence at her Auburn home through farming and a modest brick manufacturing enterprise. But Tubman was generous to a fault, taking in poor relatives, acquaintances, and even strangers, at least one of whom repaid her kindness by robbing her. Thanks to her generous nature and her naïveté, Tubman was frequently in need of financial assistance. Her friends occasionally organized fund-raising efforts to support her.

One method devised to provide her with economic aid took the form of a Tubman biography. Written by Sarah Hopkins Bradford, the book was published in 1869. The cost of printing was underwritten by local benefactors, and all proceeds were earmarked for Tubman. The book sold well and royalties were used to pay off many of Tubman's debts, including her mortgage to Seward, which was paid off in full by 1873.

Tubman herself was known to organize fund-raising drives, always for the benefit of others—namely, poor former slaves. Her old friend William Seward was chagrined by her limitless generosity. "You have worked for others long enough," Seward admonished her. "It is time you should think of *yourself*." Seward would gladly make donations to assist Tubman, but, he said, "I will not help you to rob yourself for others."

One night in 1873, two white men showed up at her door with an interesting proposition. These men claimed to know of a secret cache of Confederate gold worth about five thousand dollars. In return for two thousand dollars in cash, the men would lead Tubman to the site. With money fronted by a wealthy white businessman, Tubman set off with the men. All she got for her efforts—and the two thousand dollars—was a bump on the head and a rather expensive lesson.

Tubman was also actively involved in the woman's suffrage movement, speaking at various conventions. Though she would not live to see the vote extended to women, Tubman was an inspirational voice in the movement and helped to advance the cause, along with white suffragists Susan B. Anthony, Elizabeth Cady Stanton, and Lucretia Mott.

Poor health had plagued Tubman and her family for years. Her second husband, Nelson Davis, suffered from tuberculosis, making it difficult for him to play a significant role in supporting an extended family that tended to gravitate toward Tubman, seeking care and sustenance. In addition to blood relations, Tubman's home was often filled with poor and feeble neighbors and acquaintances. Sarah Bradford, the author of Tubman's biography, visited her once near the turn of the century. She was appalled to find an overwhelmed Tubman "surrounded by a set of beggars who I fear *fleece* her of everything sent her." The paternalistic Bradford decided to manage Tubman's royalty earnings for her, making direct payments to Tubman's creditors and meting out small payments at a time. Tubman's only other steady income at this time was a monthly government pension of twenty dollars. It had taken the U.S. government thirty-five years to finally begin compensating Tubman for her service to the country during the Civil War.

Considering Tubman's compassionate nature, it was altogether fitting that she would seek to establish an institution to care for old and sick African Americans. She managed to raise enough money to make a down payment on a plot of land, but with no funding available for construction, Tubman donated the land to her church, which opened The Harriet Tubman Home for Aged and Infirm Negroes in 1908. Just a few years later, Tubman herself became too feeble to care for herself. She spent the last two years of her life in the home named in her honor, finally dying in 1913, at the age of ninety-three.

Loose Ends

- Harriet Tubman's first husband, John, was actually a freedman living near the Maryland plantation where Harriet was enslaved. He stayed behind when Tubman fled North and eventually remarried. John Tubman was murdered in 1867 by a white neighbor over a petty dispute.

- After passage of the Fugitive Slave Law, it became unsafe for runaways like Harriet Tubman to live in the free northern states, so she moved for a time to St. Catharines, Ontario. There she met John Brown, who was developing his plans for inciting a slave revolt. She also recruited black soldiers from the Canadian fugitive community to join in Brown's raid, but none of them ultimately took part in it.

John Brown's Trial, Execution, and Apotheosis

On October 31, 1859, two weeks after his stunningly ineffective raid on the Harpers Ferry arsenal, John Brown sat in a Charles Town, Virginia, jail cell composing a letter to his wife, Mary.

"I suppose you have learned before this by the newspapers that two weeks ago today we were fighting for our lives at Harpers Ferry," he begins. "That during the fight Watson was mortally wounded; Oliver killed." Watson and Oliver were the Browns' sons.

Brown continued, "I have since been tried, and found guilty of treason, and of murder in the first degree." Before mailing the letter a few days later, he appended what might be the most understated postscript in history: "P.S. Yesterday Nov 2d I was sentenced to be hanged on 2 Decem next. Do not grieve on my account. I am still quite cheerful."

Brown bore his own hardships with ease, but he was clearly anxious about the consequences to be suffered by his surviving dependents, which included his wife, three young daughters, and a crippled son. "They have suffered much," he wrote from jail, "and it is hard to leave them uncared for." Without her husband around anymore, the soon-to-be-widowed Mrs. Brown would have to rely on others for financial support.

Many of the letters Brown wrote from jail included pleas for financial support for his family—as well as the families of his widowed daughters-in-law. Focusing entirely on his wife's future without him, until they could be reunited in heaven, Brown rebuffed Mary's offers to visit him in jail. He worried that her safety could be compromised by the high-strung proslavery mobs surrounding the jail. He also knew that a trip from North Elba, New York, to Virginia would strain his family's tenuous finances. Financial considerations also led Brown to suggest that Mary leave her loved ones' bodies in Virginia, rather than bearing the expense of shipping them to New York.

"Do not let that grieve you," he wrote her in his characteristically unsentimental manner. "It can make but little difference what is done with them."

As he often did, Brown found solace in his faith, saying that "God will be a husband to the widow, and a father to the fatherless." He also knew that several wealthy supporters had already pledged donations to support his family.

Otherwise, Brown almost seemed to enjoy his imprisonment and trial. In numerous letters he wrote from jail, Brown claimed to be "of good cheer."

"No part of my life has been more happily spent than that I have spent here," he claimed. Part of this he attributed to the "kind" and "humane" treatment received from his jailer, one Captain John Avis.

Brown went so far as to discourage accomplices from plotting an armed jailbreak, in part because he feared Avis might be injured or killed in such an attempt.

Brown derived most of his good cheer from a profound sense of having done God's work, of having performed a service to humanity. Brown may have planned and executed an armed insurrection against the United States of America, but his felonies were perpetrated to topple the evil institution of slavery, in adherence to a higher law. In his final address to the court, just before his sentencing, Brown noted, "This court acknowledges, as I suppose, the validity of the law of God. I see a book kissed here which I suppose to be the Bible, or at least the New Testament." The most important law contained in that book, according to Brown, was the Golden Rule: Do unto others as you would have them do unto you. "It teaches me, further to 'remember them that are in bonds, as bound with them.'"

Of course, in military terms the raid was a dismal failure. Of the twenty-one soldiers Brown had assembled (sixteen white, five black) to ignite what he hoped would be a widespread slave insurrection, ten were killed during the raid. Several others later died of their wounds. John Brown was wounded in the final scuffle—stabbed in the abdomen and slashed across the head by an officer's blunt sword. In his haste to join the battle, the army officer had accidentally grabbed a ceremonial weapon; otherwise Brown probably wouldn't have survived his ill-fated escapade.

But Brown was confident in the eventual success of his enterprise. Even though he failed to accomplish any of his military objectives, Brown hoped to score a public relations victory that would propel the nation toward a day without slavery. Others were less convinced. Today, it's commonly accepted that Brown's raid played a key role in the run-up to the Civil War and, ultimately, the abolition of slavery. At the time, however, many abolitionists were appalled by Brown's attack on Harpers Ferry. One by one, prominent abolitionists publicly disavowed Brown. William Lloyd Garrison, William Seward, Salmon Chase, and Abraham Lincoln among others deplored the attack as folly and possibly treason. Even Frederick Douglass—who consulted with Brown for years—and Henry Ward Beecher—who shipped rifles to Brown during the Bleeding Kansas campaign—publicly censured Brown.

From the start, Brown realized that he was worth more to the abolitionist cause dead than alive. He discouraged any talk of an armed rescue, "being fully persuaded that I am worth inconceivably more to hang than for any other purpose." Beecher—Harriet Beecher Stowe's brother and one of the most renowned preachers of his day—agreed.

"Let no man pray that John Brown be spared!" Beecher declared from his pulpit. "Let Virginia make him a martyr!" Sure, Brown's attack was misguided, Beecher was saying, but "a cord and a gibbet would redeem all that, and round up Brown's failure with a heroic success." The court obliged, handing down a death sentence.

Brown's execution had the desired effect. Even southerners present, like J. E. B. Stuart and Thomas (soon to be "Stonewall") Jackson, admired Brown for mounting the scaffold in a calm, courageous manner. Just before he died, Brown handed a note to one of his jailers. In it, he predicted the inevitability of the Civil War, saying, "I John Brown am now quite certain that the crimes of this guilty land will never be purged away, but with Blood."

After the execution, Northern sentiment for John Brown blossomed, in large part thanks to the Concord Transcendentalists, especially Henry David Thoreau, who championed Brown's courage and the nobility of his armed resurrection from the start. Ralph Waldo Emerson was soon swayed. The more famous and influential Emerson declared that Brown made "the gallows glorious like the cross."

One group of people who Brown might have expected to stand by him during his imprisonment and trial were conspicuously silent. Like wavering disciples, most of the so-called Secret Six, a cabal of Northern abolitionists who helped fund and plan the Harpers Ferry Raid, acted as if they had had nothing to do with Brown and his plans to foment a slave insurrection. Samuel Howe, Franklin Sanborn, and George Stearns fled to Canada, while Gerrit Smith found refuge in an insane asylum. Only Theodore Parker, convalescing and then dying at a safe distance in Rome, and Thomas Wentworth Higginson stood firm in their support for Brown. Scolding Sanborn in a letter, Higginson wondered, "Is there no such thing as *honor* among confederates?" Higginson was one of Brown's supporters who tried to organize an escape for Brown and some of the other jailed conspirators, but each plan fell through, due to a lack of funds or feasibility.

Even though he acquitted himself better than most of the Secret Six, Higginson never forgave himself for his role in the Harpers Ferry raid. Not that he abandoned Brown the way some of the others had—more that he subconsciously knew that he was sending Brown into a suicide mission. Higginson attempted to make up for it, in part, by commanding the first all-black regiment of Union soldiers in the Civil War.

LOOSE ENDS

- A third son, Owen Brown, escaped into the hills of Pennsylvania, along with six other Harpers Ferry conspirators. He died of pneumonia in California in 1889. Two of the fugitives who escaped with Owen Brown were later captured and hanged along with two others found guilty shortly after Brown's execution.

- The only black survivor of the raid, Osborne Perry Anderson, fought for the Union during the Civil War and later wrote a book about the Harpers Ferry raid.

- Mrs. Brown never remarried. She moved to California with her daughters and got by fairly well. The people of Red Bluff, California, raised funds to build a house for them.

- John Brown's other surviving sons, Salmon and Jason, were a different story. They squandered money on foolish investments. Jason died of old age in Akron, Ohio, in 1912. Seven years later Salmon committed suicide.

- The U.S. Marine Corps colonel who quelled John Brown's armed insurrection later earned some fame in the Civil War as a Confederate general. His name was Robert E. Lee.

- Another prominent actor in the Civil War drama also claimed to have played a role in the "capture and execution of John Brown." While it's true that John Wilkes Booth was present at Brown's execution, he merely witnessed the event, having bribed some members of a local militia into letting him tag along with them.

- One of the hostages John Brown took during the raid was Lewis W. Washington, a great-grandnephew of General George Washington. Washington's descendent, a wealthy Virginia slave owner, survived the raid and later lent support to the Confederate war effort. After the war he was granted a pardon, based largely on the assistance of George Custer, a friend of Washington's second wife.

- Among the Bostonians raising funds to cover John Brown's legal expenses was a descendent of Salem witch trial judge Samuel Sewall (also named Samuel Sewall).

- A once stalwart Brown supporter, James Redpath, soon veered drastically in his sympathies relating to the issue of slavery. Though he aided Brown's activities in Kansas and at Harpers Ferry and also wrote a worshipful biography of John Brown, Redpath later coauthored the memoirs of Confederate President Jefferson Davis.

The Assassination of Abraham Lincoln

At about 10:15 p.m., April 14, 1865, a lead bullet fired from John Wilkes Booth's derringer flattened itself within Abraham Lincoln's skull. The wound would prove fatal nine hours later. Almost simultaneously, Lewis Powell burst into Secretary of State William Seward's sickroom, stabbing him in the face and neck. As part of the coordinated attack, coconspirator George Atzerodt was supposed to kill Vice President Andrew Johnson. He went to a tavern and got drunk instead.

Within three months, almost all of the perpetrators of our nation's first presidential assassination were dead or imprisoned. John Wilkes Booth and David Herold rode furiously out of Washington, to the house of Dr. Samuel Mudd, where the doctor set Booth's badly broken leg, injured in his leap from balcony to stage. For the next five days, Booth and Herold hid out in the thick woods of Maryland, waiting for the right time to cross the Potomac River into Virginia. Maryland farmer Thomas Jones brought the assassin provisions and also gave him a boat, with which Booth and Herold arrived on the Virginia side of the Potomac on April 23. Several days later, federal soldiers tracked the two fugitives to a tobacco shed on the Garrett Farm in Virginia. When soldiers set fire to the wood structure, Herold surrendered, but Booth was determined to make a dramatic exit. An overzealous Union soldier, ignoring orders to bring Booth back alive, poked his gun through a crack in the shed and shot him in the back of the neck. Paralyzed and dying, Booth uttered his last words, "Useless, useless."

Herold was transported back to Washington, DC, where he was reunited in prison with fellow conspirators Powell, Atzerodt, and Mary Surratt, as well as Dr. Mudd, Samuel Arnold, Michael O'Laughlen, and Edman Spangler. On July 7, 1865, the first four of the assailants found summary justice at the end of the hangman's noose. Convicted of lesser charges, Mudd, O'Laughlen, Arnold, and Spangler were shipped off to Fort Jefferson on a desolate remote island in the Dry Tortugas, about seventy miles west of Key West. An outbreak of yellow fever provided an unwelcome means of clemency for O'Laughlen, who died, but it also led to early pardons for the remaining three prisoners, in part because of the medical treatment Dr. Mudd provided to fever-stricken prisoners and guards alike. In all, these conspirators served less than four years in prison for their roles in President Lincoln's assassination.

At least two conspirators got away. A reputed Confederate supporter, Jones was arrested but released for lack of evidence. For eighteen years, he kept the secret of Booth's whereabouts during the so-called lost week. In 1883 he sold the story of his role in Booth's escape to journalist and author George Alfred Townsend for $60. Jones also wrote his own account of his exploits: *J. Wilkes Booth: An Account of His Sojourn in Southern Maryland after the Assassination of Abraham Lincoln, His Passage Across the Potomac, and His Death in Virginia.* The book was published in 1893. He was seen peddling copies at the World's Columbian Exposition in Chicago. Jones died the following year.

Another conspirator, John Surratt, slipped into Canada and eventually made his way to Europe, seeking anonymity in an unlikely place: as a member of the Vatican's papal guards. Ratted out by a suspicious fellow guard, Surratt was arrested but made a second escape, this time by leaping off a seaside cliff into a garbage dump. He scurried to Naples and boarded a steamer to Alexandria, Egypt, where he was again apprehended—still conspicuously clad in his papal guard uniform. Surratt was shipped back to the United States to face justice. But the slippery Surratt had one more escape left in him—a slow, exceedingly mundane one made via the judicial system. Surratt may have been a well-known associate of John Wilkes Booth and the child of convicted conspirator Mary Surratt, but the prosecution could provide no evidence that he helped plan the assassination or that he was even in Washington, DC, on the night of the assassination. (In fact, he had been in Elmira, New York, planning a jailbreak for Confederates held in a Union prison.) Two trials later Surratt was freed in November 1868, three and a half years after Lincoln's assassination.

At one point Surratt set out on a lecture tour, but an engagement in Washington, DC, almost resulted in a riot. The event was canceled, and Surratt slipped into middle-class obscurity, working for most of his remaining days as an auditor at the Baltimore Steam Packet Company. The last surviving member of the assassination plot, Surratt died in 1916.

Though split in their sympathies to the Confederacy and Union, all members of the Booth family suffered for their association to the assassin. Booth's sister, Asia Booth Clark, moved to England with her husband, a renowned comic actor, and wrote two biographies of her famous acting family as well as a sympathetic memoir of her brother John, which was hidden away and published posthumously, seventy-three years after the assassination.

The eldest Booth sibling, Edwin, was forever haunted, and initially stigmatized, by his brother's horrendous act. An even more famous stage actor than John Wilkes, Edwin suffered public insults and was even shot at during a Chicago performance of *Richard II*. As the years progressed, the famed Shakespearean actor experienced a professional and personal renaissance. By the time he died in 1893, Edwin

Booth—a friend of president-elect Grover Cleveland, no less—was so thoroughly respected and loved that his funeral drew thousands, including:

> actors, artists, men of letters, men whose names are known as fore-most in their professions on both sides of the Atlantic, men of mil-lions, men whom the great crowd outside the quaint churchyard pushed and squeezed and craned their necks to see—all were there to join in the ceremony . . . of the greatest Hamlet of them all.

In one of those queer historical coincidences, on the same day as Edwin Booth's funeral, tragedy struck at the site of Lincoln's assassination. Ford's Theatre, which the War Department had purchased in 1866 and transformed into office space, collapsed under the weight of thirty years' worth of records, killing twenty-two and injuring another sixty-eight.

For Mary Lincoln, life after the assassination was a barely tolerable series of tragedies and indignities. Not only was she widowed under the most horrific of circumstances but she was also broke. Her creditors were closing in, but her husband's estate was tied up in court. More gallingly, whereas government pensions and private foundations were taking care of generals—Grant alone was given two houses—no one was stepping forward to help the former first lady. Her only consolations were her two remaining children, Robert and Tad. Before long Robert fell from favor. First, he married a strong-willed woman. Second, he scolded his mother for begging Congress for a pension but more mortifyingly for conducting a public auction of her old clothes. Third, he had the audacity to question her outlandish shopping habits, a chronic problem of hers that had recently become an obsessive compulsion.

After an extended estrangement, spent mostly in Europe with her beloved Taddie, Mary returned to Chicago in 1871 to meet her first grandchild. Almost as soon as they arrived, on July 15, Tad died at the age of eighteen, probably of medullary thyroid cancer. Then, in 1875, a mere decade after she was widowed, the nation's former first lady— beset by financial insecurity, loneliness, and paranoia—was branded a lunatic and imprisoned in a mental hospital. Worst of all, it was her son Robert who had orchestrated her commitment. One suicide attempt and a short stay at an asylum later, Mary was out on her own again.

On the positive side, she did come into some money, as her late husband's estate was finally settled. The financial freedom enabled her to shop and travel (far away from Robert, "that wretched young man"). She died on July 16, 1882, at her sister's house in Springfield, Illinois. The family rummaged through sixty-four trunks of clothing and baubles but was unable to find a single appropriate dress in which to bury her.

Lincoln's assassination traumatized many others, including the two closest witnesses, Clara Harris and her fiancé, Major Henry Rathbone, the man Booth stabbed in the presidential balcony, before leaping to the stage. The couple married in 1867 and later moved to Germany. Moody, temperamental, and insanely jealous in the years after the assassination, Rathbone made a lousy husband and father. On Christmas Eve 1883, Rathbone staged a bizarre reenactment of Lincoln's assassination, shooting his wife and stabbing himself. As he had eighteen years earlier, Rathbone survived the stab wound, but once again the gunshot victim succumbed. Rathbone was committed to an insane asylum, where he lived out the remainder of his life.

Robert Lincoln's life after the assassination was that of a living, breathing bad luck charm. Despite professional success and vast wealth, he managed to figure in several of the worst tragedies of the late nineteenth century. His Chicago mansion was one of the thousands of homes destroyed in the Chicago Fire of 1871. He also served as a legal adviser to railway tycoon George Pullman during the deadly rail strike of 1894, later taking over as president of the Pullman Palace Car Company after the owner's death. Most ominously, Robert Lincoln played a role in the country's first three presidential assassinations. He was bedside when his father died; he was present in 1881 when Charles Guiteau shot President James Garfield; and he was in attendance at the Pan-American Exposition in Buffalo, New York, when Leon Czolgosz assassinated President William McKinley in 1901.

Robert Lincoln died on July 26, 1926, at the age of eighty-two. Plans were being made to transport his body to Springfield, where he was to join his son, mother, father, and three brothers at Oak Ridge Cemetery's Lincoln Memorial Tomb. But it was not to be. Robert's wife, Mary Harlan Lincoln, overruled her husband's wishes and decided to bury him at Arlington National Cemetery instead. Because she planned to be buried beside her husband, perhaps Mary Harlan Lincoln found the prospect of spending eternity so near her mother-in-law unappealing.

CHAPTER SEVEN

DISASTER RELIEF

DISASTERS have a way of bringing out the best and worst in people. In the following entries, you'll see how a fire, a flood, and an earthquake triggered massive outpourings of sympathy in various forms of relief aid. But these disasters also stoked smoldering class anxieties, resulting in fear, distrust, and even violence. Ultimately, though, lessons were learned, and the three stricken cities—Chicago, Johnstown, and San Francisco—rebuilt themselves in grander fashion and with safeguards in place to prevent future disasters. However, the damage to some individuals' reputations and fortunes were beyond recovery.

Mrs. O'Leary's Cow Exonerated

When the Great Chicago Fire swept away two-thirds of the burgeoning Midwestern city on October 8 and 9, 1871, it became the most devastating urban catastrophe in U.S. history. An unstoppable wall of flames bulldozed the city, consuming almost $200 million in property and terrorizing countless citizens. Considering the scale of destruction, a surprisingly small number of people lost their lives. Including the missing, who were presumed to be completely incinerated or perhaps trapped under tons of debris, the death toll was set at approximately three hundred.

The fire left a hundred thousand Chicagoans homeless, but not the O'Learys, owners of the barn where the fire originated. Although the barn was a total loss—including the cow that allegedly kicked over the lamp—the arid southwesterly winds sent all the destruction north and east of their home and detached boardinghouse. The fact that Patrick and Catherine O'Leary's house survived the devastating fire did not add to their popularity among newly homeless Chicagoans. Nor did the rumor that the fire was the result of a careless, nocturnal milking session.

Whether the product of neighborhood rumormongers or of an imaginative journalist, the story of the O'Leary cow and the lamp was first published in the October 9 *Chicago Evening Journal*. In the days after the fire, reporters from various newspapers descended on the O'Leary home, seeking to verify the story. What they found was a proud and willful woman who steadfastly denied any knowledge of how the fire began in the family's southwest side barn. Yes, the fire started in the barn, and yes, the family owned several cows, which Mrs. O'Leary milked twice daily, but never at night. Mrs. O'Leary had fed the family's horse at seven o'clock, she said, and then retired the animal to the barn. That was two hours before the fire, and she had no lamp with her at the time. The O'Learys went to bed sometime between seven-thirty and eight o'clock that Sunday night, a fact that was corroborated by a neighbor who attempted to pay them an evening social call. It was this man, Daniel "Peg Leg" Sullivan, who later testified that he noticed the smoke coming from the barn at a quarter to nine.

An official fire department inquiry failed to pinpoint the true cause of the fire, but thanks to the persistent legend of the cow kicking over the lantern, Mrs. O'Leary suffered perennially. Reporters hounded her on every anniversary of the fire. They called her an old Irish hag—even though she was in her forties at the time of the fire. They accused her of being on the dole—even though she earned her living by selling the milk of her family's five cows and through rental income, and her husband, Patrick, worked as a deliveryman. They concocted stories about how she may have intentionally started the fire in vengeance after being denied aid by the church.

No matter how hard they tried in the years after the fire, reporters failed to get Mrs. O'Leary to comment or pose for a photograph. There is no known photographic image of Catherine O'Leary, but there is at least one amusing forgery, in which an old, stern-faced Caucasian woman stands beside a cow—actually, the bovine impostor was a handy steer, most likely fetched from one of the nearby stockyards.

The reporters weren't the only ones hassling Mrs. O'Leary. Once, a representative of P. T. Barnum knocked on her door, offering her a job in the traveling circus. Legend has it she chased him away, brandishing a broomstick (though this final detail may well be yet another journalistic embellishment).

Patrick and Catherine O'Leary had a son, James, who was two years old at the time of the fire. Later known as "Big Jim" O'Leary, he worked for a time in the stockyards, before opening a saloon on South Halsted, a short walk from his former workplace. By the 1890s he emerged as one of the city's preeminent gambling kingpins. Along with Mike McDonald and Mont Tennes, "Big Jim" O'Leary headlined a generation of vice lords preceding the likes of Jim Colosimo and Johnny Torrio, who were followed by Al Capone and other Chicago mobsters. O'Leary was a brash impresario of the gambling industry, notorious for taking any bet imaginable, including the weather and presidential elections; he reportedly lost a half million dollars when Woodrow Wilson beat Charles Evans Hughes in 1916. But he obviously won more than he lost, if his brownstone mansion and palatial gambling house were any indication.

O'Leary's gambling den was occasionally raided by the police and bombed by rivals, but the easygoing—and well-connected—Irishman shrugged it all off. He certainly greased the right palms and probably kept the right people well supplied with free booze and female companionship. However he managed it, O'Leary was never jailed, but he did have his business licenses revoked from time to time, and he was obliged to pay several fines—whenever the "goo-goos" (good government reformers) started making noise.

O'Leary's devil-may-care nature was perhaps most adroitly on display in 1908, when he bet fellow gambler, Pat O'Malley, a thousand dollars that O'Malley could not travel from Chicago to County Limerick, Ireland, in a week. O'Malley arrived just in time, sending O'Leary a telegram that read simply, "You lose." For the colorful O'Leary, it was a lark well worth the price.

O'Leary also never missed an opportunity to defend his mother from the charge of burning down the city of Chicago. Over the years he granted several interviews with newspapers, offering his opinion that the fire started as a result of spontaneous combustion. This might sound like a lame attempt to divert blame, but it turns out that densely layered green hay does have a tendency to burst into flames when the conditions are right. Earlier on the day of the fire, the O'Learys had just filled their barn with several tons of hay.

When he died in 1925, O'Leary was eulogized by notoriously crooked alderman Mike Kenna as a "square shooter" who "never welched on a bet." Nine years later, O'Leary's gambling hall and saloon burned down in the Stockyards Fire of 1934, thereby associating the O'Leary name with the first- and second-largest fires in Chicago history.

The story of the cow and lamp weren't the only wild rumors flying around Chicago in the immediate aftermath of the fire. Reports of widespread looting and arson were compounded with tales of vigilante justice. Panicky citizens and imaginative reporters fabricated stories of looters shot dead and arsonists hung from lampposts. The tall tales helped create an atmosphere of chaos and fear, especially among members of the moneyed class. Relegated to homelessness, if only briefly, Chicago's captains of industry found themselves sharing open-air tent cities with the rabble of Chicago. Personal safety concerns combined with an irrational fear of worker unrest led to an overreaction among Chicago's business and social elite. A cabal of private citizens, including Marshall Field, George Pullman, and *Chicago Tribune* owner and the city's next mayor Joseph Medill, asked Mayor R. B. Mason to call in federal troops under the command of General Philip Sheridan. Soldiers were stationed throughout the city, with orders to shoot anyone breaking the law.

A couple weeks after the fire, the city's prosecuting attorney, Thomas Grosvenor, was on his way home. It was a little after midnight, and Colonel Grosvenor, a decorated veteran of the Civil War, had just exited a streetcar near the University of Chicago. A volunteer sentry in the University Patrol called for him to halt. Grosvenor told him "to go to hell and to bang away." The overzealous student took him at his word and shot him dead. The incident provided much-needed ammunition to Governor John Palmer, who was outraged that federal troops would be permitted to usurp his authority over any part of the state of Illinois. Palmer wrote nasty letters to Chicago officials and eventually petitioned the Illinois legislature to censure President Ulysses S. Grant and Secretary of War William Tecumseh Sherman for violating states' rights.

LOOSE ENDS

- In 1915, a former reporter for the *Chicago Republican*, Michael Ahern, claimed that he was present when the story of Mrs. O'Leary's cow and the lamp was invented by Jim Haynie, a reporter for the *Chicago Times*. But if the story had been invented by a *Times* reporter in the presence of a *Republican* reporter, why was it initially published only in the *Evening Journal*? It's more likely that a reporter for the *Journal* overheard a rumor circulating in the neighborhood and got it past his editors, whereas other papers, if they even heard the story, found it too dubious to print. As historian Richard Bales has pointed out, Ahern's story evolved over the years, with his own role expanding in each retelling. So, if not the cow, who did start the fire? Pointing out numerous inconsistencies in the testimony offered by Daniel Sullivan, Bales puts the blame for the fire on the O'Learys' peg-legged neighbor. Partly in response to Bales's sleuthing, the Chicago City Council passed a resolution in 1997 that officially absolved Mrs. O'Leary—and her cow—of any blame for the Chicago Fire.

- In terms of financial losses, the fire's biggest loser may have been William B. Ogden, Chicago's first mayor. Ogden had created a vertical monopoly on Chicago's primary construction material, lumber. Not only did he own the lumberyards in Chicago but he also owned lumber mills in Peshtigo, Wisconsin, as well as the railroads that connected the two cities. He lost it all on the same day. At the same time that the Chicago fire was ravaging the Midwest's largest metropolis, a prairie fire was also consuming Peshtigo, Wisconsin. The less famous of the two fires claimed closer to a thousand lives and completely decimated the town's infrastructure. As devastating as his financial losses were, they represented only about one third of his overall wealth, and of course, he still had his life. To his credit, Ogden helped resurrect the Wisconsin town before retiring to his New York estate.

- Despite profound post-fire labor strife in Chicago, including the Haymarket bombing and the subsequent execution of four "anarchists," the city still managed to rebuild itself in the years after the fire, to a much grander degree. This was in large part due to the opportunity presented by the clean slate created by the fire. From 1871 to the World's Columbian Exposition in 1893, the city experienced a building surge that included gems such as the Home Insurance Building, Auditorium Building, the Monadnock Building, and the Rookery. An influx of architects, financiers, and workers resulted in a population explosion as well, from three hundred thousand to more than one million. Chicago's rebirth culminated in the World's Columbian Exposition held at the glimmering White City designed under the direction of Daniel Burnham.

Johnstown Flood

When it occurred on May 31, 1889, the flood of Johnstown, Pennsylvania, resulted in the largest death toll from a natural disaster in U.S. history, claiming more than two thousand lives. The heavy rains that inundated the hills and valleys of southwestern Pennsylvania could not be helped, but, the scale of the disaster was amplified by the poor design and questionable location of the dam fifteen miles upriver from Johnstown and six hundred feet higher in elevation.

Unequipped with release valves, the surface level of the man-made lake swelled to overflowing. When it inevitably burst, the dam released a twenty-ton wave measuring forty feet high that virtually swept the entire town of Johnstown off the map.

The results were grim. With so many of the town's residents killed—including ninety-nine entire families—identification of the victims was difficult. What's more, many of the bodies were severely battered or stripped of clothing, further complicating identification. More than seven hundred fifty bodies were eventually buried in a plot for the unknown dead. Some bodies drifted as far downstream as Pittsburgh and even Cincinnati.

Over fifteen hundred homes were destroyed. The town's economic engine, the Cambria Iron Company, suffered extensive damage, but the company president, John Fulton, vowed to repair and reopen as soon as possible. In the meantime, surviving Cambria employees would be paid to help with the overall cleanup of the city. Widows and orphans would receive the pay due their late husbands and fathers.

Word of the disaster spread rapidly throughout the nation, as did the de rigueur rumors of lawlessness and vigilantism. If you were to believe the *Chicago Tribune*, lynched thieves caught scavenging jewelry from dead bodies adorned lampposts throughout the flooded city. Of course, the *Trib* also exaggerated the number of dead by a factor of five.

The charitable outpouring was impressive for its speed and generosity. Trainloads of clothing, food, building materials, and medicine arrived daily, along with ample supplies of embalming fluid and coffins. Cincinnati sent twenty thousand pounds of smoked meats.

Pittsburgh sent thousands of loaves of bread, provided by the S. S. Marvin Company. Cities around the world organized fund-raising drives. Chicagoans raised over $100,000. Philadelphia, $360,000. New York, $750,000. In all, nearly $4 million was raised in the wake of the tragedy.

The job of delivering care and relief supplies was spread across many different ad hoc committees and organizations. Most notably, the emergency brought Clara Barton and the fledgling American Red Cross to Johnstown from Washington, DC. Established as a field hospital during the American Civil War, the Red Cross proved in its response to the Johnstown Flood that it was equally prepared to respond to peacetime disasters. Under Barton's direction, the Red Cross arrived within days of the disaster, providing tens of thousands of survivors with shelter, furniture, and other supplies.

Dazed by the enormity of the disaster and consumed with grief, survivors, up until this point, were mostly preoccupied with the most basic needs—potable water, food, and shelter. Then something happened to change the tenor of their reaction to the flood. Johnstown residents started to wonder what had caused the South Fork Dam to fail. Was it the result of a storm of unfathomable proportions? Or was the fallible hand of human artifice in some way to blame?

On June 9, a crowd gathered for an informal prayer meeting. After two local ministers delivered their sermons, John Fulton, who had fortuitously been out of town when the flood struck, rose to address the crowd. The head of the Cambria Iron Company, Fulton offered uplifting words: The company was committed to helping widows and orphans of employees killed in the flood, it would rebuild bigger than ever, creating jobs for remaining residents. What he said next solidified a suspicion harbored by many of the town's survivors: "I hold in my possession today . . . my own report made years ago, in which I told these people, who, for purposes for which I will not mention, desired to seclude themselves in the mountains, that their dam was dangerous. I told them that the dam would break sometime and cause just such a disaster as this."

Who were "these people" and what were the nefarious-sounding purposes vaguely alluded to?

The report Fulton stood clutching had been commissioned in 1880 by Fulton's boss at the time, Daniel J. Morrell, the previous head of the Cambria Iron Company. Getting wind of construction work taking place on the old dam at the South Fork of the Conemaugh River, Morrell decided to investigate. He sent Fulton up to the dam, where he was to make a formal inspection of the structure and report back to his boss.

The dam was originally constructed by the state of Pennsylvania to create a reservoir to feed a nearby shipping canal, but railroads soon rendered the canal obsolete, making the dam unnecessary. It was neglected for years and fell into disrepair. But this didn't present a threat to the communities downriver, because the leaky dam was not now retaining enough water to cause significant damage during major storms.

What Fulton learned during his inspection disturbed him. The new owners of the dam, the South Fork Fishing and Hunting Club, an amalgamation of wealthy Pittsburgh industrialists and their ilk, had purchased more than 160 acres of land near the confluence of the Conemaugh River and the South Fork Creek. They planned to flood a portion of the land to create a private summer resort for upscale leisure activities. To do so, they would need to repair the dam. But for reasons unknown, the club hired a contractor who lacked engineering credentials for the job.

The rebuilt dam had several worrisome features. The height had been lowered, and the low point of the structure was in the center, making spillover and failure much more likely. The previous owner had removed the iron release valves, selling the metal for scrap, making it impossible to release excess water to make repairs or in the event of an unusually large storm. Most gallingly, the owners of the club had installed a screen designed to keep precious game fish from escaping downstream. During the flood of 1889, the screen became clogged with heavy debris, creating even more pressure on the earthen dam.

Newspapers seized on the story, inflaming class resentments. Mastheads were splashed with headlines like: "The Pittsburgh Fishing Club Chiefly Responsible," "The Club Is Guilty," and "May Be a Lynching."

Members of the club didn't stick around long enough to test this last theory, so "the rabble" resorted to vandalizing their luxurious cottages. From the safety of Pittsburgh, the members mostly kept mum. After the negative publicity broke, they decided to supplement their initial contribution to the relief effort, which had been a thousand blankets. As a group, the club donated thousands of dollars. Steel magnate Henry Clay Frick ponied up $5,000, banker Andrew Mellon gave a thousand. Several lawsuits were brought against the club, but none of them proved successful. The club itself had, by design, few assets, and no individual member was ever found to be legally liable for the disaster.

One member who managed to keep his association with the club a secret was Andrew Carnegie, the multimillionaire steel magnate. The flood occurred right around the time Carnegie was beginning to initiate his plan of distributing his vast wealth. He pledged $10,000 in cash and promised to cover the costs for a stately new gothic limestone library. This new building was among the first of some 250 newly constructed libraries Carnegie financed throughout the world.

The new library building and the city of Johnstown as a whole have survived two more floods of lesser impact, in 1936 and 1977. Today the former library building houses the Johnstown Flood Museum.

LOOSE ENDS

- One of the reporters who descended on Johnstown to cover the story was rookie correspondent Richard Harding Davis. Davis went on to cover numerous major stories, from the first electric-chair execution in 1890 to Queen Victoria's Diamond Jubilee in 1897. His most famous war reporting occurred during the Spanish-American War, in which his dispatches were manipulated by William Randolph Hearst to make the case for war with Spain. Davis wrote nearly fifty books, including novels, collections of reportage, and travelogs.

- Sylvester Stephen (S. S.) Marvin, the owner of a large bakery in Pittsburgh, donated tons of bread to the surviving citizens of Johnstown and served on a committee to organize relief efforts. His immense baking enterprise, which included bakeries in Pennsylvania, Ohio, Indiana, and Michigan, became the centerpiece of the newly amalgamated National Biscuit Company, known today as Nabisco.

- John Fulton remained in Johnstown, serving as a member of the city and state boards of health. Fulton was instrumental in securing access to clean drinking water for the city of Johnstown.

San Francisco Earthquake and Fire

Striking at about five o'clock in the morning, the Great Earthquake of 1906 caught most San Francisco residents in their beds, including Fire Chief Dennis Sullivan, whose third-floor apartment collapsed in a heap. Pinned beneath tons of loose bricks, splintered furniture, and the remnants of the building's roof, Sullivan would be of no help in putting out the ensuing fires that ravaged the city over the next four days. In all, the fire consumed about three-quarters of the city, approximately twenty-eight thousand buildings, worth between $350 and $500 million. Entire neighborhoods—Nob Hill, Telegraph Hill, and Chinatown—were wiped out. Of course, many of the structures that burned had already been demolished by the 8.3-magnitude earthquake, and many others were dynamited in an effort to deprive the fire of fuel—with varying degrees of success.

The job of handling the ongoing crisis fell to a hastily assembled Committee of Fifty, made up of elected officials, administrators, and private citizens dedicated to putting out the fires, preserving order, and administering aid. The committee was headed by Mayor Eugene Schmitz and included interim fire chief John Dougherty as well as prominent San Franciscans, such as capitalist James Phelan and real estate mogul Rudolph Spreckels. At the same time, the military force stationed at the Presidio also took swift and decisive action, under the command of Brigadier General Frederick Funston, a decorated veteran of the Spanish-American War and the Philippine-American War. Although martial law was never officially declared, Mayor Schmitz issued a proclamation ordering troops "to KILL any and all persons found engaged in Looting or in the Commission of Any Other Crime."

Wild rumors of criminality abounded—that one man cut the hand off a dead woman to get her rings and that another man threw himself onto the prostrate form of his dead mother, only it wasn't his mother and he wasn't really kissing her face, but chewing off her ears to get at her diamond earrings. These certainly apocryphal stories were supplemented with tales of widespread military atrocities—that soldiers shot hundreds for looting, or for merely failing to follow random orders, covering their tracks by throwing the corpses into the fires or weighing them down and dumping them into the bay.

Unlike the Chicago Fire of 1871, there was no individual to pin the blame on for the San Francisco Fire of 1906. In this case, it was of course the earthquake that severed gas lines. The temblor also ruptured the water main connecting the city to its only source of fresh water. But San Franciscans attempted to deny or at least downplay the earthquake's role in starting the fire—as hard as that may be to believe. Their motive was financial. Insurers would cover fire damages but not losses occurring as a result of an act of God like an earthquake. In fact, some less scrupulous insurance companies tried to deny all claims, arguing that what had burned were not intact structures but worthless piles of rubbish demolished by the earthquake.

Lacking a convenient scapegoat for the disaster, San Franciscans would eventually find a vessel for their collective anguish in Mayor Schmitz, along with his wily political ally, Abraham Ruef. Even though he was popular among the working classes and did a fairly admirable job of responding to the crisis (notwithstanding the heavy-handed shoot-to-kill order), Schmitz was opposed by well-to-do members of San Francisco society, in part due to his pro-union sympathies but also because of his fairly obvious penchant for corruption. An effort to oust the mayor had actually begun even before the earthquake and fire. Special prosecutor Francis Heney hired private detective William Burns to investigate reports of bribes paid for preferential treatment. In one scheme the United Railroad Company was said to pay

$200,000 in return for an exclusive city contract to build and operate the city's streetcar system. The alleged ringleader was kingmaker and political insider Ruef, who distributed the bribes to Schmitz and members of the board of supervisors, keeping $85,000 in "legal fees" for himself.

Less than a year after the fires burned out, a grand jury indicted Ruef and Schmitz for numerous counts of bribery. Ruef cut a limited immunity deal with the district attorney and pled guilty. In return for his testimony against his former ally Schmitz, Ruef hoped for leniency from the court. The jury in the Schmitz trial found the mayor guilty and sentenced him to five years in jail. But each man's fortunes changed dramatically: Schmitz's conviction was overturned on appeal, but Ruef was sentenced to fourteen years in prison. With his name cleared, to a certain extent, Schmitz ran for mayor again but never again attained that office. He settled for a seat on the board of supervisors. After almost five years in prison, Ruef was released on good behavior, and the governor of California eventually pardoned him in 1920.

Phelan and Spreckels, two of the crusaders who helped engineer the downfall suffered by Ruef and Schmitz, were also behind an effort to beautify and bring order to their ravaged city. Even before the disaster of 1906 they had spearheaded an effort to overhaul the city, which had grown organically but erratically, resulting in a built environment largely without logic, grace, or distinction. Wealthy, civic-minded boosters created the Association for the Improvement and Adornment of San Francisco. They hired architect and urban planner Daniel Burnham to submit a master plan for a wholesale redesign of the city.

Known for his urban planning skills, as well as for building skyscrapers of muscular grandeur, like The Rookery in Chicago and the

Flatiron Building in New York, Burnham modeled his plans for San Francisco on elements borrowed from Paris and Washington, DC, including a centrally located city hall, from which broad avenues extended like spokes, and connecting streets formed radiating concentric circles. Copies of Burnham's plan arrived at City Hall on April 17, 1906, the day before the calamity struck. History seemed to be repeating itself, in urban planning terms, as much like what happened in Chicago, catastrophe had provided a young, rapidly growing city with a blank canvas upon which to construct a new, more beautiful and more logical city.

It was not to be. A large faction of the city's merchant class, eager to resume business as soon as possible, desired to rebuild quickly, using the existing city layout. Aesthetics lost out to commercial interests, and the city beautiful movement bypassed San Francisco.

Unfortunately for the Chinese residents of San Francisco, many citizens united behind another unique opportunity created by the disaster: to get rid of Chinatown—or at least move the Chinese enclave to another—that is, less desirable—part of the city, opening up valuable real estate for development. The consensus objective, voiced in an editorial, was to "preserve this fine hill for the architecture and occupation of the clean and moderate Caucasian."

Immediately after the devastation, the surviving Chinese were shunted into an ad hoc refugee camp on Fort Point, thereby enabling the city's "clean and moderate Caucasian" population to loot the remnants of hard-hit Chinatown. Military troops stood idly by—or partook in the free-for-all themselves. Meanwhile, city planners were trying to figure out if it was feasible to relocate Chinatown to Hunters Point—or even on the more distant and secluded Angel Island. The Chinese government intervened, pointing out that they owned a good deal of real estate in the area and that they had no intention of rebuilding their consulate building in any other part of the city. The city knuckled under pressure from the Chinese government and Chinese Americans who made a strong stand for their rights.

LOOSE ENDS

- Fire chief Dennis Sullivan spent three days trapped beneath the debris of his demolished apartment building. Splayed across a ruptured steam radiator, he suffered extensive burns and later died of his injuries.

- Frederick Funston later became Woodrow Wilson's pick to lead U.S. troops in World War I, but Funston died before he got the chance, on February 19, 1917. The assignment went instead to General John Pershing.

- During the prosecution of Abraham Ruef, assistant district attorney, Francis Heney, was shot in the head by a disgruntled jury candidate. Heney recovered and later ran for district attorney but lost.

- Private detective William Burns went on to open his own agency in 1909. Long a rival of Allan Pinkerton, Burns was involved in a number of high-profile cases, including the strangulation murder of Mary Phagan, a teenage Georgia factory worker. Her boss, Leo Frank, was found guilty in a trial that many regard as a mockery of justice. Frank was sentenced to hang, but when the sentence was commuted to life in prison, a mob of vigilantes stormed the jail, abducted Frank, and lynched him. A Jewish man, Frank's death led to the founding of the Anti-Defamation League. Burns later became the head of the Bureau of Investigation (now the FBI), but his career was derailed thanks to his involvement in the Teapot Dome Scandal.

- Rudolph Spreckels remained active in business and politics. His vast fortune, which peaked at approximately $30 million, was wiped out in the Great Depression. By 1938, he was reduced to selling off "all the worldly goods" in his possession to settle an outstanding income tax debt.

- James D. Phelan was elected U.S. Senator representing California in 1915. His unsuccessful reelection campaign slogan, "Keep California White," neatly summarized his position on Chinese and Japanese immigration.

- One of the more celebrated visitors who fled San Francisco after the earthquake was famed tenor Enrico Caruso, who kept his promise never to return to the scene of such horrific destruction. His operatic contemporary, Luisa Tetrazzini, was less skittish. She returned to San Francisco in 1910 to rave reviews. A local chef ensured the soprano's legacy by creating a new dish in her honor— you guessed it, Chicken Tetrazzini.

CHAPTER EIGHT

WILD WEST OUTLAWS
AND SHERIFFS

AFTERMATH stories about outlaws of the Wild West are usually brief or nonexistent. Gunslingers typically led short, eventful lives that ended early and violently. But some of those who lived long enough eventually went straight and led somewhat productive lives. And many of the lawmen who tracked and shot down robbers of trains, banks, and cattle ranches lived to tell the story. Some found less dangerous ways to make a living, but others fell victim to the harsh brand of justice meted out in the lawless West.

Billy the Kid's Killer Gets His

Live by the sword and die by it—a lesson demonstrated repeatedly in the Wild West but rarely heeded. True, Pat Garrett was the Lincoln County Sheriff, which made it his job to bring Henry McCarty, aka William Bonney, aka Billy the Kid, to justice. But he didn't have to kill him, especially not the way he did.

Acting on a tip, Garrett tracked Billy the Kid down to Pete Maxwell's place at Fort Sumner, New Mexico, where Billy was known to seek the accompaniment of Maxwell's younger sister, Paulita. Garrett could have given word to a go-between that he was there to bring the Kid in for the numerous murders he committed, most recently two guards killed during the Kid's escape from Lincoln County jail, two weeks ahead of his scheduled execution, but he didn't. Instead, on July 14, 1881, Garrett crept into Maxwell's room late at night, asked him about Billy's whereabouts and then, when Billy unexpectedly entered the room, Garrett shot him without warning.

Garrett couldn't have been proud of the manner in which he earned his fame. He had violated the unwritten gunslingers' code, which proscribed that you never shoot an unarmed man, and you never shoot a man in the back. In his defense, Garrett claimed that he did not feel obligated to offer the Kid a fair fight. Here's how he put it in his book *The Authentic Life of Billy the Kid*, first published in 1882: "Whenever I take a contract to fight a man 'on the square,' as they put it . . . , that man must bear the reputation, before the world and in my estimation, of an honorable man and respectable citizen." Garrett also claimed that the Kid was armed with a butcher knife in one hand and a revolver in the other. Witnesses have corroborated the knife, with which some have surmised the Kid intended to retrieve a piece of beef jerky from Pete's supply. Most other accounts of the events say there was no gun, however.

Afterward, things didn't go terribly well for the man who shot Billy the Kid. First, he had a hard time collecting the bounty offered by outgoing New Mexico governor Lew Wallace. The attorney general of New Mexico Territory argued that the wording of the governor's proclamation made it sound like a personal offer, not one sanctioned by the government. Wallace, the private citizen, wasn't offering a reward from his own pocket, so the matter was set aside. Meanwhile, other private citizens who benefited from the Kid's demise—cattle ranchers and the companies that insured them—stepped in, making donations that totaled approximately $5,000, enough money to help Garrett get into the cattle business himself.

But the restless Garrett didn't stick with anything for long. He later ran an unsuccessful campaign for a legislative seat in New Mexico Territory. He also dabbled in farming, a nursery, and a dairy operation. He invested in real estate developments, a hotel, and Thoroughbred racehorses. Most of these schemes ended in failure. Eventually Garrett accepted an offer to hunt down rustlers in Texas. But the money he made from that didn't come close to covering his gambling losses and rising debts. With more and more mouths to feed—Garrett and his wife eventually had nine children—the erstwhile lawman decided to return to doing what he did best. He ran for Chaves County sheriff in 1889 but lost to one of his former deputies. Garrett settled for a deputy sheriff position back in Doña Ana County, New Mexico. By the time he became head sheriff, he found himself in the middle of the county's most sensational murder case.

In the years after Billy the Kid's death, one of his defense lawyers, Albert J. Fountain, had made a name for himself as a successful legislator and prosecutor. He was also good at making enemies, including an outfit of cattle rustlers he had recently helped bring to justice. On his way home from one such prosecution, Fountain and his eight-year-old son were bushwhacked. The bodies were never found, but an abandoned wagon and two pools of dried blood were proof enough that they met a grisly end. Garrett was called on to track and capture the murderers. His posse cornered the main suspects, Oliver Lee and James Gililland, but his deputy got shot and needed medical attention, so they backed off. Lee and Gililland surrendered several months later and engaged influential attorney Albert Fall to represent them. Garrett's case failed to sway the jury, and the defendants were set free.

Garrett had had enough of law enforcement. Between the public criticism and the danger, he decided to pursue his many business opportunities. Unfortunately, he still had the same gambling habits and poor business instincts, which meant more hard times, increasing debts, and unpaid back taxes.

What he needed was a steady paycheck, and he found it in his new benefactor, none other than president of the United States Theodore Roosevelt. It was no secret that Teddy was infatuated with the Wild West and had a deep admiration for rugged lawmen like Garrett, Bat Masterson, and Wyatt Earp. Some of Garrett's friends (and even frequent adversary Albert Fall) endorsed Garrett for the El Paso customs inspector position, but Roosevelt was worried about Garrett's gambling and drinking. Against his better judgment, he ignored the many opponents to the appointment. Using language the frontier sheriff and gambler well understood, Roosevelt told him, "Mr. Garrett, I am betting on you." Garrett replied, "Mr. President you will win that bet." As usual Garrett was overplaying a weak hand.

Problems surfaced almost immediately. Garrett refused to hire an experienced rancher to appraise cattle imported from Mexico, preferring to do the job himself. Importers were rankled not only by what they considered excessive duties levied on cattle, but also by Garrett's rigid, imperious nature. Complaints reached Garrett's boss, Secretary of the Treasury Leslie M. Shaw, who pulled rank and hired an independent appraiser, George Gaither, on a thirty-day trial basis. The situation seemed to improve, but after thirty days Garrett summarily dismissed the temporary inspector.

The animosity between Garrett and Gaither reached the boiling point during a chance meeting on the street. Garrett called Gaither a "god-damned liar," and Gaither hauled off and cracked Garrett in the jaw. It took a crowd of passersby to separate the two men, Gaither bleeding from injuries received in the scuffle. The local newspaper reported on the fracas, calling it "more or less ludicrous."

Somehow, Roosevelt still had faith in his appointment, enough to invite Garrett as a special guest at a reunion of Rough Riders taking place in San Antonio. Garrett foolishly brought with him a friend named Tom Powers, the proprietor of a tawdry saloon and gambling house. Unaware of Powers's notorious reputation, the president was photographed with Garrett and his dubious friend. It was the last straw. Roosevelt stripped Garrett of his appointment.

Once again without a steady income, Garrett's life quickly unraveled. Several of his properties were foreclosed on and auctioned off by his creditors. He tried to pull together several deals, but his reputation was equally bankrupt. There was a time in Garrett's life when he wanted to diminish his role in the killing of Billy the Kid, but now it seemed as if his reputation as a frontier sheriff was all he ever had going for him. His last chance to pull himself from debt and resurrect his dignity was a new book, *The Story of the Outlaw*, which he worked on with ghostwriter Emerson Hough.

Garrett would never live to see it published. Between Hough's poor health and difficulties finding a publisher, the project was delayed repeatedly. In the meantime, Garrett had gotten himself into another imbroglio, this time with a tenant leasing one of the ranches he still owned. The tenant, an odd bird named Jesse Wayne Brazel, had imported a herd of goats, which were decimating his landlord's property. Garrett and Brazel agreed to meet in order to hash out a deal with a third party who offered to buy the property from Garrett. On their way to the meeting, Garrett and Brazel's paths crossed. With Pat Garrett, unexpected meetings between adversaries usually ended in violence. This was no exception. This time Garrett was the loser, though no one ever found out exactly how, why, or by whose hand. The only certain facts were that Garrett was shot twice—once in the back of the head and once through the stomach. Also, his pants were unbuttoned, leading some to believe that he was executed while relieving himself on the side of the road. Brazel was tried for murder but found not guilty, thanks in great part to the legal defense mounted by his attorney Albert Fall.

LOOSE ENDS

- Pete Maxwell never lived down his role in the Billy the Kid slaying. Billy's large contingent of friends and sympathizers derided Maxwell for cowardice. After the shots were fired at Billy in his bedroom, Maxwell was seen fleeing the building shouting, "Don't shoot! Don't shoot!" His nickname from that day on was Don Chootme.

- When New Mexico was granted statehood in 1912, Albert Fall was elected one of its first two senators. Later, he was appointed secretary of the interior by President Warren G. Harding. Convicted of fraud during the Teapot Dome Scandal, he served a one-year prison term in federal jail.

- Lew Wallace, the former governor of New Mexico Territory, had a second career as an author of fictional works. His most notable contribution to American letters was undoubtedly *Ben-Hur: A Tale of the Christ*, the number one bestselling American novel of the nineteenth century—selling more copies than *Uncle Tom's Cabin* and *The Adventures of Tom Sawyer*.

After the Smoke Cleared at the O.K. Corral

When people hear the name Wyatt Earp, most immediately conjure an image of a fearless sheriff, a hero of the law-abiding Wild West who gunned down a gang of vicious desperadoes. That's the legend anyhow, the story invented by hack writers of Earp's day and popularized by Hollywood. The truth is a little bit more complicated, the line dividing bushwhacker and constable a bit fuzzier.

The Gunfight at the O.K. Corral happened on October 26, 1881, in Tombstone, a small mining town in the Arizona Territory. At the time, Wyatt Earp wasn't even an official lawman, though he longed to be one. Earp had recently vied for the county sheriff appointment, but territorial governor John C. Frémont gave the job to Johnny Behan instead. The only reason Earp was even present at the gunfight that would later make him famous was that he was temporarily deputized by his brother Virgil, the town marshal, to help him run off a small gang of ne'er-do-wells.

The Clanton and McLaury brothers were part of a loose network of cowboys—the word carried a pejorative connotation back then—of cattlemen who traded in stock of dubious provenance. They readily conducted business with known cattle rustlers, like Johnny Ringo and Frank Stilwell, who were not above other illicit activities, such as robbery and, on occasion, murder. The cowboys were welcome in town, as long as they spent money and stayed out of trouble. On this occasion, Ike Clanton was having a hard time doing the latter. On a two-day drinking and gambling binge, he had been making threats against not only the Earps but also their friend and associate Doc Holliday. Virgil and Morgan Earp observed Ike carrying a Winchester rifle and a six-shooter, in open violation of a law requiring visitors to check their guns at designated locations. The Earps disarmed Clanton and roughed him up a bit before taking him to the justice of the peace. Ike was fined for the weapons violation and was released on bail.

In hindsight, the gunfight doesn't appear to have been a prearranged showdown at high noon or anything like that. In fact, having concluded their business, the Clanton and McLaury boys were in the process of leaving town. Virgil, Wyatt, and Morgan Earp along with Doc Holliday confronted them as they were preparing their horses, not too far from the O.K. Corral. Nobody knows for sure what triggered the fight or who shot first, but when the smoke cleared Tom and Frank McLaury and Bill Clanton were dead. Ike had somehow scurried to safety. Virgil and Morgan Earp were shot but survived. Holliday had been grazed by a bullet, and Wyatt Earp was completely unharmed.

Far from receiving plaudits for their zealous law enforcement, the Earps were accused by many in Tombstone of being the real outlaws. A huge number of local citizens turned out for the cowboys' funerals, showing their sympathy for the victims of the gun battle. Before long, county sheriff Behan arrested the Earps and Holliday on charges of murder, but the local judge determined that there wasn't enough evidence to bring them to trial—despite seemingly damning testimony by witnesses. Some testified that the lawmen fired first, without provocation, and that the McLaurys and Clantons had their hands in the air, and that two of the victims were unarmed.

Ike Clanton wasn't satisfied with the verdict, and neither were many of his cohorts. The Earps and Doc Holliday had avoided the hangman's noose, but they now became targets for assassination. No sooner had Virgil Earp, who had since lost his job as town marshal, recovered from his gunshot wound than he was assaulted again. He was walking home one evening about two months after the gunfight when shots rang out from a partially constructed building on the opposite side of the street. Virgil took three shotgun blasts to his back, leg, and arm. He survived but lost most use of his left arm. Wyatt sent him to the family's California hometown to recover. Nobody witnessed the shooting, but Virgil had seen Frank Stilwell near the empty building just before the shooting, and Ike Clanton's hat was found near where the shooting took place. Wyatt also suspected several other cowboys of complicity, including "Curly Bill" Brocius, Johnny Ringo, and Pony Deal.

The suspects turned themselves in but were released due to a lack of evidence. Three months later, Morgan Earp was shooting pool in Tombstone when he was shot in the back and killed by unseen assassins. Wyatt determined that the only way to get his revenge was to take out his brother's killers personally. He formed a posse and tracked down Frank Stilwell in Tucson, shooting him to death. Next was "Indian Charlie" Cruz.

By this time, Johnny Behan had formed a posse of his own, this one to track down and arrest Wyatt Earp, Doc Holliday, and the rest of Earp's posse for the murders of Stilwell and Cruz. Remarkably, one of the men that Behan recruited for his posse was none other than "Curly Bill" Brocius. When Behan's posse caught up with the Earp fugitives, another shootout erupted, leaving Brocius dead. Behan and his men backed off, leaving the fugitives to their remote stronghold.

Eventually, Johnny Behan lost his job as Cochise County Sheriff, and the political will to bring charges against Wyatt Earp fizzled out. So, too, did Tombstone's fortunes. Devastating fires and diminishing returns from local mines spelled the slow steady decline of the former boomtown.

Wyatt Earp never did manage to get revenge on Ike Clanton. Clanton had moved away from the Tombstone area but never gave up his cattle rustling habit. In 1887, deputies shot and killed Clanton when he refused to surrender during a botched arrest. In the same year, Doc Holliday died of tuberculosis in Colorado. He had been sick for some time, subsisting near the end on a bottle of whiskey per day. The youngest Earp brother, Warren, was killed in a saloon argument in 1900. In the years after the famous gunfight in Tombstone, Virgil Earp, the real sheriff of Tombstone, recovered from his gunshot wounds. Without the use of one arm, he still managed to work as the marshal of Colton, California, and briefly ran his own detective agency. He later moved to Goldfield, Nevada, where he was a deputy sheriff for a short time before he died of pneumonia.

By this time Wyatt had deserted his common-law wife, Mattie Blaylock Earp, and taken up with actress and singer Josephine Marcus. Wyatt and Josephine lived a nomadic lifestyle, traveling from town to town, where the now famed lawman earned a living through gambling, operating saloons, investing in mining and real estate—even refereeing the occasional prizefight. Along the way, he built and lost several small fortunes in San Diego; San Francisco; Nome, Alaska; Goldfield, Nevada; and Los Angeles.

Late in life Earp embarked on an effort to publish his memoirs. He had seen several other books published about his exploits and longed to set the record straight—and make a little cash while he was at it. But conflicts with his collaborators and ill health got in the way, and he died broke in 1929.

The process by which Wyatt Earp and Doc Holliday became legendary heroes of the Wild West began with a series of articles written by his old friend, the Dodge City marshal turned journalist, Bat Masterson. It continued after Earp's death, when a biography based on interviews with Wyatt was finally published in 1931. *Wyatt Earp: Frontier Marshal* became a bestseller in spite of the Great Depression and in spite of Josephine Earp's objections. She wanted the book to tell "a nice clean story," but her publisher finally convinced her that a grittier tale would sell more books. Hollywood movies and television programs took it from there. Played by Henry Fonda in *My Darling Clementine* and Burt Lancaster in *Gunfight at the O.K. Corral*, Wyatt Earp posthumously earned a reputation that he didn't quite deserve: as the squeaky-clean marshal who cleaned up Dodge City and Tombstone.

Loose Ends

- After Wyatt Earp deserted her, Mattie was forced to fend for herself—not an easy task for an aging, single pioneer gal. To make ends meet, she resorted to prostitution and later to booze and laudanum to dull the misery of her new profession. She committed suicide in 1888.

- In 1882 Johnny Ringo was found dead in the Arizona desert, shot in the head either by highwaymen (his boots and horse were missing), a personal enemy, or himself. Ringo was known to be moody and had a perverse obsession with death. Later in his life, Wyatt Earp claimed that he had done the deed himself, but most considered it a tall tale.

Frank James Goes Straight

By the end of 1881, after more than a decade of bank robberies, the once-fearsome James-Younger Gang was decimated by six-shooters and jail sentences. Three Younger brothers, Cole, James, and Robert, were serving lengthy jail sentences for their roles in a Northfield,

Minnesota, bank robbery. Only Jesse James, who was believed to have murdered one of the bank tellers in Northfield, and Frank James remained living and unincarcerated. The rest were dead.

Frank had decided to quit the holdup business, but Jesse was planning his next heist with a couple of new gang recruits, Robert and Charlie Ford. On April 3, 1882, Jesse reportedly paused to straighten a crooked wall hanging in his parlor, when Robert Ford shot him in the back of the head. The Fords had schemed with Missouri authorities in order to collect a $5,000 bounty on Jesse's head.

Jesse was buried in the yard of the family farm in Kearney, Missouri. The Ford boys, much to their surprise, were immediately jailed and charged with first-degree murder. Instead of protesting their innocence, they pled guilty to the charges and were sentenced to be "taken to some convenient place and hanged by the neck until . . . dead." Hours later, though, they received a full and unconditional pardon from the governor. However, they collected only a small portion of the reward—there was some confusion about whether the bounty would be paid for Jesse dead or alive. The unpopular Fords soon left town.

Some said that Jesse's brother Frank was likely to seek revenge against the Fords, but that wasn't the case. By the time Jesse was killed, Frank was trying to figure out the smartest way to surrender to the authorities. He sought a pardon from the governor but was rebuffed. Basically, the governor told him that he couldn't be pardoned until after he was found guilty. Without any guarantees of leniency, Frank still decided it was best to face the charges against him and let the chips fall where they may. He was tired of running from the law.

Of course, in the age of vigilante justice, a prisoner's safety was never certain. One newspaper dared to wonder in print why Frank James, "the most hardened criminal in the United States," was not "taken out of the jail in Independence and lynched." But no noose was ever placed on Frank's neck, not by vigilantes, nor by the government. Frank was acquitted of murder and robbery for holdups in Missouri and Alabama but wasn't even tried by Minnesota authorities. Never convicted of any crime, Frank was released from jail in 1885.

The James Gang reportedly stole hundreds of thousands of dollars. Whatever happened to all that money, Frank's share was not enough to sustain him and his family. After prison, his first honest job was as a farmer. Tracked down by a newspaper reporter at his farm outside of Independence, Iowa, Frank claimed that he was "quite poor" and not sure "just how he would get through the long winter." He adamantly refused, he said, to attempt to profit from his notoriety as a bandit.

"I have received a bushel of letters from managers of first-class theatres who wanted to get blood and thunder plays written for me, and from managers of dime museums who wanted to place me on exhibition, but I have paid no attention to their offers." James flatly refused "to become an actor" or to be reduced to a sideshow "curiosity."

Asked if he ever intended to write his memoirs, James again demurred, asserting that the true story of his and Jesse's life was far tamer than the exploits depicted by dime novelists of the day. Any accurate account of his life would show "how little we did and how entirely lawful our acts were" and therefore sell poorly. Nope, James said, "I have chosen a farm life and I'm going to stick to it through all the rest of my days."

Whether James himself believed these statements, not one of them turned out to be true. When farming proved unprofitable, he became a salesman at a shoe store in town. He later applied his sales skills to a dry goods store. Other jobs included working as a starter for horse races at county fairs, as a traveling agent in the employ of a horse importer, and most demeaning of all, as a doorman at a St. Louis theater specializing in girlie shows. At one point, Frank attempted to transfer his doorkeeping skills to the Missouri legislature, but the Democratic leadership wisely voted against him.

The Ford Boys, on the other hand, had no scruples preventing them from trying to profit from their role as the killers of Jesse James. Unfortunately for them, their stage production dramatizing the event couldn't sugarcoat the fact that they shot an unarmed man in the back. Beset by depression, a case of tuberculosis, and a morphine addiction, Charlie Ford committed suicide in 1884.

Bob worked for a brief time as a police officer, of all things, in Las Vegas, New Mexico. But he could not escape his reputation as a coward. "If any citizen of the meadow town hereafter disobeys the law," one newspaper quipped, "Bob will bring him a sense of his duty to good government when said citizen may be hanging a picture." Challenged to a duel by an old accomplice of Billy the Kid, Bob did the sensible thing and skipped town. He turned to the tavern business but that proved equally perilous. A customer seeking his own notoriety blasted him with a sawed-off shotgun, killing him.

Frank James's career scruples receded with age. Faced with diminishing opportunities, he actually took to the stage but shunned plays about bank robbers and train holdups. He even sued the producers of "The James Boys of Missouri" because it "glorifies these outlaws and makes heroes of them."

Nevertheless, by 1903, James gave in to the inevitable and teamed back up with the last surviving member of the Younger gang, Cole, fresh from serving twenty-five years in prison for his part in the Northfield, Minnesota, robbery. Together the former outlaws staged "The Great Cole Younger and Frank James Historical Wild West Show." Reviews were mixed and the production was plagued by criminal parasites common to road shows of the age: pickpockets, sharpers, loose women, and con men. The show was a sensation in the District of Columbia but it didn't go over so well in Huntington, West Virginia, where the gang had robbed a bank twenty-eight years earlier.

The show closed down a year later and Frank returned to farming, inheriting the family farm in 1911 after his mother's death. For "two bits," Frank James would give curiosity seekers a tour of the family farm, regaling them with tales of daring robberies and shoot-outs. When Frank James died, his old comrade in arms, fellow gang member and business partner Cole Younger cleared up what had been a mystery for years. He told reporters that it was Frank, not Jesse, who had shot and killed the teller in the disastrous Northfield, Minnesota, bank robbery. Unarmed, the teller posed no threat to the bandits. Frank shot him on their way out of the bank, in spite for not opening the safe. So much for scruples.

LOOSE ENDS

- Jesse James Jr. found himself making headlines on both sides of the law. For a time he fell in with an aspiring outlaw who idolized the young man's namesake father. In 1898 young Jesse was even implicated in a train robbery but was later acquitted for a lack of evidence. In 1900 Jesse Jr. married a descendant of Daniel Boone. The couple had a tumultuous marriage, but they ultimately stayed together, raising four children. Jesse Jr. graduated from law school with honors and sometimes distinguished himself in his legal career, taking one case all the way to the Supreme Court. He also suffered from a nervous condition and experienced serious financial setbacks, including a poorly received silent film, which he produced and acted in, starring as his father. In his later years he was dogged by impostors claiming to be his father. Jesse James Jr. died in 1951.

- Zerelda James Samuel, Jesse and Frank's mother, was the first family member to turn the family farm into a tourist attraction, which one newspaper reporter described as "the strangest of summer parks and the weirdest of freak shows." The freak show reference probably had to do with Mrs. Samuel's readiness to show visitors the remaining stub of her right arm, the other half having been blown off by a bomb tossed into the house in 1875 by Pinkerton agents attempting to smoke out Jesse and Frank James. The bomb also killed the James's boys' younger half brother, Archie.

CHAPTER NINE

INVENTORS

WHAT is it about geniuses that makes them so inadequate in other areas of life? Several of America's most prominent nineteenth-century inventors displayed a pronounced lack of business acumen. Maybe those who trade in the lofty currencies of intellectualism are loath to wallow in the gutters of capitalism. Regardless, the inventors of the modern world's premier technological advances—the telegraph, telephone, and airplane—showed varying levels of incompetence in or indifference toward the business side of their inventions.

Telegraph Connects Baltimore and Washington, DC

On May 24, 1844, a tall wiry man, aging but still possessing the intensity of a Romantic painter, sat in a basement room of the U.S. Supreme Court building in Washington, DC, tapping out a seemingly random series of clicks on a strange little machine. At the same moment, the man's assistant was stationed in Baltimore, Maryland, monitoring the automated motions of an odd-looking contraption of his own, a device spitting out a thin stream of paper displaying a series of dots and dashes. Translating the code, the assistant announced the message instantaneously transmitted over the forty miles of telegraph wires: "What hath God Wrought!"

Indeed.

The occasion marked the official opening of the first long-distance telegraph line in the United States. Inventors in England had previously experimented with telegraph systems of their own, sending messages up to thirteen miles. The difference with the American system, developed by Samuel F. B. Morse, was that the message was recorded on paper. Messages sent using the English system developed by Charles Wheatsone and William Cooke were transient. If not for an operator standing by, the message would be lost forever.

The historic moment in the history of telecommunications was celebrated far and wide. As one newspaper put it, the telegraph was "the greatest revolution of modern times and indeed of all time, for the amelioration of Society." Some prophesied that Morse's invention would mysteriously reduce crime and even produce unprecedented levels of immediate and easy understanding, thereby reducing the likelihood of future wars. Perhaps it never occurred to any of these people that this amazing new technology could just as easily be used for less dignified and even suspect purposes. But the telegraph did in fact revolutionize communications. By making long-distance communication immediate, it had an enormous impact on all areas of modern life.

Morse had every reason to believe that his invention would make him a rich and famous man. It did eventually, but at an immense cost. Morse never could have predicted the scope and intensity of the problems caused by his subsequent attempts to profit from his intellectual property and secure his place in history. Actually, his troubles had started earlier, back in 1837, when he first registered his new invention with the U.S. Patent and Trademark Office. From that moment on, for the rest of his life, Morse was besieged by challenges to his patent from rivals who claimed to have beaten Morse to the punch or who subsequently developed unique variations on telegraph technology.

Morse brought some of these problems on himself. Because he loathed the business side of creating a large-scale, profitable telegraph system, Morse entered into one of the most disastrous partnerships of his life. He granted Francis O. J. Smith, a former U.S. congressman from Maine, rights to a portion of all future profits stemming from the telegraph. Morse believed that Smith's government connections and experience would open all the right doors. To some extent he was right. Smith helped Morse get his first deal with Congress, a $30,000 appropriation to pay for the wires connecting Baltimore and Washington, DC. Unfortunately, Smith never passed up an opportunity to demand more than his fair share of, well, every aspect of the business.

In charge of negotiating contracts for the construction of the Baltimore-Washington line, Smith insisted on hiring his brother-in-law to dig trenches for the underground wires. (This was before they decided it was more cost-efficient to string the wires high overhead on wooden poles.) Smith's brother-in-law subcontracted the work to a man named Ezra Cornell, who had devised a machine that would dig the trench and lay and bury the pipes all at once. Delays and shortages of material led to still more delays. Even though the work was nowhere near complete, Smith and his brother-in-law demanded payment in full. When Morse refused, Smith publicly accused Morse of incompetence and malfeasance.

These squabbles were over a fairly small amount of money, but the patterns established in this dispute were played out over and over again. Equipped with the moral code and fighting style of a hyena, Smith attacked his enemies at every angle. He never hesitated to make incendiary accusations, file lawsuits, enlist foes of his enemies—anything to win and profit.

Smith even joined in lawsuits filed against Morse by rival telegraph companies. Morse had to defend himself against more than a dozen legal challenges to his patent on the telegraph. Finally, in 1854, the U.S. Supreme Court, with Justice Roger Taney presiding, ruled unanimously in Morse's favor, putting all challenges to rest.

The outbreak of the Civil War proved that the telegraph would not necessarily facilitate the preservation of world peace. Quite the opposite, it turned out, as both sides used the telegraph to advance their military objectives. The Confederates seized control of the telegraph network in its territory, depriving Morse of any associated rights or profits.

The war also highlighted an extremely unsavory facet of Morse's belief system. Despite being a Northerner—born no less in Charlestown, Massachusetts, the cradle of American liberty—Morse harbored acute proslavery sympathies. Astounding to modern sensibilities, Morse based his support of the peculiar institution on lessons he took from the Bible. Master decoder that he was, Morse gleaned from the Old Testament a hierarchy of obedience based on four pillars of authority: the government's rule over its citizens, a husband's dominion over his wife, a parent's rule over its child, and finally, an owner's authority over its slaves. Any violation of these essential foundations was an affront to God. Morse thus arrived at a philosophy that put serious limits on personal liberty.

Like many antebellum supporters of slavery, Morse went so far as to argue that slavery was in the best interests of slaves, in that it provided them with "protection and judicious guidance" as well as the provision of food and shelter. Not to mention spiritual guidance. As a sign of slavery's value to the enslaved, Morse pointed to higher Christianity conversion rates among slaves than among free blacks living in Africa.

"Slavery to them," he concluded, "has been Salvation, and Freedom, ruin."

When the war ended, Morse refused to celebrate the preservation of the Union, saying, "I should as soon think of applauding one of my children for his skillful shooting of his brothers in a family brawl." Even if it had not turned out to his liking, the war had also precipitated an accelerated expansion of the telegraph system, connecting the nation from sea to sea, and making the septuagenarian Morse a vastly wealthy man. When he died in 1872 at the age of eighty, Morse was celebrated in obituaries as "the most illustrious American of his age."

LOOSE ENDS

- Before he became an inventor, Morse was a respected artist—a painter of portraits, landscapes, and historical scenes. When he decided to focus his efforts on telegraphy in the 1830s, Morse turned his back on a promising artistic career. In fact, he left behind a never-finished tableau, *The Gem of the Republic*, a representation of the signing of the Mayflower Compact. Previously, Morse was also commissioned to create portraits of important historical figures such as John Adams, the Marquis de Lafayette, and James Monroe. He even created some of the first portraits ever made using a new technology invented by Louis Daguerre. Morse operated his daguerreotype studio from 1839 to 1840, making portraits of wealthy customers and teaching pupils like Mathew Brady the new art form.

- Morse's assistant, Alfred Vail, never earned the recognition or remuneration that he deserved, even though he helped develop the technology of telegraphy in profound ways. Trained as a machinist in the family-owned shop, Vail engineered major improvements to Morse's hardware—the transmitter and receiver—as well as enhancements to the code that most famously bears Morse's name. Feeling squeezed out, Vail quit the telegraph business in 1848, just as the industry was coming into its own. Morse minimized Vail's contributions even after his loyal assistant's death in 1859. At the unveiling of a monument to Morse in 1871, the inventor mentioned Vail's name only in passing, a snub that infuriated Vail's widow, who was in attendance.

- Morse fathered eight children with two wives. None of them really amounted to much. One was convicted of murdering an Indian, but was later exonerated and became a cowboy in Buffalo Bill's Wild West show. Two of Morse's children appear to have committed suicide, though there was no definitive proof. His daughter Susan disappeared during a ferry ride, and his son Arthur "fell" onto railroad tracks moments before an approaching train crushed him to death. There's no doubt about the suicides of two of his grandchildren—one a son of Susan's, the other a son of Charles's.

- Dr. Charles Jackson was one of the people who claimed that he and not Morse had come up with the idea for the telegraph. His credibility was later called into question when he made similar claims about several other discoveries, including the use of ether as an anesthetic and the digestive functions of the stomach. He also claimed to have made advances in ballistics technology.

Bell Covers His Tracks

The story of how Alexander Graham Bell invented the telephone is a familiar one. On March 10, 1876, he and his assistant, Thomas Watson, were testing a new method for carrying vocal signals across a metal wire. Watson was in one room down the hall, setting up the receiver. Bell, positioned in an adjacent room housing the transmitter, inadvertently spilled some acid.

"Watson!" he exclaimed, "come here—I want to see you!" To his everlasting shock, Watson heard his employer's words emanating from the receiver. Over a century later this quaint story continues to define this milestone in technological history, but an examination of the events that unfolded in the coming months and years belies a far murkier, potentially nefarious truth. At least that's the conclusion reached by several experts and journalists who have studied the details of the telephone's invention, including a bewildering series of events at the U.S. Patent Office.

From the time Bell made his discovery, he behaved strangely for a man who had just invented a revolutionary new technology potentially worth millions of dollars. Did he take the story directly to the press? As a matter of fact, Bell himself never publicly told the story of the first telephone conversation. The story was unknown to the world at large until related in a history of the telephone published in 1910. Did he rush to the patent office to stake his claim to this invention? It turns out he didn't have to, because Bell had already been granted a patent three days earlier. This was highly unusual. To be granted patent applications typically required that an inventor submit a working model of the invention in question. To stake a claim to a technological advance still in the conceptual stage, Bell should have filed a document known as a caveat. A patent caveat, essentially, grants the inventor dibs on his intellectual property for a one-year period, ample time to build a working prototype. More about this later.

Having made his revolutionary discovery, Bell seemed oddly reluctant to publicize it. He squirreled himself away in his laboratory, along with Watson, presumably in an effort to perfect his contraption before making public demonstrations. The upcoming International Centennial Exposition of 1876 in Philadelphia would seem to be the ideal forum to unveil this new technology to the world, but Bell showed no interest in attending. His partner, Gardiner Hubbard, implored Bell to change his mind, but Bell was adamant, claiming that he needed to make additional refinements. Eventually, Hubbard played his trump card—his fetching daughter.

A year earlier Bell had declared his intentions toward Mabel Hubbard, one of Bell's deaf students and sixteen-year-old daughter of his employer and business partner. But her parents deemed the girl too young to get married to a young man of modest means and pedigree, however potentially brilliant he might be, especially since he was now proving inexplicably slow to capitalize on what seemed to be a potential gold mine. The Hubbards did not completely discourage Bell's interest in Mabel but asked him to hold off on his advances for the time being.

At first, Mabel had no more luck than her father in encouraging Bell to attend the Centennial Exposition, so she resorted to trickery. An innocuous carriage ride in the park ended up at the train station. Mabel shoved a packed suitcase into Bell's hands and told him she wouldn't marry him if he didn't go. He did, complaining that he would "be glad when the whole thing is over."

So, what in the world was Bell so afraid of? An accomplished public speaker, it couldn't have been stage fright. There was a deeper, more substantial source of anxiety, at least according to Seth Shulman, the author of *The Telephone Gambit: Chasing Alexander Graham Bell's Secret*. Bell's secret, Shulman says, was that Bell stole a key element of his invention from a rival scientist, Elisha Gray. Worse, Gray was expected to attend the Centennial Exposition, where he was scheduled to exhibit his own "musical telegraph" at the same forum. Surely Gray would presumably learn of the intellectual theft.

Let's back up a little bit. In 2004, Shulman was doing research on a related topic when he stumbled across an illustration from Bell's lab notebook. The image, which featured a variable resistance transmitter—essentially a wire suspended in a vial of mercury—was uncannily similar to one Shulman had recently seen in Elisha Gray's patent caveat filed on February 14, the same day Bell submitted his patent application. Two things struck Shulman as odd: Bell's lab notebook schematic was dated March 9, just two weeks after his trip to Washington. Even more suspiciously, Bell's notebooks contain no other indications of this idea's evolution. Up until this point Bell had been experimenting with a metal reed transmitter, with which he was only able to produce muffled sounds but not clear speech.

Could it be, Shulman wondered, that Bell somehow learned of Gray's innovation and slipped it into his own design, essentially adding the final puzzle piece to an invention he was on the verge of making? Shulman sure seems to think so, making the stunning accusation that Alexander Graham Bell committed "a clear and discernible act of plagiarism . . . on the crucial eve of his success with the telephone."

On top of that, Shulman learned that Bell had met privately with an officer at the patent office, who later testified that he not only told Bell about Gray's breakthrough but also permitted Bell to review Gray's caveat, a serious breach of professional ethics. As if that were not enough, the officer, Zenas Wilber, said he even lied about which inventor had submitted his documentation first, placing Bell's ahead of Gray's. Considering that the patent Bell was granted has been called the most valuable patent in American history, this was larceny of the highest order.

Bell denied the charges—especially that he had given Wilber a $100 bribe. However, documentary evidence suggests that some sort of irregularities may have occurred. Bell's patent application contained a description of a liquid transmitter uncannily similar to Gray's. However, that passage appears under an asterisk, suspiciously appended to the margin of Bell's application. Under oath Bell later admitted that Wilber permitted him to amend his application after their secret meeting. It certainly seems plausible that Bell may have based his added footnote on intelligence gathered illegally from Gray's caveat.

Shulman's iconoclastic accusations have induced an equal and opposite reaction among a cadre of Bell apologists, including Edwin S. Grosvenor, the editor in chief of *American Heritage* magazine and Bell's great-great-grandson. They point out that Shulman is not the first to question Bell's stature as the lone inventor of the telephone. Far from it. Over the years, Bell defended himself against hundreds of legal challenges to his telephone patent. Significantly, he never lost a single one of these court cases—though Bell Telephone did settle out of court with Gray's company, Western Electric, in 1879. Bell loyalists also assail the testimony of patent office clerk Wilber, who they say was an aging, impoverished alcoholic at the time he filed his affidavit impugning Bell. Wilber was put up to it by the founders of a newly formed company, Pan-Electric, who also paid off the U.S. attorney and several U.S. senators involved in the investigations. For what it's worth, in his affidavit Wilber claimed that poverty and alcoholism had induced him to accept Bell's bribe back in 1876.

It's unlikely that anyone will ever know just what happened back in that patent office. Several things are clear: Bell and Gray were both brilliant scientists who were heading in the same direction at the same time. Whether through accident, good fortune, or chicanery, Bell beat Gray to the punch and enjoyed the spoils of victory. But Gray fared pretty well himself. As the president of Western Electric he continued to innovate, taking numerous patents under his own name and others for his company. In 1887 he invented the teleautograph, a precursor to the fax machine. Gray died in 1901 shortly after collaborating on a device for sending long-distance underwater signals.

Bell, too, continued to invent, but thanks to his Bell Telephone stock he had the luxury to operate on the basis of a gentleman-scientist. When President James Garfield was shot by an assassin in 1881, Bell answered the challenge of devising a metal detector to locate the bullet lodged in Garfield's body. Unfortunately the bullet was buried too deeply, and Garfield died several weeks later of infections introduced by his doctors' probing—and unsterilized—fingers.

Bell was also inspired by the prospect of human flight. One of his companions in this endeavor was his friend Samuel P. Langley, the director of the Smithsonian Institution. The two spent countless hours at Bell's summer home, discussing and experimenting. Bell focused on a horizontal propeller system, a kind of predecessor to the helicopter, while Langley developed a biplane similar in design to the Wright brothers' "aeroplane." Bell later recruited Lieutenant Thomas Selfridge and Glenn Curtiss to his camp of aviation pioneers, two names that would figure in the history of human flight.

LOOSE ENDS

- Gardiner Hubbard, Bell's business partner and father-in-law, later established the National Geographic Society in 1888. The society sponsored meetings and published a magazine featuring technical articles targeted to experts. When Hubbard died in 1897, Bell took over as president. Two years later Bell hired his future son-in-law, Gilbert Grosvenor, to edit the magazine. Over the next fifty-five years, Grosvenor turned *National Geographic* into the internationally respected publication it is today. Bell helped shape the magazine's photographic bent, prodding his new editor in one letter to "run more dynamical pictures—pictures of life and action—pictures that tell a story 'to be continued in our text'!!"

- Thomas Watson, like Bell, made a fortune from Bell Telephone Company stock. After retiring from the Bell Company, Watson tried farming for a while but then turned to shipbuilding. His Fore River Ship & Engine Company built some of the U.S. Navy's first battleships capable of shooting torpedoes. Watson and Bell were reunited by telephone in 1915, when they were invited to conduct the first transcontinental telephone conversation in the United States. Bell sat at a phone in New York and Watson was stationed in San Francisco. Bell repeated his famous phrase, "Mr. Watson, come here. I want to see you." This time, Watson replied that it would take him a week to get there.

- Hubbard's granddaughter Grace Hubbard Fortescue, was convicted of manslaughter by a Hawaiian court in 1932. Her daughter, Thalia Massie, had accused several local Hawaiian men of rape. After a mistrial, Fortescue masterminded the abduction of one of the defendants, Joe Kahahawai, in the hopes of getting him to confess to the crime. She and several others were found later in the act of disposing of Kahahawai's dead body. The killers were found guilty, but their sentences were reduced to one hour of jail time.

Wright Brothers, Wronged

As the sun set in Dayton, Ohio, on December 17, 1903, Bishop Milton Wright settled into his study, but his thoughts were in Kitty Hawk, North Carolina, where his two youngest sons were testing their first powered flyer. Just then the Wright family's cook was at the front door signing for a telegram that would forever change the lives of the Wrights and the rest of the world as well. In telegram shorthand, the message read:

> Success four flights thursday morning all against twenty one mile wind started from Level with engine power alone average speed through air thirty one miles longest 57 seconds inform Press home Christmas. Orevelle Wright

Orville's name was misspelled, and two seconds were inadvertently shaved from the length of the longest of their four flights, but everything else was correct. And, by the way, they did make it home for Christmas. Good thing, as Wilbur was in charge of stuffing the turkey.

On that fateful day on the Outer Banks of North Carolina, younger brother Orville made the first-ever human flight unaided by wind. It lasted all of twelve seconds. Wilbur took the controls for the minute-long flight, which covered 852 feet. The Wright Brothers had discovered the secret to human flight. For the next two years, they were the only human beings capable of what had been until then an unimaginable feat in the minds of most people. During these halcyon

days the Wrights were relatively unencumbered by external expecta-
tions, complicated business relationships, administrative red tape, and
patent challenges. Sure, they were lampooned by those who doubted
their claims, but the Wright brothers possessed a serene confidence,
as well as a prescient knowledge of the eventual importance of their
discoveries—a self-assuredness that would carry them through the
adversities they would soon experience.

Forsaking their bicycle shop, Orville and Wilbur Wright immediately began tinkering with their design, building a new more powerful, sturdier, and more easily maneuvered airplane. Advancing ever
beyond gliding technology, in favor of powered flight, they no longer
relied on the gusts provided by the Atlantic's coastal winds. The following season's test flights were conducted in an open field near their
Dayton home. With each flight, they set a new record, traveling farther, flying higher and longer. Orville flew 1,760 feet on November 16,
1904. Later that day, Wilbur piloted the plane on a two-mile flight. A
year later, they were flying twelve miles in twenty minutes, then twenty-
four miles in forty minutes.

The world was waking up to the practical applications such a flying
machine might have, but slowly. Wilbur and Orville were confident
that the government would want to commission the building of planes
for military and governmental uses, but they got a chilly reception.
Instead of relying on reports of successes, the government demanded
proof, in the form of a demonstration, as well as detailed drawings of
the aircraft and a firsthand inspection. The only problem was that the
Wrights were still concerned about their hold on the intellectual property. The Wright brothers' patent, applied for in 1903, still had not been
granted. They were concerned that others would copy their designs and
beat them to market, so all demonstration flights were grounded for
two years, and the brothers refused to disclose proprietary information,

even to the U.S. government. Without a contract in hand, they were content to sit on their invention.

Finally, in 1906, the U.S. Patent Office granted patent protection for the brothers' "alleged new and useful improvement in Flying-Machines." Stung by the U.S. government's previous lack of faith, the Wrights decided to demonstrate the value of their airplanes to several governments simultaneously, including France, Great Britain, and Germany. Orville headed to Fort Myer, Virginia, to show the U.S. Army Signal Corps what their airplane could do, while Wilbur took to the skies in Pau, France. Each captivated his audience with flights that far exceeded any of the other rivals then competing for aeronautical superiority.

Even though there had been several mishaps and minor crashes, the Wright brothers had to this point escaped any significant injuries, but their luck would soon run out. In 1908, the government sent a number of representatives to Fort Myer to monitor Orville's flights, inspect the machines, and report on their potential utility. One of these men, Lieutenant Thomas Selfridge, boarded the Wright Flyer II for a test flight with Orville. After a smooth takeoff, the plane had barely reached its cruising altitude when a loud popping noise signaled a major problem. The plane nose-dived into the ground. Orville sustained a head wound as well as a broken leg and broken ribs. Selfridge was dead, the first person ever to die in a powered plane crash. Pinpointing and fixing the mechanical failure, the Wrights still earned the government contract of $30,000, a small fortune at the time.

The next few years saw their share of frustrations and outrages. The Wrights were repeatedly forced to defend their patent rights in court, as other companies began to manufacture their own planes using technology developed by the Wrights. It wasn't that the Wrights were insisting on a monopoly on airplane technology. They just believed that as inventors who invested so much time and money and who assumed so many risks to life and limb that they were entitled to a share of the profits. Ideally, they hoped to earn enough through royalty and licensing arrangements so that they could focus on what they truly loved to do: researching new technologies. They sought injunctions on companies selling competing airplanes and conducting paid exhibitions until they came to terms.

At the same time the Wrights were obliged to defend their reputations from attacks by aviation rivals who questioned the brothers' claims of being "first in flight." A cabal of scientists and inventors associated with the Smithsonian Institution closed ranks in an effort to diminish the discoveries made by the bicycle repairmen turned aviation pioneers. Octave Chanute and Alexander Graham Bell— friends of the late Samuel Langley, aerodynamics pioneer and onetime head of the Smithsonian—each added to the myth that the Wrights were acolytes of Langley and Chanute. They made it seem like the Wrights merely put into practice theories developed by their alleged predecessors. Subsequent studies have proven, however, that not only were the Wright brothers' innovations original to them but also that Langley's theories on aerodynamics were largely flawed.

Commercial and legal disputes drained Wilbur's energies. A notoriously taciturn and often morose man, naturally wary and reluctant to trust, Wilbur spent much of his time steadfastly protecting the Wrights' intellectual property rights around the world.

"Orville and I have been wasting our time in business affairs and have had practically no time for experimental work or original investigations," Wilbur complained. These were dark and vexing days for a man who would rather be confronting the challenges of aerodynamics in a workshop than haggling with lawyers in a boardroom. But what choice did he have? After all, "the world does not pay a cent for . . .

inventions unless a man works himself to death in a business way also." And that's just what he ultimately did. Wilbur died May 29, 1912, at the age of forty-five, of typhoid fever, his last days spent in febrile disorientation. Two years later, the Wright Company won a civil lawsuit that officially legitimized their patents.

Orville, even less inclined toward business affairs, sold the Wright Company shortly after his older brother's death. He maintained a role as a research consultant but never made any other truly groundbreaking inventions for the rest of his life. Like Wilbur, Orville never married. For much of his life, his closest female companion was his sister Katharine, who lived with him and his father for most of their lives. Their father died in 1917, and in 1926 Orville's then-fifty-one-year-old sister married a widower she had previously dated in her college years. Orville was distraught and furious, refusing to attend the wedding ceremony or to even speak with his sister, despite numerous attempts at reconciliation. It took a grave illness before Orville would relent. He visited Katharine on her deathbed just before she died of pneumonia in 1929.

Orville lived long enough to see his invention used for great accomplishments, such as Charles Lindbergh's Atlantic crossing in 1927, and the Lockheed Constellation's record-time-setting cross-country flight in 1944. He also saw his invention used to horrifying effect, first in World War I, then in World War II, when the Japanese bombed Pearl Harbor and then the atom bombs were dropped on Nagasaki and Hiroshima, Japan. He died of a heart attack on January 30, 1948.

LOOSE ENDS

- After its historic first flight, the original Kitty Hawk Flyer was never flown again. Damaged by winds, it was placed into storage where it remained for years. The Smithsonian Institution would have seemed the proper place to display this important relic, but Orville could not bring himself to add his invention to an exhibit that he believed misrepresented the history of human flight. Designed by employees loyal to former Smithsonian secretary Samuel Langley, the exhibit gave precedence to Langley's rival flying machine, the Aerodrome, even though it never achieved manned flight. Instead, Orville sent the Kitty Hawk Flyer to the London Science Museum in England in 1928. The dispute with the Smithsonian outlived Orville, but the museum eventually agreed to terms with the Wright estate to display the Kitty Hawk Flyer in an exhibit that accurately represented the Wrights' primary role in the pursuit of human flight. Today, the flyer can be viewed in its rightful place beside Lindbergh's *Spirit of St. Louis* at the Smithsonian's National Air and Space Museum.

- The Wright brothers were famously shy and reserved. As one contemporary said, "You have never heard true silence until you have talked to Wilbur Wright." On one occasion, when the Wrights were the guests of honor at an awards ceremony, they were asked to share some insights about their aeronautical feats. Wilbur reluctantly approached the bank of microphones. "Thank you, gentlemen," was all he said before returning to his seat. The even less gregarious Orville was content to let his big brother do all the talking, so to speak. He routinely shunned reporters and public speaking opportunities.

CHAPTER TEN

GANGSTERS AND G-MEN

W HAT did Al Capone, Eliot Ness, John Dillinger, and Melvin Purvis all have in common? Regardless of what side of the law they were on, they all relished the attention they got for their exploits. They were media savvy at a time when newspapers, radio, and newsreels were broadcasting their derring-do to an international audience. The intense publicity contributed to the downfall of Capone, Dillinger, and Purvis and did little to assuage the professional and personal failings of Ness—at least during his lifetime.

After the Valentine's Day Massacre

On February 15, 1929, George "Bugs" Moran could consider himself a lucky man. After all, he was still alive. The same could not be said for the seven men who the day before, lay sprawled in puddles of their own blood, having just been sprayed by a barrage of machine gun bullets and shotgun pellets. Moran would have been lying right next to them if he hadn't been late for the morning meeting with his associates. As his car approached the nondescript garage on Chicago's north side, he saw several men dressed in police uniforms enter the building. Moran retreated to a nearby coffee shop, at a safe distance as the most famous massacre in gangland history took place.

Most assumed the massacre was the handiwork of Moran's bootlegging rival Alphonse Capone. The two had squabbled over turf for most of the Prohibition era, attempting to control the liquor markets, gambling, and other illegal rackets. Some speculated the massacre was retribution for the recent murder of two Capone associates, most likely ordered by Moran. But definitive proof never materialized. Capone was in Florida when the shooting erupted in the north-side garage, and his go-to hit man "Machine Gun" Jack McGurn also had a plausible alibi. Even though no one was ever found guilty of the gruesome crime, the event marked a turning point in Chicago's gang warfare; the fortunes of all those involved—or suspected—would suffer greatly from this point forward.

No matter who was to blame, the Chicago Crime Commission and the FBI were alarmed by the intensity and boldness of violence in organized crime, and they decided to do something about it. While Eliot Ness was staging raids of Capone's breweries, the authorities began to look for other ways to bring down the underworld kingpin. The U.S. attorney in Chicago, George E. Q. Johnson, summoned Capone to Chicago for questioning in the St. Valentine's Day massacre. When Capone ignored the summons, Johnson charged him with contempt of court. Meanwhile IRS agent Frank Wilson was working up a tax evasion case on Capone, and the Chicago Crime Commission invented the Public Enemy list, naming Capone their number one target.

Collaborating on the tax evasion angle, Johnson and Wilson

eventually got their man. Although they had no proof of income, they built a largely circumstantial case based on the testimony of those who witnessed Capone's lavish spending. A man who spends $30,000 on a bulletproof limo and $50,000 on a diamond-encrusted ring must have gotten the dough from somewhere. Legal or not, income was income, and Capone had not paid taxes on it. The jury found Capone guilty on five counts of tax evasion, and the judge imposed a harsh sentence of eleven years in prison and $50,000 in fines. A mere three years after the St. Valentine's Day massacre, Al Capone's criminal reign had come to an end.

Capone began his sentence at a federal prison in Atlanta, where he suffered indignities like group showers and menial jobs. It went from bad to worse when he was transferred to the new maximum-security prison called Alcatraz, on a foreboding island off the coast of San Francisco. The man who once sat atop a criminal kingdom was now reduced to pushing a mop around the prison floor. They used to call him Scarface, now they called him the "wop with a mop." A fellow inmate stabbed Capone in the back with a pair of scissors. Capone also started to lose his marbles. Largely due to the effects of an untreated case of syphilis, Capone could often be found shuffling around the cell block muttering nonsensically.

Capone had lost his freedom, his health, and finally his wits. His shockingly precipitous fall was consummated one day when an argument between Capone and an inmate in an adjacent cell degenerated into a feces-throwing fight. Shortly after that episode, Capone was transferred to a federal prison on Terminal Island and finally released from prison on November 16, 1939. A shell of his former self, Capone no longer presented a threat to society. He lived out the rest of his years in his Florida home, subsisting on criminal revenues squirreled away before his prison sentence, supplemented by his brother Ralph's management of gambling and prostitution rackets. Capone's favorite pastime was fishing, but as his mental capacity deteriorated, even this pleasure was robbed of all significance, as he usually just sat by the waterside idiotically dipping a bare hook in the water.

Capone died of a heart attack on January 25, 1947, at the age of forty-eight. His wife, Mae, outlived him by almost forty years, dying in 1986 at the age of eighty-nine.

Things also went south for Bugs Moran after the St. Valentine's Day massacre. He went underground for a time. By the time he came back up for air, Prohibition was repealed, robbing him of the conditions that made bootlegging so profitable. Moran returned to his old ways, pulling small-scale heists and garden-variety burglaries. His lack of criminal versatility rendered him a small-time player for the rest of his career, which pretty much ended when he began serving the first of two prison sentences in 1946. While doing a stretch in federal prison, Bugs Moran succumbed to lung cancer in 1957. Any secrets he may have had about who perpetrated the St. Valentine's Day massacre and why died with him.

Though Capone hit man "Machine Gun" Jack McGurn was long a suspect in the mass murder, he never faced charges, mostly thanks to testimony provided by Louise Rolfe, the sultry girlfriend dubbed the "blonde alibi" by local reporters. But as with Capone, the authorities were hell-bent on getting the violent thug McGurn off the streets. When McGurn retreated to Florida with Rolfe, the authorities picked him up on a trumped-up charge of violating the Mann Act. Also known as the white slavery act, the law made it a federal crime to transport unwilling females across state lines to force them into prostitution. Not only did Rolfe travel willingly with McGurn, by this time she was actually his wife. Unbelievably, the jury still returned a guilty verdict. In a strange application of justice, they also convicted

Rolfe, presumably for being complicit in her own abduction. The defendants challenged the rulings in the Supreme Court, which threw out the convictions.

McGurn continued to live in the Chicago area, but with Capone in jail he no longer had an employer who appreciated his skill set. He even attempted—unsuccessfully—a career in professional golfing. An expendable hit man is a dangerous thing to be. On the seven-year anniversary of the St. Valentine's Day massacre, McGurn was bowling with friends at a north-side alley. Shortly after midnight, gunmen shot him down, leaving behind a greeting card that read:

"You've lost your job, you've lost your dough, your jewels and handsome houses. But things could be worse, you know. You haven't lost your trousers." The murder was never solved.

The police in Chicago, meanwhile, were having no luck solving the mystery of the St. Valentine's Day massacre. A major break in the case seemed to come in December 1929 on the other side of Lake Michigan. What started as a routine fender bender in St. Joseph, Michigan, turned into a high-speed chase and a shoot-out. St. Joseph police officer Charles Skelly was shot and killed. The gunman turned out to be Fred "Killer" Burke, a Capone henchman. Authorities searching his home found contraband and a huge arsenal of weapons, including two machine guns. Ballistics tests indicated that these were the guns used in the St. Valentine's Day massacre. Maybe Capone had hired the hit after all.

But it wasn't that simple. Several witnesses placed Burke in Calumet City on the morning of the massacre. And no one could say for certain how many times this pair of weapons changed hands on the black market since the killings. Burke was never charged with the St. Valentine's Day massacre, but he did spend the rest of his life behind bars for Officer Skelly's murder.

It turns out that the most plausible explanation for the massacre was in the hands of the FBI for almost eighty years. But the information didn't come to light until 2010. While doing research for his new book, *Get Capone*, reporter and author Jonathan Eig discovered what he deems "the most logical and satisfying solution to the crime." It was a letter dated January 28, 1935, written by a man named Frank T. Farrell addressed to J. Edgar Hoover. The letter details a series of plausible events leading up to the slaying. One night in 1928, a few of the Moran gang's boys were whooping it up in a north-side tavern when one of them got into an altercation with William Davern Jr. Davern was shot in the stomach. He died six weeks later, but not before he told his cousin William White who the shooters were.

A lifelong hood, White had pulled jobs in the past with two of Moran's cronies, the Gusenberg brothers, so he had the connections required to orchestrate the meeting at the S.M.C. Cartage Company garage. Eig pieces the motive and the means together with a heretofore ignored piece of eyewitness testimony provided by a passerby:

"Just about the time I arrived in front of the place, an automobile I thought was a police squad car stopped in front of the garage. There were five men in it. The fellow who stayed at the wheel had a finger missing." Sometimes referred to as William "Three-Fingered Jack" White, the crook had two fingers missing on his right hand.

So what would prevent Hoover from acting on this information? For one thing, White was already dead. It turns out that White had been acting as a federal informant, feeding the FBI useful information about other Chicago gangsters. But White's cover was blown in 1934, and the mobsters he betrayed had him rubbed out. If Hoover knew about White's involvement in the St. Valentine's Day massacre, he decided that it wasn't worth losing White as an informant. After he died, there was no point in pursuing the matter.

Loose Ends

- During his post-prison convalescence Al Capone was reunited with a long lost brother, James Vincenzo Capone, who had run away from home as a young man. Out west he adopted a new name and identity. He came to be known as Richard "Two Gun" Hart, a Prohibition agent who ironically specialized in bootlegging raids, not unlike the ones Eliot Ness performed on Al Capone's operations.

- Having inherited his father's genes—not to mention a case of syphilis—Al Capone's only child, Albert "Sonny" Capone, would seem to stand little chance of leading a law-abiding and productive life. He was a sickly youth who underwent treatments and operations for various ailments, but he pretty much recovered by the time he reached adolescence and actually lived a fairly honest and humble life. His only encounter with the law occurred in 1965 when he was arrested for shoplifting $3.50 worth of merchandise at a neighborhood grocery store. The previous year Sonny had made headlines for suing his old high school classmate Desi Arnaz. Desilu Studios was one of the producers of *The Untouchables*, the highly fictionalized television program that glorified Eliot Ness and, the Capone family said, violated the privacy of the Capone family. The Capones lost their case in federal court.

The Untouchables Disband

Anybody who knows the name Eliot Ness most likely associates him with the Untouchables, his team of loyal bribery-proof Prohibition agents operating in Chicago during the 1920s. But it turns out that Eliot Ness wasn't as instrumental in taking down Al Capone as once believed. Most of the credit belongs instead to the pencil pushing deskbound agents in the Internal Revenue Service. The Untouchables certainly did their part, raiding illegal breweries and distilleries, always making sure that reporters were close by to snap photos of agents smashing casks of beer and dumping thousands of gallons of spirits down the drain. But because the Untouchables never figured out a way to pin the bootlegging crimes on the mob bosses, their headline-grabbing efforts amounted to little more than a persistent but ultimately harmless nuisance.

So where did the legend of the Untouchables come from? Mostly from the imagination of a skilled coauthor, Oscar Fraley, who recorded and embellished the boozy memories of an aging and dispirited agent, rehashed a quarter century after they had occurred. The resulting book, also titled *The Untouchables*, bore this misleading tagline: "The thrilling story of the handful of incorruptible men who smashed the bootleg empire of 'Scarface' Al Capone as told by their leader."

But Ness's reputation as a Chicago crime fighter overshadows some of his biggest public service successes, as well as his biggest failure—all of which took place in a city that he is rarely associated with, Cleveland, Ohio.

With Al Capone in jail and Prohibition repealed, Eliot Ness moved from the spotlight in Chicago to the hills of Kentucky and Tennessee, where he continued his mission against illegal intoxicants in relative obscurity, this time targeting small-time moonshiners. But he quickly grew weary of performing on such a small and remote stage. His next opportunity to regain the spotlight came in 1935 when he was recruited to take over as Cleveland's director of public safety. At the time, Cleveland's police squad was rife with corruption. Precinct captains were on the take, permitting crime bosses to run their gambling, prostitution, and drug-running operations with little interference.

Who better to reform the system than the "incorruptible" Ness?

The former Prohibition agent applied the same zeal and skill that he used in Chicago to root out corruption in the police squad. Several high-ranking officers were indicted, convicted, and sentenced to prison terms. Others were fired or reassigned, breaking up the cycle of apathy and criminality. Having cleaned up the police force, Ness focused his energies on the rackets, securing indictments for a number of the city's top mob figures. Ness didn't wipe out organized crime altogether, but he did turn the city around, making it a less amenable place for the mobsters to operate their illegal enterprises.

Early on in Ness's administration, an event occurred that jarred the nerves of Cleveland residents and initiated a bizarre series of events that would represent the biggest failure of Eliot Ness's crime-fighting career. Two youths were playing along a deserted stretch of railroad tracks. Overgrown with weeds and littered with trash, the area known as Kingsbury Run was home to transients and other down-on-their-luck types. One of the boys came across something strange. Taking a closer look, he realized it was the decapitated and castrated remains of a murder victim.

It was the first of at least twelve similar victims, all beheaded and others more thoroughly dismembered. The majority of the victims were reduced to armless, legless, headless torsos. The killer seemed to prey on people residing on the lower rungs of society, derelicts, prostitutes, and misfits. For the next three years, the so-called Torso Murderer of Cleveland scattered his victims throughout the city, often varying his patterns to send cryptic messages or perhaps simply to keep the authorities off balance. As the number of victims piled up, Ness and the rest of the police were completely confounded. By the time the tenth victim was discovered, Ness was no closer to cracking the case.

"About all we have to go on," he confessed, "is that one of the victims we have been able to identify was a pervert and another was a prostitute."

Responding to criticism in the press about a lack of progress in the Torso investigation, Ness fell back on a tried-and-true tactic. He conducted a high-profile, large-scale police raid on the shantytown region where most of the victims were found, rounding up hundreds of hobos and burning down their makeshift homes. When all you have is a hammer, the saying goes, everything starts to look like a nail. The operation didn't bring Ness any closer to finding a killer. It merely traumatized members of the class that had been victimized by the Torso killer and now by the police authorities. The absurdly misguided act of aggression proved to be a public relations disaster for Ness. Changes in his personal life would soon add to his public problems.

Throughout the early years of his public safety directorship, Ness had lived a relatively sedate existence. When he punched the clock at the end of the day he retreated to the quiet suburban home shared with his wife, Edna. When the couple split up in 1938, Ness's social life changed drastically. Instead of home-cooked meals and beach walks, Ness now spent most of his evenings on the town, boozing and carousing into the wee hours. Some worried that his new social life might be problematic for such a high-profile goody-two-shoes like Ness. They would eventually be proven right.

Still smarting from the fallout caused by the shantytown raids, Ness reasserted himself to rooting out organized crime. He conducted a series of raids on gambling dens, which eventually led to nearly two dozen arrests of Cleveland's top mob figures. Ness also found time to overhaul the juvenile offenders system and enacted an extremely successful campaign for automobile safety.

In addition, Ness found a new wife. Ten years his junior, Evaline Ness was an independent career woman working in the fashion industry—not a homemaker, waiting for her husband to come home after work. After a long workday, the newlyweds liked to meet downtown for dinner and drinks and then go dancing at swanky social clubs. It was a very different marriage than Ness's first, as he now had an accomplice who abetted rather than discouraged boozy late nights on the town.

On their way home after one particularly late night of partying, Ness's car spun out of control on some icy roads, crashing into another vehicle. Ness left the scene of the accident before police arrived. A passerby took down his license plate number. It didn't look good that the city's foremost proponent of auto safety was involved in a hit-and-run accident, and it didn't help that the man who made his reputation as a Prohibition agent was driving under the influence of alcohol. No charges were ever filed, but Ness was pressured into resigning. He moved to Washington, DC, and worked for a time at the Federal Social Protection Program, a governmental initiative to limit sexually transmitted diseases in the U.S. military. Two years later Evaline left him and moved to New York, where she hoped to further her career as a fashion illustrator and designer.

Ness then had a string of jobs in the private sector, distinguishing himself at none of them. Five years after he left Cleveland in disgrace, he returned to run for mayor. It didn't go well. Ness suffered the worst electoral defeat in the city's history.

Finally, he ended up in Coudersport, Pennsylvania, a small town in the north-central portion of the state, where he eked out a modest living, along with his third wife and their adopted son. Ness spent much of his evening hours in one of several Coudersport taverns, spinning tales of his G-man days to skeptical patrons and bartenders. Virtually unknown outside Chicago and Cleveland, Ness was anything but a national celebrity.

Around this time, he had a chance meeting with a man who would change all that. A business associate introduced Ness to Oscar Fraley, a sports reporter for United Press International. Instead of shrugging off Ness's stories as dubious bluster, Fraley suspected that he had discovered a potential gold mine. Fueled by scotch whiskey, the former agent told Fraley colorful stories of stakeouts, raids, and busts. Fraley lent his writing expertise, punching up the stories with dramatic details. The resulting book, *The Untouchables*, would eventually sell more than a million copies and make Eliot Ness a household name across the country. But Ness would not live to see the day. A couple months before the publication date, he died of a massive heart attack.

Of course, it was the subsequent TV series based on the book, with Robert Stack in the title role, that really made Ness's name. The story lines for that show were entirely fictional, as was most of the plot in the 1987 motion picture starring Kevin Costner as Ness.

LOOSE ENDS

- Evaline Ness remarried in New York and eventually became an award-winning illustrator and writer of children's books.

- In 1998, the last surviving member of the Untouchables, Albert "Wallpaper" Wolff, died. He had continued his work as an undercover cop in New York, busting narcotics rings and even an illegal racehorse drugging operation. He was tapped to provide technical expertise for the 1987 movie, *The Untouchables*, showing Kevin Costner how to handle a gun and talk like an agent.

Punishing John Dillinger's Killer

On July 22, 1934, John Dillinger was shot down in an alley after watching a movie at the Biograph Theater in Chicago. Double-crossed by a madam friend who accompanied him to the movies that evening—she wore a bright orange dress so that federal agents could easily identify her fugitive companion—Dillinger met his end after a yearlong manhunt.

In the months after John Dillinger's death at the hands of the FBI, the notorious bank robber's main pursuer, special agent in charge of the Chicago office, Melvin Purvis, became one of the most famous men in the country and even the world. In 1934, along with Franklin Delano Roosevelt, Purvis was voted one of the most influential people in the United States by *Literary Digest*. The debonair agent's exploits were noticed by prominent Europeans, including the likes of Adolph Hitler and Herman Göring. In prewar days, Göring hosted the "beeg G-man" at his country estate, where the two unlikely companions hunted for wild boar.

Purvis certainly capitalized on his fame. He became a popular pitchman for Gillette safety razors, Dodge automobiles, and even Post Toasties cereal. Hollywood courted him as a consultant for gangster films. There was talk of a movie being made about his exploits, starring Cary Grant in the Melvin Purvis role. Purvis was even offered a role in one movie. He dated movie stars.

So what happened? How did his fame recede so thoroughly, to the point where he was virtually unknown to all but hard-core gangster fans, up until the recent motion picture *Public Enemies* reintroduced him to the general public? The answer stems from his complicated relationship with his FBI boss and mentor, J. Edgar Hoover. Up until Dillinger's death the two G-men enjoyed a warm friendship, and in

the immediate aftermath of the successful manhunt, Hoover was con-
gratulatory and warmly appreciative, writing Purvis, "I am particularly pleased, because it again confirms the faith and confidence which
I have always had in you. . . . My appreciation of the success with
which your efforts have met in this case is lasting and makes me most
proud of you." Hoover's letter also included the following comments,
especially significant, considering his subsequent attitude toward Purvis and the role he played in Dillinger's death:

> The shooting and killing of John Dillinger, by Agents of your office
> under your admirable direction and planning are but another ex-
> ample of your ability and capacity as a leader and an executive. . . .
> This would not have been accomplished had it not been for your
> unlimited and never-ending persistence, effective planning and in-
> telligence, and I did want you to know how much I appreciate it.

But in the coming months, the warm and fuzzy relationship
quickly soured. In its eagerness to sell papers the local and national
press heaped praise on Melvin Purvis as the singular hero who took
down public enemy number one. Bristling with envy at the press attention garnered by his subordinate, Hoover forbade Purvis from discussing the case with the media. Hoover tried to counter the generally
accepted script with his own version of events—a version that didn't
just diminish Purvis's role but completely eliminated it. In his book
Vendetta, an undeniably biased but interesting account of the Purvis–
Hoover conflict, Melvin's son Alston argues that "Hoover insisted
the focus be on the Bureau's cutting-edge scientific methods and
streamlined organizational system—structures that he had introduced," rather than on the "integrity and bravery" and the "good old-
fashioned police work" of "individual agents" like Purvis.

Of course, one could make the argument that Hoover was right—that there were legitimate reasons to discourage hero worship of individual agents; it could compromise the anonymity of agents, making it more difficult for them to operate in stealth, or it might be detrimental to bureau morale, in that praise focused on one person diminished the important contributions by other members of the team. Hoover, in fact, did make these arguments in letters and memos. However, his actions proved that it wasn't so much that he wanted to tamp down praise for any single agent, but for Agent Purvis in particular. Hoover didn't mind it when he was the subject of media attention. He also tried to undercut Purvis's reputation by feeding the media information that made it seem like another agent was the real hero.

Sam Cowley was, after all, the agent Hoover had nominally put in charge of the Dillinger case. In reality, Cowley and Purvis worked in tandem without jealousy or competition. But the fact remains that it was Purvis who arrested Dillinger's girlfriend, Evelyn "Billie" Frechette, it was Purvis who developed contacts with informants that led to his meeting with Anna Sage, the so-called Woman in Red who betrayed Dillinger at the Biograph Theater, and it was Purvis on the scene, giving the signal for his agents to close in on Dillinger, while Cowley manned the phones at local FBI headquarters.

Less than a week after Dillinger's death, Hoover brokered an interview of Sam Cowley in *American Detective Magazine*, in which Cowley was quoted as saying, "One man alone is responsible for the end of John Dillinger, and that man is J. Edgar Hoover." Hoover had read the article before it was published and gave it his blessing, proving again that he didn't mind individual praise for agents, as long as it was directed at him or those he anointed to receive it. And especially as long as that agent was not named Melvin Purvis.

Though confused and perhaps somewhat disillusioned, Purvis had more important things to worry about. With Dillinger on ice, he turned his attention to the manhunt for Charles "Pretty Boy" Floyd, the new public enemy number one. Once again, even though Purvis did not personally shoot Floyd, it was his detective work and his coordination of the team that led to Floyd's demise. This latest accomplishment brought more plaudits from the media, ratcheting up Hoover's distaste for his protégé.

Hoover was determined to run Purvis out of the bureau and to tarnish his reputation. He forbade Purvis to interact with the media and also sent agents out to perform a top-to-bottom inspection of the Chicago office, with the clear expectation that he would receive a negative report. The inspector obliged, but it was obvious that he had to strain to find anything wrong. His report was filled with trivial violations, for example, that Purvis checked into the office late one morning, that "dirty dishes were found behind a radiator in the store-room," and that the cell rooms were littered with "dirty underwear and shirts." It's hard to believe that the agent responsible for bringing down the top two public enemies in three months should be excoriated for lax housekeeping. As unbelievable as it might sound, the inspector concluded that Purvis "has not been exercising proper supervision over his office." Hitting on themes scripted by Hoover himself, the inspector attributed it to an excess of ego, suggesting that Purvis "had been giving more time to his own personal interests and to his social activities than he had been giving to the office which he represents."

Weeks later, when the opportunity to take down George "Baby Face" Nelson arose, Sam Cowley told Purvis to sit tight in the office, so that he could personally dispatch the next big crook on the list. He and another agent cornered Nelson in Barrington, Illinois, halfway between Chicago and Nelson's Wisconsin hideout. In the ensuing gun battle, Cowley and Nelson shot each other. Each died of his wounds shortly after.

Hoover, in the meantime, officially demoted Purvis, stripping him of his duties as special agent in charge of the Chicago office and relegating his star agent to routine tasks, like interviewing potential recruits and doing paperwork. Clearly, Hoover did not want Purvis to get anywhere near the action. Receiving Hoover's message loud and clear, Purvis quit the FBI, less than one year after bringing down Dillinger.

As disappointing as it was to resign from his dream job, Purvis made up for it by living the high life for a while. No longer restricted by a jealous boss, Purvis could do as he pleased. Publishers, movie studios, and advertising agencies all bombarded the famed agent with offers. He moved to California and dated Jean Harlow for a time, followed by rising starlet Janice Jarrett to whom he became engaged. Purvis wrote a book about his FBI exploits, *American Agent*. He was also the star of a new board game and comic strip.

Purvis may not have worked for Hoover any longer, but he never managed to escape his former employer's surveillance. Hoover assigned agents to monitor Purvis's business and social activities, even conducting covert operations designed to scuttle business opportunities.

Ultimately, though, the superficial, media-centric lifestyle did not agree with the sensibilities of a small-town, southern gentleman. Purvis closed his San Francisco law office and broke off his engagement to Jarrett. He moved back to South Carolina, where he eventually married his high school sweetheart, Rosanne Willcox, a mere month after she secured a divorce from her first husband. The couple had three boys and settled into a middle-class lifestyle.

World War II intervened, and Purvis enlisted as an officer. Despite more behind-the-scenes interference from Hoover, Purvis managed to wrangle a position in a unit tasked with ferreting out war criminals.

At the end of the war, Purvis helped establish legal procedures for trying Nazis at Nuremberg. He had an awkward reunion with his old
hunting pal, Hermann Göring, who appealed to Purvis for leniency.
Purvis, of course, offered none. Rather than face sentencing, Göring
committed suicide.

Back in the States, Purvis vied for several high-profile government
jobs, but Hoover managed to influence people behind the scenes, preventing Purvis from attaining a federal judgeship as well as other posi-
tions in the federal courts.

Things went downhill quickly for the former crime fighter. Suffering from ill health and depression, Purvis resorted to heavy drinking
and developed a dependency on morphine. On February 29, 1960,
Melvin Purvis shot himself in the head with a gun that once belonged
to a Chicago thug named Gus Winkler. Before any official ruling was
reached about the death, the FBI rushed out a press release calling
the death a suicide. Hoover did not attend the funeral. In fact, he
never even sent a letter of condolence to the family. The Purvis family,
however, did send Hoover a telegram, which read, "We are honored
that you ignored Melvin's death. Your jealousy hurt him very much
but until the end I think he loved you."

A handwritten note recorded on a copy of the telegram in FBI files
states, "It was well we didn't write as she would no doubt have distorted it."

Loose Ends

- Dillinger's bullet-riddled body was taken first to the hospital and then to the morgue. Although he was supposedly carrying thousands of dollars in cash when he left for the movies that night, investigators found less than $10 on him when they searched his pockets at the morgue. Without permission from the FBI, the Cook County Coroner permitted reporters and curiosity seekers to view Dillinger's corpse. By some estimates, more than fifteen thousand spectators streamed through the morgue, getting one last glimpse of the infamous bank robber.

- Evelyn "Billie" Frechette, Dillinger's sweetheart, was sentenced to two years in jail for harboring a fugitive. According to FBI files, Miss Frechette later joined a traveling circus, appearing in a sideshow called "Crime Doesn't Pay."

- Anna Sage, the Woman in Red, who betrayed John Dillinger outside the Biograph Theater, received reward money totaling $5,000, but she was denied her second condition, U.S. citizenship. She was told she could stay in the country as long as she stayed out of trouble and away from Chicago. Having blown all her money she returned to Chicago and was summarily deported to Romania, where she died of liver disease in 1947.

CHAPTER ELEVEN

GAMES OVER

WITH their astronomical salaries, today's superstar athletes can usually expect to enjoy comfortable retirements—and endless rounds of golf. But it wasn't always that way. Unfortunately, the ability to run fast, hit a baseball, or field grounders is poor preparation for life after sports. Jesse Owens, Lou Gehrig, and Jackie Robinson each faced major challenges in their retirement years, but all three yearned to make a difference in the lives of others.

Jesse Owens's Race to His Finish

In 1942, during World War II, a German soldier stationed in North Africa penned what he feared to be the last letter he would ever write. He addressed it to U.S. Olympic sprinter and long jumper Jesse Owens, the man who had won four gold medals in the 1936 Summer Olympics held in Berlin.

I beg one thing from you. When the war is over, please go to Germany, find my son and tell him about his father. Tell him about the times when war did not separate us and tell him that things can be different between men in this world. Your brother, Luz.

"Luz" was Carl Ludwig Long, the German long jumper who took the silver medal in the 1936 Olympics. Though a blond-haired, blue-eyed incarnation of Hitler's Aryan ideal, Long did not share Hitler's ideology, and he showed that in part by befriending Owens at the 1936 Olympics. When Owens made his gold-medal-winning jump, silver-medalist Long was the first to congratulate Owens, throwing an arm around his shoulder. The two competitors became friends, corresponding in the years after the Olympics. But the war got between them and ultimately claimed the life of Luz Long, who died in an Allied prison hospital in 1943. Eight years later, Owens would make good on Long's request, meeting up with his son, Kai Long, in Hamburg.

It was the first time Jesse Owens had returned to the site of his athletic triumphs. By winning four gold medals in the long jump, hundred meters, two hundred meters, and the four-by-hundred-meter relay, Owens dealt a dramatic blow to Hitler's theories about Aryan superiority. Things had not gone so well for Jesse in the ensuing years. The celebrations over his Olympic performance were short lived. Right after the closing ceremonies, Owens and his teammates were schlepped across the Continent on a series of barnstorming track-and-field meets organized by the American Athletic Union (AAU). It was a grinding schedule. Just two days after winning the gold medal for the relay, Owens was obligated to compete in an exhibition meet in Cologne, Germany. After a lackluster performance, the exhausted Owens was put on a plane for Prague and expected to compete again the very next day. After stops in Bochun, Germany, and London, the AAU team competed in five meets in less than a week. It's no wonder that Jesse became "pretty sick of running."

In addition to the exhaustion, Owens was worried about missing opportunities to cash in on his fame. He had received telegrams with promises of big paydays for various gigs. The AAU insisted that Jesse had an obligation to run in these meets. If he refused, they would strip him of his amateur status. That might not seem like a big deal, but there was no professional track-and-field circuit. The AAU and National Collegiate Athletic Association (NCAA) were essentially the only games in town. Without an international stage on which to perform, Owens would have to find creative ways to earn a living.

Still, Owens couldn't escape the feeling that he was being exploited by the AAU. He decided to head back to the United States, while the rest of the team proceeded to Stockholm, Sweden. The only problem was money. Jesse was so broke that he couldn't afford passage back to the United States, so a previous employer arranged to wire him the cash to cover his ocean liner ticket.

Owens received a hero's welcome in New York, where he met entertainer Bill "Bojangles" Robinson and Robinson's agent. After more homecoming parades in Cleveland and Columbus, Owens returned to New York to capitalize on his fame, but the outlandish offers of money turned out to be empty promises. Jesse's biggest windfall came when Republican boosters paid him to publicly support Alf Landon in his presidential run against the incumbent, Franklin Roosevelt. Estimates on the fee Owens received varied from $10,00 to $15,000. Jesse would only say that it was "a lot."

During the Depression, when a large population was out of work and when a decent workingman's salary topped out at around $2,000, Jesse should have been set for a while. But his overly generous nature got the best of him. He bought a house for his parents as well as expensive gifts for friends. He squandered much of the money clothing and bejeweling his wife and spent the rest on fancy clothes and cars for himself.

It was common for successful white Olympic athletes, like Johnny Weissmuller and Buster Crabbe, to receive lucrative Hollywood contracts, but the only show-business opportunities open to a black man were on the so-called chitlin circuit, nightclubs catering to African American clientele. Jesse Owens—and those who paid to see him perform at nightclubs—quickly learned that athletic prowess does not necessarily endow one with the ability to sing and dance.

Dogged anew by financial pressures, Owens resorted to low-paying jobs, serving at various times as a bathhouse attendant, playground director, and clothing store salesman. Unlike other black teammates who competed in the Olympics with him, Jesse had never earned a college degree, so his opportunities were limited. But he still had his name, and he could still run. One of the gambits Owens fell back on periodically was to run a footrace against a horse. He needed a head start to win, and it didn't hurt that the starter's gun usually frightened the horse. Demeaning as these exhibitions may have been, Owens had no other choice. As he said, you "can't eat gold medals," and he had a family of five to support.

Offers to race horses were too few and far between, so Owens took it upon himself to create a platform for his talents. He sponsored a basketball team, the Olympians, that toured the nation, taking on local basketball teams. At halftime Jesse would speak and perform athletic exhibitions. In the summer months, Owens's softball team, the Olympics, picked up the slack, with Jesse putting on long jump and sprinting clinics between innings. It was during these barnstorming tours that Owens and the other black athletes were reminded that their physical skills, though they could bring in paying customers, didn't shield them from racial prejudice. They were often turned away from whites-only restaurants and hotels.

In an attempt to secure long-term financial stability, Owens opened a chain of dry cleaning stores in the Cleveland area. The enterprise quickly went belly-up, saddling Owens with huge debts. To make matters worse, the federal government charged him with failing to pay income taxes. Owens declared bankruptcy and worked hard over the next few years to pay off his debts, primarily by touring with the Indianapolis Clowns, an all-black baseball team modeled after the Harlem Globetrotters.

Owens got back on his feet during and after World War II. Ineligible to fight, he was hired by the government to help improve physical fitness among the nation's youth. He later landed a job at Ford Motor Company, as director of Negro personnel. In the 1950s, Owens was hired by the U.S. government to conduct a series of goodwill ambassador tours in Asia. But the tax man came calling again, and this time Owens was convicted of tax fraud in 1966. He received no prison term and was fined $3,000, a fraction of the maximum penalty.

In 1967, when there was talk among African American athletes of boycotting the upcoming summer Olympics to be held in Mexico City, Owens did his best to persuade U.S. athletes that "the Olympics should not be used as a battleground for civil rights." Ultimately, a boycott was avoided and the games went on—but not without controversy.

Owens did his best to understand the younger athletes, but he found himself largely out of step with them, primarily because of his fundamentally conservative personality. He clearly sympathized with those who suffered racial injustice, but he was squeamish about the more radical elements of the civil rights movement—even deeming the relatively moderate Martin Luther King's tactics overly confrontational. Though branded an Uncle Tom by the more radical wing of the civil rights movement, Owens remained a hero to many Americans. It's not surprising that his stance on the Olympic boycott improved his reputation among white Americans, earning him lucrative arrangements with a number of prominent corporations.

Like too many athletes of yesteryear, Owens was a heavy smoker. It caught up to him in 1979, when he was diagnosed with lung cancer. Owens died three months later on March 31, 1980, at the age of sixty-six. Many of his Olympic teammates attended Owens's funeral, including Marty Glickman, a Jewish sprinter from the Bronx.

Memories of the 1936 Olympics were not so positive for Marty Glickman or Sam Stoller, the only two Jewish sprinters on the team. Stoller and Glickman performed well enough to qualify for the U.S. Olympic four-by-one-hundred relay team, but they were pulled from the team at the last minute, replaced by Ralph Metcalfe and Jesse Owens—even though Glickman and Stoller each posted better trial times than the two other sprinters who retained their spots on the relay team. Avery Brundage, chairman of the U.S. Olympic Committee, allegedly caved in to Hitler's wishes. It was bad enough, the theory went, that a black man threatened the superiority of the Aryan race. That two Jews would beat Germans at Berlin was unacceptable.

Glickman went on to play professional basketball and football, but he was best known as the sports announcer for the New York Knicks, where he coined terms like the *swish shot*. Stoller enjoyed minor success as a Hollywood actor. Avery Brundage would go on to become the president of the International Olympic Committee in 1952, a position he still held through the 1972 Summer Olympics, in which eleven Israeli Olympians were murdered by Palestinian terrorists.

LOOSE ENDS

- It's surprising that a number of Jewish athletes—as well as others belonging to groups persecuted by the Nazis—competed for the German Olympic team in 1936. Helene Mayer won a silver medal in fencing and later emigrated to the United States, as did Gretel Bergmann, the Germans' best high jumper, who was kicked off the team just before the Olympics. Werner Seelenbinder, a pro-Communist, anti-Nazi wrestler planned to protest the Nazi Party by making an obscene gesture on the medal podium, but his plans were foiled when he finished fourth. During World War II Seelenbinder was imprisoned in a concentration camp and later executed by beheading.

- Sprinter Ralph Metcalfe, who took silver in the hundred meters, behind Owens, and a gold medal as part of the four-by-one-hundred relay team, later moved to Chicago where he was elected an alderman. He also served in the Illinois and U.S. Congress. Another member of the relay team, Foy Draper, died during World War II on a bombing mission to Tunisia.

- The silver medal in the two-hundred-meter dash went to Matthew "Mack" Robinson, who finished just four tenths of a second behind gold-medal-winner Jesse Owens. Mack's younger brother, Jackie, would challenge some of Jesse's collegiate records during his years at the University of California at Los Angeles, before going on to break the color barrier in Major League Baseball with the Brooklyn Dodgers.

Lou Gehrig's Luck Runs Out

Most people recollect Lou Gehrig in one of three ways: as the power-hitting first baseman who led the New York Yankees to seven championships between 1927 and 1939, in the process, setting the record for the most hits in Yankee history (until Derek Jeter came along), and for the longest uninterrupted streak of games played in the history of Major League Baseball (until Cal Ripken Jr. came along).

Or they remember him as the baseball hero stricken with amyotrophic lateral sclerosis (ALS), whose "Today I consider myself the luckiest man on the face of the earth" speech on July 4, 1939, represents the high watermark in grace and humility.

Yet few know how Gehrig spent the last two years of his life after he made that echo-suffused speech at Yankee Stadium on Lou Gehrig Appreciation Day. After splitting the doubleheader with the Washington Senators on July 4, the Yankees stood atop the American League standings with a record of 52–17. Though he never played another inning, Gehrig still suited up for almost every game, both home and away. From his usual dugout perch, he watched alongside his beloved manager, Joe McCarthy.

The Yankees went on to win the American League pennant and the World Series, too, in a four-game sweep of the Cincinnati Reds. But Gehrig was visibly withering as the season wore on. His hands shook and his gait was wobbly. Once considered the embodiment of strength and durability, Gehrig now had difficulty dressing himself. Before the year was out, he even had to surrender the only ceremonial responsibility he had been able to perform. As captain, it had been his job to deliver the day's lineup card to the umpires, but the short walk from dugout to home plate became too much for him.

In the off-season, Gehrig had a decision to make. It wouldn't do to tag along with the team any longer. Besides, the Yankees made it clear that there was no place for Lou in the organization. Owner Ed Barrow—whom Gehrig had mentioned warmly in his farewell speech—informed Lou's wife that it was time for Lou to move on. As if suggesting that he retire and take it easy, Lou's teammates gave him a fancy new fishing rod and tackle box. But it wasn't Lou's nature to be idle. Besides, he still felt the need to provide for his wife, so he went looking for a job.

He also held out hopes of making a full recovery from this strange and little-known disease because he never truly understood how hopeless his cause was. Doctors told his wife, Eleanor, the truth—that he probably only had months to live—but as a favor to her they never told Gehrig the unvarnished truth. Not that he didn't ask for it. In one letter to his doctor and friend, Dr. Paul O'Leary of the Mayo Clinic, Gehrig said, "Paul, I feel you can appreciate how I despise . . . false illusions." Having said that, Gehrig told O'Leary about an acquaintance of his who made an astounding recovery from a similar condition. Gehrig wanted to know if O'Leary was familiar with this particular case and what hope if any he should take from it.

Following Eleanor's orders to "lie like mad" to her husband about his prospects, O'Leary replied that the case Gehrig mentioned "is just one of a group that have been improved and I trust that in seeing him you have been reassured that there is a damn good probability that you will do likewise." What O'Leary neglected to tell Gehrig was that this other person had recovered from a similar but less virulent form of sclerosis. Ignorant of the distinction, Gehrig naturally concluded that he would be "well on the way to recovery very shortly."

Buoyed by his doctor's dissembling, Gehrig was eager to find a job that would enable him to do some good with his remaining years. He accepted an offer from New York Mayor Fiorello LaGuardia to take a position as a parole board officer. Either LaGuardia was in the dark about the seriousness of Lou's condition or he was in on the ruse. Either way he offered Gehrig a ten-year term. Lou's job was to review cases and make recommendations to the commission about whether an offender deserved parole. One noteworthy person whose appeal Gehrig rejected was future world middleweight boxing champion Rocky Graziano. At the time, Graziano would later say, he "felt like killing him," but time and perspective helped the boxer realize that Lou probably made the right call.

Before the 1940 season, the Major League Baseball Hall of Fame, in an unprecedented move, waived the five-year waiting period and inducted Lou Gehrig on December 7, 1939. The Yankees also retired his number 4 jersey.

With virtually the same lineup, the Yankees could safely expect to contend for the championship in 1940 as well. But as the season progressed, it was clear that something was amiss with the world champion Yankees. As they fell back in the standings, some might have wondered if the anemic start was due to Gehrig's absence. *Daily News* sportswriter Jimmy Powers offered a different theory. In a story published on August 18, 1940, Powers suggested that Gehrig's disease may have been contagious and that the current players were suffering from the same mysterious lack of strength that slowed Gehrig down in the latter half of 1938. An infuriated Gehrig sued the newspaper for making negligent and inaccurate statements that caused the former slugger undue anguish and damaged his reputation. The paper ran an apology and paid Gehrig $17,500 in an out-of-court settlement.

Meanwhile, Gehrig's health deteriorated steadily. His wife drove him to work each day, where he sat in his chair watching helplessly as Eleanor performed all the physical aspects of the job for him. He dictated letters that she typed for him. She guided his hand in writing signatures on documents and even had to light his cigarettes for him, placing them gently between his lips. A heavy smoker even during his playing days Lou was unable to kick the habit, and his wife must have known how pointless it would be to deny him any remaining pleasures.

In letters to his doctors, Gehrig expressed frustration at the dissonance between the optimistic prognoses he was receiving and his rapidly worsening condition. He began:

> From what I am going to write, please don't judge me a cry baby, or believe me to be losing my guts, but as always I would like to know the actual truths and not continue to receive encouraging reports which have little or no chance of materializing, or to continue to live in false hopes. There is definitely something going on within my body which I do not understand.

After enumerating various setbacks—violent tremors, numbness in extremities, extreme weakness—Gehrig again beseeched his doctor for his "honest opinions."

If O'Leary at all regretted the decision to sugarcoat Gehrig's chances for recovery, the following paragraph of Gehrig's letter must have struck his conscience like a dagger:

> I hate like hell to bother you with these additional burdens of mine, for the Lord knows you have enough misery out there [at Mayo Clinic] each day and week, but I know you will also appreciate the confidence I have in you and your organization, and for that reason an honest opinion coming from you people is of vital importance to me.

Regardless of how it pained him, O'Leary resolved to maintain the charade. He hated to lie to his friend, he wrote Eleanor, "but I feel that with Lou we must keep his morale up, not only for the benefit and help it may be to him, but also in order to save him the shock that accompanies such discussions."

Good intentions and white lies could not disguise the facts, however, and Gehrig reached the conclusion that he could not go on working at the parole board. Instead of quitting, though, he characteristically requested a leave of absence on April 14, 1941. Just two months later he was dead—on June 2, 1941, sixteen years to the day after he replaced Wally Pipp at first base, at the outset of his record-setting consecutive games streak.

Lou and Eleanor Gehrig never had any children, so Gehrig left behind no descendants, and Eleanor never remarried. Like a latter-day Elizabeth Custer, she devoted herself to elevating and preserving her husband's reputation in the public consciousness. She signed a contract with Samuel Goldwyn for a motion picture to be made about her husband's life. *The Pride of the Yankees*, released in 1942, starred Gary Cooper in the title role. Masterfully replicating Gehrig's famous farewell speech—with minor revisions—the movie was a huge hit, earning eleven Academy Award nominations, including Best Actor (Cooper), Best Actress, and Best Picture.

Eleanor also wrote a memoir, *My Luke and I*, in which she described their romance and married life as well as her squabbles with Lou's overbearing mother. Lou's parents, Henry and Christina, always had a chilly relationship with their daughter-in-law, but the rift deepened after Lou got sick. At one point, the elder Mrs. Gehrig criticized her daughter-in-law's care for Lou. When Eleanor told Lou about it, he vowed never to see his mother again. But as his health faltered even more, he relented, and all three were there at his deathbed. Animosity between Eleanor and her parents-in-law intensified after Lou's death. His parents disputed the validity of their son's will. Ultimately, the parties settled out of court, but they never reconciled.

Eleanor was a loyal supporter of efforts to find a cure and treatments for ALS, which has of course come to be known as Lou Gehrig's disease. She died in 1984 at the age of eighty.

LOOSE ENDS

- Wally Pipp was the player that Lou Gehrig replaced at first base on June 2, 1925. Pipp had been playing poorly and made the mistake of taking his manager up on the offer of a day off. Gehrig stole the position, playing the next 2,128 games. Wally Pipp sat on the bench for the remainder of the 1925 season, pinch-hitting on occasion, but he never started another game for the Yankees. Sold the following year to the Cincinnati Reds, Pipp played a couple more years, then retired to play the stock market in October 1929—ever the master of bad timing. He wrote a book called *Buying Cheap and Selling Dear* and even wrote a few pieces for a fledgling magazine called *Sports Illustrated*. When World War II broke out, Pipp worked in a Detroit factory that produced military aircraft. After the war, he took a job selling parts to automakers. Pipp died of a heart attack in 1965. To this day, the baseball terminology used to describe a veteran's replacement by an upstart rookie is *getting Pipped*.

- Lou Gehrig was himself Pipped when he surrendered his place in the lineup to Ellsworth "Babe" Dahlgren on May 2, 1939. In his first game Dahlgren hit a home run and a double in a lopsided Yankee victory. Dahlgren batted only .235 that year, but his fifteen home runs and eighty-nine runs batted in contributed to another

Yankees world championship in 1939. Apparently he got on the bad side of manager Joe McCarthy who arranged for his trade between the 1940 and 1941 seasons. Dahlgren bounced around from team to team, all the while trying to live down a rumor that he was a marijuana smoker. A recent book by Dahlgren's grandson, *Rumor in Town*, makes the case that McCarthy was the source of the rumor. Perhaps the manager's loyalty to Gehrig permanently distorted his attitude toward the Iron Horse's replacement.

Jackie Robinson, Civil Rights Leader, Nixon Pal

As civil rights icons go, some might consider Jackie Robinson a fairly benign figure. Sure, he broke Major League Baseball's color barrier, and he did it with class and dignity, despite the ignorance he was routinely confronted with. But few would consider him a controversial or antagonistic figure. He never advocated separatism or violence. He was no Malcolm X or Stokely Carmichael. And as far as most people know, Jackie never committed any overt acts of civil disobedience. In other words, he was no Martin Luther King or Rosa Parks, either. No, in most people's memories, Jackie Robinson was a baseball player— but what a player.

Despite the death threats and the malevolent abuse heaped on him by ignorant fans, by opposing players and managers, and even by some teammates, Robinson excelled on the field. The Brooklyn Dodgers infielder played well enough to be voted Rookie of the Year in 1947. He was voted the league's Most Valuable Player in 1949, when he led the league in batting average (.342) and stolen bases (37). In his stellar career, he batted .311 and stole 197 bases, with an amazing 19 steals of home plate—straight up steals, not double steals, wild pitches, or pass balls. He led the "boys of summer" to six pennants and one World Series championship in his ten-year career.

But there was another side to Jackie Robinson, a far more complex and sophisticated side that is often overshadowed by the feel-good story of his athletic career and successful desegregation of America's pastime. This other side of Jackie's character emerged almost as soon as he retired from baseball after the 1956 season: Jackie Robinson, the business executive, civil rights leader, political campaigner, entrepreneur, and columnist.

The first thing Robinson did after retiring from baseball was to accept a job as head of personnel for the Chock Full o' Nuts chain of coffee shops. He also began his lifelong association with the National Association for the Advancement of Colored People (NAACP). His first initiative at the NAACP was to spearhead a national membership and fund-raising campaign. Robinson was elected to the NAACP board of directors in 1958. But even while on the board, Robinson expressed frustration with what he considered the organization's conservative approach to overcoming segregation and racism. People were going to have to get used to the fiercely independent, outspoken Jackie Robinson who railed against injustices wherever he detected them and expressed his opinions no matter who they offended.

As the 1960 presidential election heated up, Jackie's independent nature was again put on display.

"I am neither a Republican nor a Democrat," he declared. "I vote for people who I believe in, regardless of their party affiliations."

For Robinson, the litmus test was always the same: Which candidate will help further the African American cause? Before the primaries, Robinson believed that person was the U.S. Senator from Minnesota, Hubert Humphrey, whose civil rights record aligned with

Jackie's dream of a country that recognized the rights and freedoms of all its citizens, regardless of race, creed, or color. But when Humphrey lost the nomination to John F. Kennedy, a curious thing happened. Instead of throwing his support behind the senator from Massachusetts—as Humphrey and countless other Democrats urged him to do—Jackie actively campaigned for the Republican nominee, Richard Milhous Nixon.

This did not come as a shock to anyone who knew Jackie. Rigidly principled and stridently independent, Robinson frequently took political stances that confounded and frustrated his friends and colleagues. He didn't judge people by their ideologies or their associations, but by their words and deeds. So, for him, Kennedy was not the champion of civil rights that Humphrey was. He was a smooth politician whose politics and alliances changed with his present company. In Jackie's estimation, Kennedy was too willing to placate the segregationist southern Democrats to get votes. When Kennedy selected Texas Senator Lyndon Baines Johnson as his running mate, it all but confirmed Jackie's suspicions.

Nixon, it's true, was a member of the Republican Party, a party that Jackie had many times chided for dragging its feet on civil rights initiatives. But Jackie had personal relationships with both President Dwight D. Eisenhower and Vice President Nixon. He carried on an active and provocative written correspondence with both leaders, never hesitating to thank them when they helped advance civil rights or to scold them when they didn't. For example, Eisenhower frequently made vague declarations of unity with the civil rights cause but also urged that Robinson and his supporters show more patience. Robinson replied that "seventeen million Negroes cannot do as you suggest and wait for the hearts of men to change. We want to enjoy now the rights that we feel we are entitled to as Americans." These are hardly the words of a complacent man.

"You unwittingly crush the spirit of freedom in Negroes," Robinson went on, "by constantly urging forbearance and give hope to those pro-segregation leaders . . . who would take from us even those freedoms we now enjoy."

In addition to his private correspondence with government leaders, Jackie used the megaphone provided by his weekly column in the *New York Post*. Topics ranged from sports to politics, but usually politics. It was in his column that Robinson first announced his support for Richard Nixon. So what, in Robinson's mind, did Nixon have going for him? As vice president, he toured Africa, making respectful statements about the prospects for self-rule in newly forming or recently liberated African nations. And Nixon rarely missed an opportunity to issue statements that were sympathetic with the civil rights agenda, even if they were equally vague in terms of action steps.

Jackie took a leave of absence from his job at Chock Full o' Nuts and put his column on hiatus to dedicate all his time and effort into getting Nixon elected. In the process, he butted heads with Republican strategists and with Nixon himself over messaging and even the campaign itinerary. Robinson's enthusiasm for Nixon was not contagious among the overall African American population, however. Nixon lost the black vote and consequently the election to Kennedy. In one of their several spats, Malcolm X chided Robinson, saying, "Evidently you were the only Negro who voted for Nixon."

In hindsight, Jackie was disappointed to say that he was wrong about Nixon, but he was ultimately glad to admit being wrong about Kennedy. After Kennedy's June 11 televised speech on civil rights, Jackie wrote the president, "Thank you for emerging as the most forthright President we have ever had and for providing us with the inspired leadership that we so desperately needed. I am more proud than ever of my American heritage." In his *Post* column, Robinson enthused, "Speaking as one person, I can honestly say that Mr. Kennedy has now done everything I hoped he would do."

Robinson's renegade ways landed him in hot water on both sides of the political spectrum. Although he was an indefatigable supporter of civil rights, he was considered an Uncle Tom by the more radical factions in the civil rights movement. At the same time some in the Republican Party considered him to be a radical. When Robinson opposed Nixon's bid for the Republican nomination in the 1968 presidential election, favoring Nelson Rockefeller, William F. Buckley wrote a column saying that "it is surely time to put an end to the mischievous national habit of taking seriously this pompous moralizer who whines his way through life as though all America were at Ebbets Field cheering him on against the big bad racist St. Louis Cardinals."

Responding to charges of race-baiting, Robinson declared, "I am proud to be black. I am also embattled because I am black; but for white Americans of the Buckley ilk, I am only one of millions of blacks who are tired of it!"

When Nixon won the Republican nomination, Robinson again threw his support behind Democratic presidential candidate, Hubert Humphrey. Explaining his flip-flop, Robinson presaged, "If Nixon is elected President, we as Negroes are in serious trouble; we would, in my opinion, be going backward." After Nixon won the election, Robinson continued to criticize the Nixon administration's actions—or lack thereof—and especially took issue with the inclusion of "known segregationists" in Nixon's cabinet, like Spiro Agnew and John Mitchell, not to mention Nixon's alliance with Senator Strom Thurmond.

To the very end, in letters written in the last months of 1972, just before his death, Robinson maintained the pressure on the Nixon administration, taking it to task for failing to show any inclination to advance civil rights any further than was politically prudent. But Jackie never gave up on Nixon the man. He seemed to harbor a personal respect for Nixon not shared by others in civil rights circles. Never one to take chances, Nixon directed J. Edgar Hoover to open a file on his old friend, Jackie. They didn't find much, except for his early involvement in a couple of organizations branded communist. If Nixon planned to use any of this information to discredit Robinson, he never got the chance. Jackie died of a heart attack on October 24, 1972, at the age of fifty-three.

LOOSE ENDS

- For the record, Jackie Robinson did perform at least one act of civil disobedience. In 1959, while waiting for a flight at an airport in Greenville, South Carolina, Jackie and some associates were approached by a security official who instructed them that they were trespassing on a whites-only waiting room. Robinson replied that he had every right to be there and he refused to leave, even though he was threatened with arrest. The standoff ended when it was time for Robinson to board his plane. He also threatened boycotts against various corporations and participated in protest marches.

- Robinson's life in baseball, business, and politics made it difficult to be an attentive father to his three children. The eldest, Jackie Robinson Jr., had an especially difficult time as the son and namesake of a baseball legend. A poor student, he joined the army and served in Vietnam, returning to the United States traumatized by the violence he witnessed. In addition to being wounded, the younger Robinson also came home a heroin user. He struggled for years with his addiction and eventually seemed to have beaten it. Unfortunately, just months after getting clean, he died in a car accident on June 17, 1971.

- Branch Rickey, the part owner and general manager of the Brooklyn Dodgers who recruited Jackie Robinson, didn't stay with the Dodgers for much longer. In 1950, he sold his share of the club and later became the general manager of the Pittsburgh Pirates. Rickey and Robinson shared mutual respect and even love for the rest of their lives—Rickey filling a fatherly void in Robinson's life.

- Pee Wee Reese was the captain of the Brooklyn Dodgers when Robinson joined the team in 1947. Without Reese's support, Robinson's integration of the league would have been much more difficult. First, Reese chose not to join other Dodger players who said they would refuse to play if Robinson joined the team. Reese's principled stand put an end to the threatened walkout. Also, during one road game the fans of the opposing team were taunting Jackie with especially offensive racial slurs. Reese came over and put his arm around Jackie. This display of solidarity again muzzled Jackie's critics. After retiring, Reese managed the Dodgers for one season. He also worked for the Louisville Slugger company and provided color commentary for television broadcasts of Major League Baseball games. Later, Reese owned a bowling alley, also in Louisville. Reese was one of the pallbearers at Jackie Robinson's funeral. He died of lung cancer in 1999.

CHAPTER TWELVE

WORLD WAR II

WARS tend to define the lives of their combatants. In this chapter you'll meet soldiers who never had a second thought about what they did and whose pride sustained them throughout the rest of their lives. You'll meet those scarred by their experiences—some who endured their pain silently and those who flamed out in self-destruction. You'll also meet those who, profoundly changed by their war experiences, dedicated their lives to promoting peace and understanding between former foes.

Pearl Harbor

The Japanese surprise attack on Pearl Harbor on December 7, 1941, is of course remembered by all Americans as the most devastating and unexpected military defeat in our nation's history—up until September 11, 2001. On that "date which will live in infamy," 2,390 Americans were killed, the great majority being sailors on the USS

Arizona. Tragic as it was, in terms of human loss and the damage it did to the nation's morale, it could have been worse. Japan failed to follow through on the victory with further attacks that would have completely crippled America's westernmost military outpost. In the lull that followed December 7, the U.S. military quickly rebuilt many of the damaged ships and replaced many of the destroyed aircraft. In doing so, it avoided a retreat to the mainland, maintaining a Pacific force that ultimately checked and then reversed the Japanese onslaught of eastern Asia. Within just six months of Pearl Harbor, the United States won the decisive and pivotal Battle of Midway. From that point on, the United States never relinquished its naval superiority over the Japanese.

One unforeseen result of the attack was the great unity of purpose that it inspired in Americans. Up until then, many were unenthusiastic, to say the least, about intervening in the world war. However, the humiliating defeat aroused a bloodlust throughout America, reflected in an unshakable determination to exact revenge against the newly hated "Japs." In words ascribed to Japanese Admiral Isoroku Yamamoto— the principal architect of the Pearl Harbor attack: "I fear all we have done is awakened a sleeping giant and filled him with terrible resolve."

Things were not so clear-cut on the island of Hawaii, where the stench of defeat lingered in the air, months after the battle was over. A pall fell over the islands' residents, fed by the fear of additional attacks, concerns about the loyalties of Hawaii's sizable Japanese population, and a sense that someone should have known what was coming and made the necessary preparations. Hawaii was not yet a state, but as a protected U.S. territory, it was still governed by a democratically elected civil government. After the attack, the military imposed martial law, requiring nightly blackouts and curfews. Habeas corpus was suspended, and military courts supplanted the civilian judiciary. Freedom of speech was severely curtailed, as Japanese-language newspapers were shut down, along with many other Japanese businesses. It wasn't even legal to speak Japanese on a long-distance phone call. The military government did not impose a wholesale internment—there were far too many Japanese living on the islands for that—but they did inter some whose loyalties were in question.

In the meantime, the military forces were placed on high alert, taking defensive measures in case of ensuing attacks—measures that should have been put in place weeks earlier, according to some. In the years after the attack, inquiries have determined that military cryptologists had deciphered messages indicating an attack was imminent. However, that intelligence was never shared with the military commanders on Pearl Harbor. Besides, the messages contained no information about the target of the attack. Navy Commander in Chief Admiral Husband Kimmel did not believe that Pearl Harbor was in Japan's range. If an attack did occur, he reasoned, it would probably befall the Philippines. As a result, the only preparations he made were offensive instead of defensive, assuming that their forces would be called on to counterattack the enemy. Kimmel and Army Commander Lieutenant General Walter Short were relieved of their duties in the weeks after the attack. Kimmel was replaced by Chester W. Nimitz, who assumed control of the entire Pacific fleet.

The battle produced heroes as well as scapegoats. When the bombs started falling, Navy sailor John Finn rushed to his base and grabbed a large-caliber machine gun. He stood in a clearing, shooting at enemy planes for two hours, stopping only to reload, even though his body had been pierced by more than twenty bullets and pieces of shrapnel. Finn was awarded the Medal of Honor for his bravery. He continued to serve throughout the war and after, reaching the rank of lieutenant. He retired in 1957. When Finn returned to Pearl Harbor in 2009 to visit a boat christened in his name, he was the final surviving recipient of the fifteen men awarded the Medal of Honor for duty in the Pearl Harbor attack. He died six months later at the age of one hundred.

The first African American to receive the Navy Cross, Dorie Miller, also distinguished himself during the attack. A navy steward, he rushed to his battle position and began firing a machine gun at Japanese planes, continuing to do so until he was ordered to take cover. After bestowing Miller with his cross, the navy called on him to fulfill a different duty. They sent him on a speaking tour of the United States where he addressed recent African American draftees. Later reassigned to the aircraft carrier USS *Liscome Bay*, Miller died along with more than six hundred other sailors when the ship was torpedoed by a Japanese submarine on November 24, 1943.

After the "dastardly attack" on Pearl Harbor, President Franklin Delano Roosevelt was determined to strike a retaliatory blow upon the Japanese mainland. Dubbed "Doolittle's Raid" after the secret mission's leader, Lieutenant Colonel Jimmy Doolittle, the plan was to launch sixteen B-25 bombers from an aircraft carrier four hundred miles off the Japanese coast. The pilots would bomb key sites in Japan and then land in safe havens in China. Unfortunately, on April 18, 1942, the carrier was detected by the Japanese six hundred miles off the coast. With their cover blown, the pilots took off anyway, determined to accomplish their mission, even though they would not have sufficient fuel to get them beyond the Japanese-controlled region of China.

The pilots successfully dropped their bombs, hitting targets in Tokyo and several other major cities. In addition to the damage caused by the bombs, the raid had a far-reaching symbolic impact on both the United States and Japan. It provided a major morale boost to Americans still smarting from the Pearl Harbor attack. Being the first attack on the Japanese mainland, it struck a devastating blow to Japan's former sense of superiority and security.

Several planes crashed, killing two crew members, but the rest of the crew successfully parachuted to the ground, ditching their planes rather than letting the Japanese take them. Most of the eighty crew members made their way to safety, but eight were captured behind enemy lines. One of them starved to death in captivity, and three were executed by their captors. The remaining airmen survived the ordeal, gaining their freedom at the end of the war.

One of the survivors, Jacob DeShazer, converted to Christianity during his captivity and later returned to Japan in the postwar years, preaching the gospel and doing missionary work. In the 1950s, De-Shazer made the acquaintance of a recent Christian convert, Mitsuo Fuchida, who had been the head pilot in the battle of Pearl Harbor. After the war, Fuchida had expressed regret for his role in the sneak attack. Fifteen years later, Fuchida actually traveled to the United States to conduct a six-month evangelical tour. Despite some protest and even a few violent threats, especially during his weeks in Hawaii, Fuchida was for the most part warmly greeted by congregations across the country. Fuchida even had an opportunity to meet Admiral Nimitz. The two former adversaries broke bread and shared stories about the war years. He also met and became a good friend of Billy Graham. Fuchida made several trips to the United States over the years, a country he came to love. With his children and grandchildren living there, he may have adopted it as his home, but ultimately returned to his homeland, where he later died at the age of seventy-three.

Mitsuo Fuchida was not the only Pearl Harbor protagonist to cause a stir in the United States after the war. Minoru Genda, the Japanese fighter pilot who devised the bombing strategy for the Pearl Harbor attack, survived the war despite participating in numerous battles. Japan's military complex was completely defeated and dismantled after the war, but in the 1950s the need for defensive forces became apparent as the Cold War progressed. Genda joined the Japanese Air Self-Defense Force, part of the limited defense forces created with the blessing and assistance of the United States. As a high-ranking general, one of Genda's jobs was to evaluate and select aircraft to be used by the new air force—a job that resulted in a scenario that most Americans—especially ones still harboring painful memories of December 7, 1941—would consider unthinkable: Genda spent several months test-flying jet fighters in the United States. Ironically, Genda also received the Legion of Merit award from the United States Department of Defense in 1962, the same year he retired from military service.

In a later visit to the United States in 1969, Genda was invited to speak at the U.S. Naval Institute in Annapolis, Maryland. As reported in the *Houston Chronicle* on the 2009 anniversary of Pearl Harbor, the visit prompted angry protests by several U.S. Navy survivors of the attack. One of them sent a telegram to the Naval Academy saying, "It is alright to forgive and forget but not to toast and honor the coward Gen. Minoru Genda who planned the sneak attack on Pearl Harbor."

After his military career, Genda served in the upper house of Japan's legislature for over twenty years, where he promoted the remilitarization of Japan, even arguing in favor of keeping the door open to future uses of nuclear weaponry. Genda died on August 15, 1989, forty-four years to the day after Japan's surrender in World War II.

LOOSE ENDS

- Isoroku Yamamoto went on to orchestrate several more victories in the months after Pearl Harbor, but he also had a target on his back. On April 18, 1943, American fighter pilots, acting on intelligence gathered by U.S. code breakers, engaged Yamamoto's aircraft in a dogfight over the Solomon Islands. Yamamoto's plane was shot down, and his bullet-ridden body was recovered from the crash site the next day.

- Disgraced commanders Husband Kimmel and Walter Short spent the rest of their lives trying to restore their reputations, but despite numerous investigations, they were never entirely exonerated for failing to protect their territory and personnel from the deadly Pearl Harbor attack.

- Japan deployed five "midget submarines" as part of the attack. The two-man sub crews were supposed to conduct a suicide mission: to torpedo American ships and then to destroy their submarines before enemy forces could capture them. One of the subs lost power and ran aground during the operation. The two sub operators attempted to scuttle the craft in the rough seas, but one drowned and the other washed up on shore, unconscious but alive. Kazuo Sakamaki became America's first Japanese prisoner of war. Sakamaki begged his captors to permit him to commit suicide, but they refused. While in captivity, the prisoner repeatedly burned himself with cigarettes to punish himself for failing to complete his mission. After the war, Sakamaki wrote a memoir, *I Attacked Pearl Harbor*, and later worked as an executive at Toyota.

- One Japanese aircraft plummeted to the ground on the tiny Hawaiian island of Niihau. The two surviving crew members took two native Hawaiians captive, but the husband and wife hostages fought back, disarming one captor and killing him. The other one shot himself in the head.

- On January 19, 1942, Franklin Roosevelt sent a handwritten note to Vannevar Bush, a scientist lobbying for government support to fund a top secret bomb in its theoretical stages. "V. B. OK-returned-I think you had best keep this in your own safe FDR." This effort, later joined by Enrico Fermi and J. Robert Oppenheimer, would eventually result in the development of two atomic bombs.

Iwo Jima: After the Flags Came Down

On January 24, 1955, a Native American man with the unlikely name of Ira Hayes was found dead on a garbage-strewn street in the Gila River Indian Community near Phoenix, Arizona. An acquaintance of the family had found the young man—he was only thirty-two—in the cold early morning hours, face down in a puddle of vomit and blood. The coroner determined the cause of death to be exposure. Apparently, Hayes had drunk too much, passed out and froze to death. It would be a sad end to any life, but it was especially pathetic in this case, because of who the man was and what he had come to represent to a nation at war.

Ira Hayes had been one of the six men during the pivotal World War II invasion of Iwo Jima, who helped raise the flag on Mount Suribachi, a volcanic crater overlooking the desolate beaches below. The moment, captured by Associated Press combat photographer Joe Rosenthal, became one of the most iconic photographs taken in U.S. history. In the following weeks, the photo was featured on the front pages of newspapers all over the country. The six flag raisers were hailed as heroes, but things turned out badly for just about every one of them.

On March 30, 1945, President Franklin Roosevelt issued orders to retrieve the six men from the battlefront and bring them back to Washington. FDR wanted the Iwo Jima flag raisers to headline a war bond tour to raise much-needed funds to finance the war's final stages. But identifying and finding the soldiers proved easier said than done. It had all happened so fast and at the time was considered such a trivial act that no one bothered to figure out just who was in the picture. In fact, Rosenthal wasn't even sure he got the shot. Distracted by trying to get into the proper position, he almost missed it altogether. Just in case, he also assembled a larger group of men to pose under the flag for a backup photo. Identification was also complicated by the perspective of the photo. All the soldiers' backs are turned, or their faces are obscured by arms, shoulders, and helmets.

By the time they figured out who was most likely in the photograph, sad news came back to Washington: Three of the men had already died in the three weeks of fighting after the flag was raised on February 23. Many people assume that the flag raising came at the end of the battle, a symbolic gesture declaring a triumph already won. But it really occurred four days into a monthlong siege. The casualties after the flag was mounted far outnumbered those that occurred before. The first to die was Mike Strank, who succumbed to friendly fire, most likely a missile fired from an offshore U.S. destroyer. Hank Hansen, identified as the guy guiding the bottom of the flagpole into its rocky base, was shot by Japanese defenders. Frank Sousley almost made it through, but he was felled by an enemy sniper on March 21.

By the time the Battle of Iwo Jima was over, the U.S. invasion force suffered its worst casualty rate of the war. Of the seventy thousand men who landed at Iwo Jima, almost seven thousand died and another twenty thousand were wounded. Of the eighteen soldiers who posed for Rosenthal's staged photograph beneath the just-hoisted flag, only four made it back relatively unscathed.

Three of them were flag raisers Ira Hayes, Rene Gagnon, and John "Doc" Bradley. They came out of the battle with their bodies intact—though Bradley required several surgeries to repair a leg injury. Their psyches, however, sustained damage that could not be fixed so easily.

Following orders from President Franklin Roosevelt, the two marines, Hayes and Gagnon, and the navy corpsman, Bradley, were whisked off the island and flown to Washington, where they began a national war bonds tour. They enjoyed the fanfare at first, but as the tour progressed, all three began to consider it a tedious grind. It was bad enough that they were living out of suitcases, spending the majority of their time on planes, buses, and cars or in cheap hotel rooms. Even worse were the constant reminders that they had survived what so many of their buddies had not. It may have also been gnawing at them that many of their friends were still in the trenches, while they sat in parades and got slapped on the back for being heroes.

Hero was a word they all came to despise. Sure, they had all fought bravely for their country in the bloodiest campaign since the Civil War, but it was their inclusion in the photo that made them heroes in the eyes of Americans living Stateside. To these fighting men, the prosaic act of hoisting a flag was nothing compared to the other things that they and the rest of the marines and navy men had done. They had faced the Japanese enemy, turned them out of their fortified bunkers, and killed or captured them. Doc Bradley had come to the aid of countless wounded and dying soldiers, treating the wounded and easing the pain and suffering of the dying. Together, the U.S. invasion force secured the island of Iwo Jima, a key strategic piece of land in the Pacific, as well as an important symbolic victory.

That's what these brave soldiers could not seem to get their heads around. That, as captors of Iwo Jima and figures in the iconic photograph of the event, they played essential roles, in both practical and psychological ways. By securing a remote airfield they established a strategic outpost used by thousands of U.S. bombers. In securing the surrounding airspace, they also improved the prospects for the most decisive bombing mission in the Pacific campaign: the atomic bombing of Hiroshima and Nagasaki.

In his bestselling book, *Flags of Our Fathers*, James Bradley shares his father's oft-repeated belief that he was no hero. "The heroes of Iwo Jima are the guys who didn't come back." Perhaps suffering from survivors' guilt and even what would be diagnosed today as posttraumatic stress disorder, the remaining flag raisers wrestled with their demons for years, especially with every anniversary of the event and of V-J Day. They all resorted to alcohol, but none more devastatingly than Ira Hayes. His excessive drinking actually got him kicked off the bond tour, and he was sent back to active duty. Stationed at Pearl Harbor, he kept on drinking—usually alone—and kept on brooding.

After being discharged from the military, Hayes returned to southern Arizona. Moving back in with his parents, Hayes worked a string of low-paying, mindless jobs. He continued to drown his demons in booze on a nightly basis. Over the years he would be arrested more than fifty times for being drunk and disorderly. In May 1946, Hayes decided to take care of some unfinished business. He hitched a ride east and didn't stop until he reached the small dusty town of Weslaco, Texas. There he sought out members of the Block family. He wanted them to know that their son, Harlon, was one of the men in the famous photo. It was Harlon, Hayes told them, who was crouched down, back to the camera, guiding the flagpole into the ground, not Hank Hansen. For months, even before she ever met Hayes, Block's mother would tell anybody who'd listen that it was her son in the photo. Most doubted that a definitive identification could be based on a picture of a man's backside, but Mrs. Block insisted.

"I changed so many diapers on that boy's butt," she said, "I know it's my boy."

Analyzing testimony from Hayes, Gagnon, and Bradley, as well as a comparison of other photos taken at about the same time, the government determined that Mrs. Block's instincts were right after all. Unfortunately, Harlon Block died within hours of Hank Hansen on the same battlefield. Even so, Ira Hayes had set the record straight, and the Block family could derive a sense of satisfaction knowing their son died a national hero.

Over the years Hayes, Gagnon, and Bradley would reunite occasionally for events related to "the photo." The three retired military men even made their Hollywood debuts in 1949, playing themselves in a reenactment of the flag raising in *The Sands of Iwo Jima*, starring John Wayne.

Like Hayes, Gagnon had a hard time finding good employment. After failing to meet the qualifications for a job in the police or fire departments, he returned to the New Hampshire mill he worked at before the war. Gagnon was thoroughly embittered by the experience, feeling that one of the famed raisers of the flag on Iwo Jima deserved better. Gagnon died prematurely, of a heart attack at age fifty-four.

The only one of the three who was able to move on with his life was Bradley, the Pharmacist's Mate Second Class who watched so many of his comrades suffer and die on Iwo Jima. Back in Antiga, Wisconsin, Bradley finished his studies in mortuary sciences and opened his own funeral home. Bradley became a model citizen, popular with his fellow residents, not because of his military fame but because of the compassionate care he extended to his customers, as well as his philanthropic endeavors. Bradley died of a stroke in 1994 at the age of seventy.

In the years after the photo was taken, Rosenthal often repeated the story of how it came together and how he almost missed the opportunity to freeze the moment in history. Considering the controversies that sprung up and that continued for the rest of his long life, he may have sometimes wished he had never ascended the volcanic mountain in the first place.

First, there were the accusations that the photograph was posed, instead of an actual, unrehearsed event. Rosenthal unwittingly contributed to the confusion. Having sent the undeveloped film to the military press office, Rosenthal had no idea how the pictures turned out. He learned secondhand that one of his photos had been featured in numerous newspapers. When asked if the image was posed, he assumed they were referring to the posed shot beneath the flag and said yes. After he learned that it was his candid shot that had been published in newspapers all over the country, he attempted to set the record straight.

"If I had posed it," he explained, "I would have ruined it. I would have [put] fewer Marines in the picture, and I would [have made] sure that their faces were seen."

Fortunately, there was documentary evidence corroborating Rosenthal's version of events. A marine film photographer Sergeant William Genaust was standing beside Rosenthal at the pivotal moment, recording the entire sequence on film. Several seconds of color film show the flag being raised spontaneously as others looked on, followed by the assemblage of marines beneath the flag for the posed shot.

Even so, the genie was out of the bottle, and Rosenthal was dogged by skeptics his entire life. The photograph made Rosenthal famous, but like the flag raisers it depicted, it did little if anything to improve his fortunes or advance his career. That's not to say that Rosenthal was unsuccessful. For years he was a beat photographer for the *San Francisco Chronicle*, where he humbly and dutifully took assignments that others may have deemed trivial to a man who once worked under such dangerous conditions and captured one of the most enduring news images ever photographed.

According to an AP retrospective of Rosenthal's life and career, years later he was asked if he regretted taking the photo.

"Hell, no! Because it of course makes me feel as though I've done something worthwhile. My kids think so—that's worthwhile."

Rosenthal was also very proud of the Marine Corps War Memorial at Arlington National Cemetery in Virginia, which is based on his famous photograph. He died in 2006, at the age of ninety-four.

LOOSE ENDS

- Bill Genaust, the marine who caught the footage of the flag raising on film, was another one of the Americans who never returned from Iwo Jima. Enlisted to help clear out an enemy cave by lighting the entrance with his camera, he was shot dead by hiding Japanese soldiers.

- Part of the confusion about the photo's legitimacy came from the fact that Rosenthal's photo captured not the first but the second raising of an American flag that day. The first flag, raised by another group of marines, was photographed by marine photographer Sergeant Lou Lowery. The photographs of that raising got lost in the shuffle for a time, probably because the first flag was smaller and the images were less dramatic.

- Because it was considered dishonorable to be captured, most Japanese soldiers either fought to their death or committed suicide late in the Iwo Jima campaign. The last two Japanese soldiers to surrender on the island of Iwo Jima emerged from their hiding places in 1949, the same year that Bradley, Hayes, and Gagnon made their on-location appearance in *The Sands of Iwo Jima*.

Little Boy and Fat Man Postmortem

It had been almost a month since an atomic bomb code-named "Little Boy" demolished Hiroshima on August 6, 1945, and "Fat Man" descended on Nagasaki three days later. By then the American public had learned many details about the Manhattan Project, the top secret initiative to develop and deploy these unprecedented weapons. They knew that the bombs had been dropped, that they'd worked, and that tens of thousands of Japanese had died, most of them civilians. They also knew that Japan surrendered on August 15, three months after Germany did. Peace in the Pacific theater was formally ensured when representatives from Japan and the United States signed the Instrument of Surrender aboard the USS *Missouri* on September 2, 1945. The Manhattan Project's leader, J. Robert Oppenheimer, had also become a scientific celebrity, appearing on the covers of *Time* and *Life* magazines.

But there was a lot about the bombings that would remain unknown for quite some time—mostly because the U.S. military was now fighting a public relations battle. Throughout the world, critics were questioning the decision to employ a weapon capable of unleashing such horrific power. Japan was already teetering on the edge of surrender, some objected. Others simply considered the instantaneous extermination of tens of thousands of civilians morally repugnant. Others worried about the potential long-term dangers stemming from radiation exposure.

In the face of these criticisms, it was imperative that the U.S. military take control of the media coverage. General Douglas MacArthur enforced a news embargo, forbidding reporters from entering Hiroshima and Nagasaki in the weeks after the bombing. Not even U.S. military occupation forces entered the bombing sites until the end of September. Two reporters, however, defied MacArthur. Australian reporter Wilfred Burchett sneaked into Hiroshima on September 3, 1945, and American reporter George Weller infiltrated Nagasaki on September 6, disguised as a member of the U.S. Army.

Meanwhile, the U.S. government organized a press junket to the bombed cities, chaperoned by military personnel. Reporters were provided with a narrow, carefully orchestrated glimpse of the damages and were forbidden to question Japanese doctors about the effects of radiation. In an attempt to focus attention on Japanese atrocities, U.S. military handlers shepherded the reporters to POW camps, which were filled with newly liberated Allied prisoners, many showing the effects of malnutrition, torture, and slavery.

While in Nagasaki, the reporters were surprised to encounter their colleague George Weller, the Pulitzer Prize–winning reporter from the Chicago *Daily News*. Slipping into the city three days before any Western journalist, Weller had been writing eye-opening firsthand stories on the bomb's awesome destructive power—of the forty thousand victims killed, many of them instantly within the mile-wide ground zero.

Weller may have ignored MacArthur's orders to keep out of Nagasaki but decided not to skirt the military news protocol entirely. He dutifully sent his reports to the military press office. Not until weeks later did he learn that all of the reports and photographs he sent were destroyed on MacArthur's orders. Burchett managed to get his uncensored story to the *Daily Express* in London, which published it under the headline "The Atomic Plague."

"Hiroshima does not look like a bombed city," Burchett reported. "It looks as if a monster steamroller has passed over it and squashed it out of existence." In addition to the people who died as a result of the initial concussive impact and heat, Burchett couldn't help but notice that the bomb continued to claim victims—a hundred a day—long after detonation.

"People are still dying, mysteriously and horribly—people who were uninjured in the cataclysm from an unknown something which I can only describe as the atomic plague."

Weller had noticed a similar phenomenon in Nagasaki. Doctors there called it "Disease X."

Meanwhile, the father of the atom bomb, Oppenheimer, was having his own misgivings about the horrors he had wrought. Associates noted that Oppenheimer was noticeably anxious and lugubrious about what the bomb meant in terms of human survival and his role in unleashing this dismal power. On October 25, 1945, Oppenheimer met with President Harry Truman, the man who authorized the bombings of Hiroshima and Nagasaki.

"Mr. President," he fretted, "I feel I have blood on my hands."

If Oppenheimer was looking to create a sympathetic bond with the only other man who could be said to share the same degree of culpability in the matter, he was mistaken. Truman dismissed the scientist's qualms and ended the meeting. Later, he privately referred to Oppenheimer as a "cry-baby" and a "son-of-a-bitch."

"He hasn't half as much blood on his hands as I have," Truman complained. "You just don't go around belly-aching about it."

Marshaling his thoughts and steeling his nerves, Oppenheimer joined with like-minded colleagues in an attempt to steward a peaceful future for nuclear science. The only way to reap the benefits of nuclear power while avoiding a nuclear Armageddon, Oppenheimer claimed, was to create an international atomic commission. This commission would perform the necessary experiments and develop nuclear energy technology, while monitoring its uses in various countries to make sure that it was being used safely and responsibly. Above all, Oppenheimer insisted, "I would say that no [more] bombs be made."

To create and maintain the governing body envisioned by Oppenheimer, individual nations would have to surrender a portion of their sovereignty. No longer would nations—the United States included—be free to make unilateral decisions regarding the development and use of nuclear energy or warfare.

"The peoples of this world must unite or they will perish," Oppenheimer concluded. With fifty years of Cold War politics in our rearview mirrors, it's tempting to scoff at the political naïveté of this proposition, but Oppenheimer was not in the minority among the scientists who developed the atomic bomb at Los Alamos.

Truman had other ideas. Foolishly believing that the United States could maintain a perpetual monopoly on atomic weaponry, Truman saw no reason to share the technology with others. Despite these differences, Truman approved Oppenheimer's appointment to the Atomic Energy Commission (AEC).

Oppenheimer served as chairman of the General Advisory Committee of the AEC, and he also returned to teaching physics at Caltech and then Berkeley. All the while, he was under surveillance by the Federal Bureau of Investigation. His phones were tapped, his movements were monitored, and his associates were scrutinized. J. Edgar Hoover took a personal interest in his case, trying to prove that Oppenheimer was a closet communist and sexual pervert. Oppenheimer freely admitted that he had once felt sympathy for communist causes, but only in terms of helping to further workers' economic rights. He was never a member of the Communist Party and would never think of sharing any secrets about the atomic bomb with the Soviets or any other country.

Somebody had, however, and it was someone on the Manhattan Project, Klaus Fuchs, who had come to Los Alamos as a member of the British scientific team. Thanks in part to Fuchs, the Soviets had their own atomic bomb by 1949. This development led to an all-out nuclear arms race. Not content to simply stockpile more and more atomic bombs of the Hiroshima and Nagasaki variety, Truman and others argued in favor of a hydrogen bomb—a technological quantum leap in nuclear weaponry. Oppenheimer was opposed to the idea on moral and strategic grounds. At odds with political leaders, as well as members of the AEC, Oppenheimer was pressured to resign, and when he refused, he became the subject of a formal investigation.

On December 23, 1953, the commission presented Oppenheimer with a list of charges. They dredged up the now-stale accusation that he was a communist. And they suggested that his opposition to the H-bomb was un-American. Thus the man who was more responsible than any other for the development of the bomb that ended World War II was forced to defend himself before an AEC security panel. After intense hearings—showing all the earmarks of the McCarthy era—the panel ultimately declared Oppenheimer an unacceptable security risk. They stripped him of his security clearance and removed him from his position.

Disgraced and dispirited, Oppenheimer refused to let this episode destroy his sense of worth or prevent him from making significant intellectual contributions to the world at large. He continued to serve as director of the Institute for Advanced Study, wrote books, and delivered lectures. He earned a degree of redemption in 1963 when the Atomic Energy Commission presented him with the Enrico Fermi Award. President Lyndon Johnson also restored Oppenheimer's security clearance. Oppenheimer died of throat cancer in 1967 at the age of sixty-two.

LOOSE ENDS

- George Weller kept carbon copies of his censored dispatches from Nagasaki, but eventually misplaced them. After his death in 2002, his son discovered the papers in an attic. Four years later, the articles were published as a book, *First into Nagasaki*.

- Colonel Paul Tibbets was the lead pilot on the *Enola Gay*, the aircraft—named for his mother—that dropped Little Boy on Hiroshima. After the war, Tibbets remained with the Air Force, where he had a varied and distinguished career of twenty-nine years. Tibbets was proud of his service and had no regrets about dropping the bomb. Tibbets was back in the news in 1995, during the controversy sparked by the Smithsonian's *Enola Gay* exhibit marking the fiftieth anniversary of the bombing of Hiroshima. He was among the military veterans who objected to the tenor of the exhibit, which placed more emphasis on the Japanese victims than on their empire's military aggression. Tibbets died in 2007 at the age of ninety-two.

- Klaus Fuchs admitted his role in sharing secrets related to the atomic bomb with the Soviet Union. He also acted as a government informant, providing the British government with information that eventually led to the conviction and execution of Ethel and Julius Rosenberg. After serving part of a fourteen-year sentence, Fuchs was released from jail in 1959. He moved to East Germany, where he continued to work as a scientist. He died in 1988.

CHAPTER THIRTEEN

HAPPY DAYS NO MORE

THE celebrations after the end of World War II didn't last long. The good feelings stoked by the conquest of fascism were doused by a new ideological threat, communism. The spiraling strength of the Soviet Union—especially worrisome in the atomic age—the Korean War, and the perceived spread of communist sentiment at home, combined to make for a complicated era in American history.

In this chapter, you'll read about what happened after the House Committee on Un-American Activities (HUAC) hearings attempted to expose subversive elements in the motion picture industry and learn about the curious retirement years of Harry Truman and Douglas MacArthur.

Hollywood Ending

In October 1947, the House Un-American Activities Committee conducted hearings intended to ferret out communist infiltration of the motion picture industry. The committee subpoenaed forty-one individuals. The first ones to take the stand were so-called friendly witnesses like Adolphe Menjou, Walt Disney, Gary Cooper, and Ayn Rand who cooperated with the committee, motivated either by patriotism, fear, or a combination of the two.

Some named names of suspected "commies," others railed against organizations they considered communist fronts, and all took the opportunity to profess their allegiance to the U.S. Constitution and enthusiastically supported any efforts to purge Hollywood of "reds."

Many of the remaining unfriendly witnesses—current or lapsed Communist Party members as well as sympathizers and civil libertarians—indicated that they would not cooperate with the committee. Eleven were called to the stand. One by one, they were sworn in, and one by one they were asked, "Are you now or have you ever been a member of the Communist Party?" Several defendants attempted to launch into diatribes of their own, questioning the legitimacy of the proceedings, but boisterous committee chairman, New Jersey Republican J. Parnell Thomas, was having none of it. He cut them off, denying them their free speech rights, issuing grandstanding browbeatings in the process. The only foreigner among the eleven, Bertolt Brecht, fled the country. The remaining ten were charged with being in contempt of Congress.

The Hollywood Ten, as they came to be called, was made up of screenwriters Ring Lardner Jr., Dalton Trumbo, Alvah Bessie, Lester Cole, John Howard Lawson, Samuel Ornitz, and Albert Maltz along with writer-director Herbert Biberman, writer-producer Adrian Scott, and director Edward Dmytryk. All were accomplished professionals with credits to their names, though some worked primarily on B movies. Among the writers, the best known were probably Oscar-nominated Trumbo (*Kitty Foyle*) and Lardner, who had won an Academy Award in 1942 for *Woman of the Year*, starring Spencer Tracy and Katharine Hepburn. With twenty-six movies to his credit, Dmytryk was nominated by the academy for best director for the 1947 film *Crossfire*.

Sentenced to jail terms of up to one year, the defendants appealed to the Supreme Court, which refused to take up their cases. Soon, they were all incarcerated in various federal penitentiaries, serving terms between six months and one year. Lardner and Cole were sent to the Federal Correctional Institution in Danbury, Connecticut, which by this time was the new home of former HUAC committee chairman J. Parnell Thomas, who managed to get himself convicted of fraud in 1949 for a ghost payroll kickback scheme. Fittingly, Thomas had refused to testify in his own trial, exercising a right denied to the Hollywood Ten.

While in prison, one of the Hollywood Ten had a change of heart. Edward Dmytryk realized that being associated with communism would make it impossible to work in the motion picture industry again. To avoid the blacklist, he requested a second hearing before HUAC, a hearing in which he promised to cooperate fully. Taking the stand during HUAC's second round of hearings Dmytryk ratted out his former comrades. He provided names of other communists and even claimed that members of the Hollywood Ten—Lawson, Maltz, and Scott—encouraged him to weave Marxist messages into his films. The use of this kind of subtle propaganda was what the committee had hoped to find.

In return for his testimony, Dmytryk was taken off the blacklist, and his career flourished. In 1954 he directed *The Caine Mutiny*,

starring Humphrey Bogart, Fred MacMurray, Van Johnson, and José
Ferrer. In the film, a principled but naive U.S. naval officer, Lieutenant
Steve Maryk (Johnson) conducts a mutiny aboard a World War II
minesweeper, based on the questionable assumption that it was the
best decision for the crew and the service. Goaded by a self-serving junior officer, Lieutenant Tom Keefer (MacMurray), into believing that
the ship's captain, Lieutenant Commander Philip Queeg (Bogart) is
mentally unhinged, Maryk takes control of the ship during a storm,
relieving Queeg of his duties. Maryk is court-martialed but he avoids
punishment thanks to his canny defense attorney, Lieutenant Barney
Greenwald who despite taking the case is disgusted by the whole matter. Played by Ferrer, Greenwald is especially disdainful of Keefer,
whom he insults in the film's climactic scene:

> I wanna drink a toast to you, Mr. Keefer. From the beginning you
> hated the Navy. And then you thought up this whole idea and
> you managed to keep your skirts nice and starched and clean, even
> in the court martial. Steve Maryk will always be remembered as a
> mutineer. But you, you'll publish your novel, you'll make a million
> bucks, you'll marry a big movie star, and for the rest of your life
> you'll live with your conscience, if you have any. Here's to the real
> author of the *Caine* mutiny. Here's to you, Mr. Keefer.

Greenwald then throws his drink in Keefer's face, before delivering
this memorable line: "If you wanna do anything about it, I'll be outside. I'm a lot drunker than you are, so it'll be a fair fight."

Pretty heady stuff coming from the mouth of a guy who three
years earlier had squealed on fellow members of the Hollywood community in an effort to save his own bacon. Ferrer's innocent associa-

tion with actor Paul Robeson landed him on a list of Hollywood subversives. Like Dmytryk, Ferrer did what he had to do to preserve his career.

Bogart's integrity didn't fare much better in the blacklisting episode. He and a crew of Hollywood's elite actors, including Lauren Bacall, Edward G. Robinson, and Groucho Marx, had flown into Washington, DC, making a showy display of their solidarity with the Hollywood Ten, but once they found themselves in the middle of the maelstrom they backtracked quickly. Bogart went as far as to formally disassociate himself with the Hollywood Ten in an article he wrote for *Photoplay* magazine, titled "I'm No Communist," saying "the ten men cited for contempt by the House Un-American Activities Committee were not defended by us. We were there solely in the interest of free speech, freedom of the screen, and protection of the Bill of Rights." Presumably, those rights took a backseat when their reputations and pocketbooks were at stake.

After the Klieg lights dimmed, the friendly witnesses went on with their lives, reputations and careers intact, though some suffered loss of face after being branded as informers. It was a different story for those who refused to testify. Once they served their sentences (many got time off for good behavior), the nine members of the Hollywood Ten who stuck to their guns found themselves blacklisted and unable to work openly in Hollywood. Some of the screenwriters were assigned to low-budget projects, written under pseudonyms or submitted by fronts. Trumbo, Lardner, and Maltz moved to Mexico for a time but each returned to the United States eventually. Lardner wrote uncredited scripts for the television series *The Adventures of Robin Hood*.

The blacklist was finally lifted in 1960 when producer-director Otto Preminger hired Trumbo to write a credited screenplay for his production of *Exodus*. Shortly thereafter Kirk Douglas made the announcement that Trumbo had also written the screenplay for *Spartacus*. It turned out that Trumbo had written numerous other uncredited screenplays during the blacklist era, including two Academy Award–winning screenplays: *Roman Holiday* (1953), which was credited to a front, Ian McLellan Hunter, and *The Brave One* (1957), which Trumbo wrote under the pseudonym Robert Rich. With the blacklist lifted, Lardner wrote his first credited script, *The Cincinnati Kid* (1965), followed by the screenplay for *M*A*S*H* (1970), for which he won the Academy Award for Best Writing.

One of the Hollywood Ten writers whose career was permanently stalled by the blacklist was Alvah Bessie. He resorted to menial jobs over the years, working at one point as a stagehand. In an article for the *New York Times Magazine* (March 25, 1973), Victor Navasky tells the story of Bessie's awkward reunion with turncoat Edward Dmytryk:

> Alvah Bessie, as militant as any member of the 10, was put to the test when, after some post-prison hard times, he finally landed a job as P.R. director of San Francisco's film festival—only to discover that he had been recommended for the job by Ed Dmytryk, the one member of the 10 who had defected and named names. . . . One day Dmytryk walked in the door, put out his hand and said, "Hello, Alvah." Bessie's jaw dropped, he stared and, speechless, left the room.

There were tiffs between other members of the Hollywood Ten, too. Trumbo caused a stir when he won the Writers Guild's Laurel Award in 1970. At his acceptance speech, he spoke of the blacklist era, saying, "it will do no good to search for villains or heroes or saints or devils because there were none; there were only victims." This was too much for Albert Maltz, who complained that Trumbo's position "makes a mockery of the struggle" for freedom of thought and expression. To dramatize his position, Maltz made a comparison with the Nazi era. "If an informer in the French underground who sent a friend to the torture chambers of the Gestapo was equally a victim, then there can be no right or wrong in life that I understand."

Informed of this position by Navasky, Trumbo replied, "Fuck Albert Maltz!" For the most part, Trumbo resolved to live and let live, rather than to hold onto the bitterness created by that dark chapter in Hollywood's history. Still, he couldn't bring himself to forgive Elia Kazan, the director who freely named names in committee hearings. "Kazan is one of those for whom I feel contempt, because he carried down men much less capable of defending themselves than he." With his immense professional stature, Trumbo suggested, Kazan could have continued to get work on some level. But those he named suffered greatly.

Trumbo's feud with Maltz continued until Trumbo died of cancer in 1976.

One by one, the Hollywood Ten passed on, the last one being Ring Lardner, who died in 2000 at the age of eighty-five.

LOOSE ENDS

- On October 23, 1947, actor and Screen Actors Guild president Ronald Reagan took the stand at the HUAC hearings. Although he was a friendly witness, he claimed that he did not know of any communists in Hollywood. His personal opinion was that it was unnecessary and even undesirable to outlaw the Communist Party. Although he despised their ideas, Reagan said, "I never as a citizen want to see our country become urged, by either fear or resentment of this group, that we ever compromise with any of our democratic principles through that fear or resentment. I still think that democracy can do it." On another occasion, he proclaimed that the SAG "will not be a party to a blacklist." It turns out, though, that Reagan was saying one thing and doing quite another. Communists and those who refused to cooperate with HUAC were subsequently denied membership to SAG. And in 1985, it was revealed that Reagan had been naming names all along, just not openly in front of the committee. He had been secretly funneling names of suspected communists to the FBI.

Not Fade Away

As the war against communism raged in Hollywood and Washington, the hero of World War II's Pacific theater of war, General Douglas MacArthur, was prosecuting the Cold War in Korea. The only problem was that MacArthur and his boss, President Harry Truman, were not seeing eye to eye. Things finally came to a head when MacArthur made public comments that contradicted the administration and jeopardized a pending peace initiative. Truman consequently relieved the popular general of his command on April 10, 1951. From that day on, there was never any love lost between the two headstrong leaders. But as they butted heads—through the media, comments and letters to friends, and finally dueling memoirs—their lives took divergent paths.

A week later, MacArthur was addressing Congress, concluding his farewell speech with the oft-quoted line, "Old soldiers never die; they just fade away." Though the phrase provided a vivid rhetorical flourish, it was an inaccurate description of what was to come, for MacArthur did neither—at least not right away.

Despite MacArthur's assertions that he had "no political aspirations whatsoever," anyone who attended his public speaking engagements might have had to wonder. After being honored with one of the largest and most enthusiastic ticker-tape parades in New York's history, MacArthur toured the United States, excoriating the Truman administration's war effort and domestic policies.

Covering one such speech, *Time* magazine described a defiant MacArthur, delivering "hard-hitting" attacks on Truman, "full of oratorical thunder." MacArthur "raked the Administration up one side and down the other," accusing it "of appeasing Soviet Russia and thus inviting World War III." Shifting to domestic issues, MacArthur groused about "high taxes, the drift to socialism, the debased dollar, the rise of bureaucracy, the decline of morals, and the way that corruption has 'shaken the people's trust in . . . those administering the civil power.'"

"If MacArthur isn't a candidate for President," quipped Senator Robert Kerr of Oklahoma, "there's not a steer in Texas."

But MacArthur's political instincts were often misguided. In November 1951 he delivered a vitriolic partisan speech at a Seattle centennial celebration. An audience that was presumably eager to laud the retired soldier for his brilliant military career was less inclined to tolerate a tone-deaf rant against the Truman administration.

Even after Truman decided against running for reelection, MacArthur continued to aim most of his barbs at the increasingly unpopular president, instead of focusing on fellow candidates for the Republican nomination. MacArthur's best opportunity to seize the nomination came at the Republican convention in Chicago, but MacArthur turned in one of his most pathetic rhetorical performances in an uncharacteristically lifeless speech. He still may have salvaged an opportunity to become vice president, but he picked the wrong horse, as Senator Robert Taft lost the nomination to Dwight Eisenhower.

His political career over as quickly as it began, MacArthur went into hibernation. Bunkered in his high-rise luxury apartment at the Waldorf Astoria Tower in Manhattan, MacArthur turned inward, receiving few guests and making no appearances for months. The only passions he indulged were televised football games and boxing matches.

Meanwhile, Truman and his wife, Bess, returned to Independence, where they would live out their remaining years. For a guy who made some of the most momentous decisions in the history of the United States and the world, Harry Truman spent his retirement years in a curiously homespun and humble way. The folksy former leader of the free world strived to live much like the average Tom, Dick, or Harry—to the extent that an ex-president can. His grandest objective was to raise funds for and build the Truman Library. Other than that he hoped to keep a low profile.

"It's almost impossible to do as other people do"—that is, lead a simple, inconspicuous existence—Truman observed, "after you've been under those bright lights." But Harry and Bess gave it their best shot. The effort was made easier, in part, by Truman's shaky finances. When he left the White House, Truman had no significant means of income. Today's former presidents receive a substantial pension, as well as an ample expense account to cover administrative costs associated with their duties as former presidents. Not so in Truman's day.

Other presidents had amassed large personal fortunes before their political careers, but Truman, a former farmer and haberdasher, had little in the way of savings, and the only pension he had was the $112 he received each month from his World War I service in the U.S. Army. This amounted to about a third of an average workingman's income.

And of course Truman had expenses that the average workingman did not. The former president received thousands of letters per month. The cost of responding to his mail came to about $10,000 a year.

Truman had offers, but he was determined not to take on any jobs or entangle himself in any business dealings that would commercialize or otherwise demean the office of the presidency. Even opposed to accepting speaking fees, Truman eventually took a page from the playbook of Ulysses S. Grant, accepting a contract to write his memoirs. For this the president received an advance of $600,000—a huge sum of money for that era. But it wasn't as good as it seemed. Those who like to rail about today's high taxes should be glad they aren't paying the same tax rate Truman did: 67 percent. Between taxes and expenses incurred to hire researchers and other assistants, Truman estimated that he netted a mere $37,000 from the project.

Still, the influx of cash enabled the Trumans to take a much-needed vacation to Hawaii. Their next vacation would be a far more modest affair—that quintessentially American expedition: the family road trip. Unencumbered—not to mention unprotected—by the Secret Service, Harry and Bess hit the road, kicking off a two-thousand-mile road trip from Independence, Missouri, to Washington, DC, and back, with stops at Philadelphia and New York City along the way. Back then, there were no laws requiring protection for former presidents. That would change after November 22, 1963.

They departed Independence with no fanfare whatsoever and hoped to remain incognito throughout the trip, staying in no-frills motels and eating at roadside diners. Each stop in a small town followed a loose script. The Trumans would pull off the highway to refuel or for a quick meal. The gas station attendant or waitress would recognize the former president and first lady and before they knew it they'd be swarmed by well-wishers, gawkers, reporters, and autograph seekers. Harry and Bess managed to go unnoticed in one or two cities, but on most occasions their every move was monitored and often chronicled in the local newspaper. One headline, from the *Decatur Review*, in Illinois, noted: "Truman 10% Tipper." The cost-conscious Truman was not above griping about an overpriced breakfast in Wheeling, West Virginia—55¢ "for tomato juice, a little dab of oatmeal and milk and toast." The following day he was pleased to see that a generous lunch of roast chicken with five sides and coffee could still be had for just 70¢.

In Washington, DC, Truman spent a week politicking with Democrats, visited the Senate floor, and did some subtle lobbying for a presidential pension. Then it was off to Philadelphia where he delivered his first post-presidential political speech. A thousand attendees on hand as well as thousands of radio listeners nationwide listened in as Truman warned against Eisenhower's plans to reduce the defense budget. The next stop on the itinerary was New York City, the new home to his adult daughter, Margaret. The Trumans lived it up in New York, staying in comped rooms at the Waldorf Astoria, which provided the former president and first lady with a complimentary five-room suite. They took in a couple of Broadway shows, dined at swanky restaurants, and managed to tour the United Nations, which was founded during Truman's presidency.

Truman did not of course pay a social call to the MacArthurs, who resided at the famous hotel. As chairman of the board at Remington Rand Corporation, MacArthur occupied a vastly higher rung on the socioeconomic ladder. Between his salary and military pension, MacArthur brought home about $90,000 per year.

On the return trip to Independence, Truman had a couple run-ins with the law. The first one occurred on the Pennsylvania Turnpike. Harry was a bit of a lead foot, but his wife—aka "The Boss"—kept a close eye on the speedometer, insisting that Harry not exceed the

posted speed limit. Harry obliged, but made the mistake of doing so
in the left lane, creating a long "car snake." A patrolman pulled the car
over and was shocked to find the bespectacled moonfaced president
behind the wheel. He let him go with a warning.

The Trumans also got pulled over by the police in Richmond,
Indiana, but this time it was by a pair of self-aggrandizing troopers
intent on capitalizing on a photo opportunity. Truman was a good
sport about it, but he was eager to be back home in Independence,
where he and Bess could go about their lives relatively unmolested by
the locals.

MacArthur meanwhile was helping his company, now called
Sperry Rand Corporation, garner hundreds of millions of dollars in
annual revenues related to defense and space programs. MacArthur
also continued to collect his salary as an active five-star general. Between those revenues and others—the Philippines gave him half a
million for his services over the years—MacArthur would never know
the financial pressures that weighed on Truman during his retirement
years. When he died in 1964, MacArthur's estate would be valued at
nearly $2 million.

Lacking a financial incentive, the most likely reason MacArthur
wrote his memoirs was to settle scores and secure his legacy. Truman's
autobiography had been sharply critical of MacArthur on many
counts. Truman claimed that he and the Joint Chiefs of Staff had
"leaned over backward in our respect for the man's military reputation," but that MacArthur repaid him with a slap in the face. MacArthur's behavior in this episode, Truman said, "had the earmarks of a
man who performs for the galleries." Summing up, Truman drew a
favorable parallel between his troubles with MacArthur and Lincoln's
with the irksome George McClellan.

MacArthur's memoir, *Reminiscences*, attempted to even the score with a man he privately referred to as "a vulgar little clown." He charged Truman with having "an uncontrolled passion." To illustrate, he trotted out the old story about how an irate Truman threatened to punch a music critic who savaged a theatrical performance by the president's daughter, Margaret. MacArthur made his own comparison with Abraham Lincoln, citing an instance in which Lincoln pledged his wholehearted support for General Grant. Truman, MacArthur implied, was no Lincoln, but it was equally true that MacArthur was no Grant, at least not in terms of obedience to his commander in chief.

Like Grant, though, MacArthur never lived to see his book published. In a negative review, a critic for *Harper's* magazine suggested that this might have been a good thing, in MacArthur's case. "He was always his worst enemy, and his autobiography will add nothing to his reputation. He should be remembered by his deeds, not his words." Douglas MacArthur died on April 5, 1964. He is buried at a shrine built in his honor at Norfolk, Virginia.

Truman's health began to falter at about the same time. Famous for his daily early-morning walks, Truman was forced to abbreviate them as he became dependent on a cane, and eventually gave them up altogether. Truman died on December 26, 1972, at the age of eighty-eight. Bess lived another ten years, eventually becoming the oldest living first lady in U.S. history before dying at ninety-seven on October 18, 1982.

LOOSE ENDS

- One of the enduring mysteries related to Douglas MacArthur is the fate of his only son. Arthur MacArthur IV was thirteen years old when Truman fired his famous father. When he accompanied his parents to the United States, it was the first time he ever set foot on American soil. In the following months, his every move was scrutinized and publicized by the media. Described by one of his teachers as a "sensitive, bright, delicate boy"—who was said to possess a gift for music—Arthur apparently disliked all the attention, for he largely shunned public appearances after his first few whirlwind months in America. He also turned his back on the military legacy established by his father and grandfather, both Medal of Honor recipients. Instead of attending the U.S. Military Academy at West Point, Arthur matriculated at Columbia University, where he earned a bachelor's degree in liberal arts in 1961. In the years after his father's funeral, Arthur MacArthur disappeared from public life. Some have speculated that he changed his name and pursued a career in music. A handful of people have tried to uncover his current whereabouts but none have succeeded. Presumably, the mystery will not be lifted until his obituary appears in the newspaper.

CHAPTER FOURTEEN

CIVIL RIGHTS AND WRONGS

T HE 1950s and 1960s were a period of massive social upheaval in the United States, as the civil rights movement picked up steam and boiled over throughout the southern states and into the urban north. Activists pressed for desegregation of public education and public transportation, as well as free and equal access to voting booths, housing, and public commercial spaces, such as restaurants and hotels.

Some of the biggest events included Rosa Parks's refusal to surrender her seat on a bus to a white passenger and James Meredith's forced integration of the University of Mississippi. In the following entries, we'll see how one of these civil rights icons was marginalized by the movement she helped to inspire and how the other one did everything he could to marginalize himself.

Where the Kennedy and Johnson administrations had supported efforts to extend civil rights to oppressed classes in the 1960s, the Nixon administration engaged in covert operations that willfully deprived U.S. citizens of their civil rights, most notably the right to privacy. Believe it or not, the government informant who helped expose the Watergate scandal was subsequently found guilty of depriving other U.S. citizens of their civil rights.

A Seat on the Bus, but Not at the Table

Some have called Rosa Parks the Mother of the Civil Rights Movement. It is an appropriate moniker, not only because her courageous stand on a Montgomery, Alabama, city bus gave birth to a larger and ultimately triumphant campaign but also because, although many claimed to love and admire her, she was often taken for granted. Parks was content to labor in the background, doing the unglamorous work of a yeoman volunteer—before and after that momentous date, December 1, 1955, when she refused to relinquish her seat to a white passenger.

There's a new myth in circulation, a supposed corrective to an older myth. The original myth was that Parks was just a humble seamstress whose feet were tired from a long day at work. A simple woman, she took the obvious yet powerful stance that the system was unfair and she wasn't going to take it anymore. Why hadn't anyone thought of this before? Well, they had. In fact, Rosa Parks was thoroughly aware of several recent instances in which other African Americans had similarly refused to give up their seats, resulting in arrest or ejection from the bus.

Parks knew about these cases because she was more than just a seamstress working at the Fair department store in downtown Montgomery. She also volunteered at the local chapter of the National Association for the Advancement of Colored People (NAACP). Parks and other members of the NAACP were looking for a good test case to challenge the city's segregated public transportation system. They thought they had their ideal case when a high school student named Claudette Colvin was arrested on March 2, 1955. But they decided not to go ahead with the challenge. It turned out that Colvin, already considered a somewhat ill-mannered teenager, was also pregnant out of wedlock, making her an easy target for the white press.

So Parks was definitely aware of the issues and active in helping to right a wrong, but she always insisted that on the day she was arrested she had no intention of becoming a test case herself. She was busily planning for the holidays and juggling competing obligations in her mind on her way home from work when the bus driver demanded that she give up her seat. She made a snap decision in the moment that she was tired of being pushed around. The other factor that sometimes gets overlooked is that the driver on that fateful day just so happened to be the same driver who ejected Parks from a city bus years earlier. Ever since, Parks had refused to ride any bus driven by this man, but preoccupied with her thoughts, Parks boarded the bus that evening without noticing the driver. Her bitter memories of that past injustice swelled within her and propelled her toward her historic encounter.

The new myth is that Parks's decision to refuse her seat was a pre-meditated act, that she boarded the bus with the express purpose of getting arrested. Of course, even if true, it's not clear how this would diminish the nobility of her actions. But it wasn't. None of her fellow activists was aware of any such plan. And when they learned of her arrest, they were just as surprised as her husband, Raymond, was when he found out. They all rushed to the police station—Raymond in a panic. It took some time to collect the bail money, as it was more than the Parkses could come up with. Bail was eventually posted by civil rights attorney Clifford Durr and local activist E. D. Nixon.

Regardless of how it came about, the Montgomery civil rights movement now had its ideal test case. Durr and Gray outlined their legal strategy. In the best-case scenario Parks would be found guilty of violating the city ordinance that required blacks to forfeit their seats to whites, they would appeal the case, taking it as far as the U.S. Supreme Court, if necessary, until they secured a decision that was binding on a statewide or federal level, thereby reinforcing the illegality of segregation that had been established in the landmark 1954 case *Brown v. Board of Education of Topeka*. Parks was indeed convicted and fined $14, but her attorneys eventually determined that the particulars of her case would not make for a precedent-setting appeal. There was a good chance that the higher court's ruling would hinge on a technicality.

But Parks's act of civil disobedience spawned another parallel offensive in the fight against segregated public transportation. The day after Parks's arrest on a Thursday, Jo Ann Robinson, the leader of the Women's Political Council composed a leaflet calling for a citywide boycott of the bus system to coincide with Rosa Parks's court date on Monday. As the clear majority of the system's riders, African Americans hoped to cripple the system by refusing to ride. Robinson printed up thousands of the leaflets, distributing them to churches, schools, and other community hubs. The flyer was also printed verbatim in the local newspaper. The boycott would ultimately last for thirteen months. Organizers, including a young minister named Martin Luther King, coordinated carpooling arrangements, negotiated reduced fares from black-owned taxi companies, and encouraged solidarity throughout the boycott.

It wasn't easy. Activists were brutalized, bombed, and arrested. Rosa Parks was indicted on February 21, 1956, along with about eighty other activists, for violating a city ordinance that prohibited boycotts. On the following day—not on the occasion of her first more famous arrest—the iconic photos were taken of her being fingerprinted by a white police officer and holding the number 7053 in her now-famous mug shot.

Ironically, Parks's attorneys decided to resurrect the case of Claudette Colvin, along with several other appellants, for their strategic appeal to end bus segregation. In *Browder v. Gayle*, the U.S. District Court found in favor of the appellants, outlawing segregation on Montgomery buses. Never ones to miss a photo opportunity, Martin Luther King and fellow rising civil rights star Ralph Abernathy arranged to have their photographs taken riding in the front seats of city buses, signaling the successful end of the boycott. Strangely, neither of them thought to invite Rosa Parks to join them. But a *Look* magazine photographer did coax Parks to pose for a picture that is probably the best-known image of the civil rights crusader. She sits gazing out the window of the bus, as a grim-faced white man sits behind her.

The day marked a turning point in the lives of Martin Luther King and Rosa Parks. From this point on the woman who inspired a successful campaign to end a major component of segregation in the American south would be overshadowed by one of the men whose reputation was first established by the boycott launched by her arrest. It's not that Parks sought out the spotlight. It wasn't in her nature to grandstand. Even so, she bristled at the male chauvinism that shunted her to the side of the movement. One local activist called Parks a "lovely, stupid woman." Abernathy considered her little more than a useful tool of the movement.

Not only that, Parks also lost her job as a result of her activism, and her husband quit his job when his workplace became a hostile environment. It wasn't easy to be the husband of Rosa Parks, always fearing for his wife's safety and often the target of insults and threats himself.

Raymond compounded bad health and psychological stress with heavy drinking.

Out of work, frustrated with the direction of the local civil rights movement, and daunted by unrelenting death threats, Parks moved to Detroit with her husband and mother. She once again found work as a seamstress, and performed behind-the-scenes volunteer work for the Detroit chapter of the NAACP. Parks participated in several more defining moments in civil rights history, including the March on Washington, where King delivered his famous "I Have a Dream" speech, and the freedom march from Selma to Montgomery. On both occasions, however, Parks felt marginalized by the other leaders of the movement. Whether they had no respect for her ideas or her public speaking abilities or whether they were disinclined to share the stage with a woman, civil rights leaders never asked Rosa Parks to speak at these events. She was considered a useful symbol of the movement, but nothing more.

Parks regained a measure of respect in 1975 when the city of Montgomery invited her to return to commemorate the twentieth anniversary of her arrest and the bus boycott. By this time she had also been working for more than a decade for U.S. Congressman John Conyers. In 1987, Parks founded the Rosa and Raymond Parks Institute for Self Development, an organization designed to help minority youth. Parks wrote several books, including *My Story* and *Quiet Strength*, both targeted to young adult readers.

In 1994 an intruder broke into Rosa Parks's home and beat her savagely. The assailant made off with $103, but was arrested shortly thereafter. A final insult, at least according to Parks, came in 1999, when the rap group Outkast released a song called "Rosa Parks." Although intended as a tribute of sorts, the song included language that

Parks considered offensive. Parks sued the band but the judge ruled that the song was protected expression under the First Amendment. Another unfortunate by-product of the lawsuit was the disclosure of Ms. Parks's medical records, which indicated the elderly activist was suffering from dementia.

On a happier note, Parks had received many tributes and rewards over the years, including the Congressional Gold Medal, bestowed by President Bill Clinton in 1999. The Rosa Parks Library and Museum in Montgomery opened in 2000.

Rosa Parks died on October 24, 2005, at the age of ninety-two.

LOOSE ENDS

- James Blake, the bus driver who had Rosa Parks arrested for refusing to surrender her seat on the bus, continued to work for the Montgomery City Lines bus company for another twenty years. Later in life, Blake remained unapologetic about his role in history. "I wasn't trying to do anything to that Parks woman except do my job," he said in a *Washington Post* interview. "She was in violation of the city codes. What was I supposed to do? That damn bus was full and she wouldn't move back. I had my orders. I had police powers—any driver for the city did. So the bus filled up and a white man got on, and she had his seat and I told her to move back, and she wouldn't do it." Blake died of a heart attack on March 22, 2003. He was eighty-nine years old.

James Meredith, Accidental Activist

On January 20, 1961, the same day that John F. Kennedy took the oath of office as president of the United States, an African American man named James Meredith submitted a written request for an enrollment application to the University of Mississippi, where no other black student had ever attended. Meredith's plan was to integrate the university, and he planned to do it by putting "pressure on John Kennedy and the Kennedy administration to live up to the civil rights plank in the Democratic platform." Unaware of the applicant's race, the university sent a stock reply, stating, "we are very pleased to know of your interest in becoming a member of our student body." They soon changed their tune. When they learned Meredith was an "American-Mississippi-Negro citizen," the university balked, claiming that the entire enrollment process had been put on hold.

With the help of Medgar Evers of the NAACP, Meredith appealed to Thurgood Marshall and the NAACP's legal defense team. But even the attorney whose brilliant handling of the *Brown v. Board of Education* case, which in 1954 resulted in the ruling that secured for Meredith the legal right to attend any school he wanted, was taken aback by Meredith's audacity. Concluding, "This guy's gotta be crazy," Marshall assigned the case to legal counsel, Constance Baker Motley.

Meredith lost his first legal battles, but Motley eventually won a federal court appeal. Despite the efforts of Mississippi's grandstanding governor, Ross Barnett, to block the schoolhouse door, Meredith was finally admitted on September 30, 1962. Many people may remember the tense but relatively peaceful public school standoffs in other southern states, for example, the Little Rock Nine and George Wallace's stand at the University of Alabama, but Meredith's enrollment triggered a massive riot. Irate segregationists attacked the five hundred federal marshals on hand with bats, rocks, and even guns. When the smoke cleared, two people were dead and more than a hundred marshals were injured. Though largely forgotten today, the riot was, according to author William Doyle, "the biggest domestic military crisis of the twentieth century." Kennedy sent another five thousand federal troops to make sure Meredith was safely enrolled, and a detail of armed federal marshals escorted Meredith on campus for the rest of his tenure.

Perhaps the reasons few know or talk about these events today have to do with the afterlife of the drama's protagonist, the inscrutable James Meredith. The same traits that enabled him to penetrate the University of Mississippi—courage, determination, and fierce independence—would take him on an unpredictable journey, confusing and sometimes alienating those who would otherwise identify and sympathize with his plight. Meredith resisted the pull of the civil rights movement from the very beginning. In an editorial printed in the Ole Miss student newspaper, Meredith claimed that his mission was personal, not social. He was merely interested in getting the best education possible for himself, he said, and professed "little concern for the phenomenon of integration and desegregation." (It's worth noting that these claims run contrary to other comments he made before and after his successful bid to integrate the University of Mississippi.)

Meredith graduated in three semesters, having transferred numerous credits earned at a variety of other institutions over the years. In a final attempt to foil Meredith, Governor Barnett attempted to block Meredith's graduation on a technicality, but the State College Board voted 6–5 in Meredith's favor.

Meredith next studied in Nigeria for a year. Returning to the United States, he enrolled in Columbia University's law school in

1966. But before classes even began, he embarked on his quixotic "March Against Fear," a one-man trek from Memphis, Tennessee, to Jackson, Mississippi, designed to promote voter registration in the African American community. He didn't get far. On the first day of the march, the lone Meredith, flanked by a handful of reporters and photographers, was shot by a white assailant. Associated Press photographer Jack Thornell snapped a Pulitzer Prize–winning image of a prone Meredith writhing in pain from buckshot wounds to the head, neck, and legs.

Meredith was visited in the hospital by a phalanx of civil rights activists, including Martin Luther King and Stokely Carmichael, who were at the time vying for opposing factions of the civil rights movement. Taking up Meredith's cause, they continued the march without him. Having recovered from his injuries, Meredith joined the march on its last day, when marchers entered Jackson. During the month-long march, more than two thousand African Americans had registered to vote.

In a sign of things to come, in 1967 Meredith ran as a Republican against Adam Clayton Powell Jr., a popular African American U.S. Representative to New York. Inexplicably, he also endorsed Ross Barnett in his reelection campaign for governor of Mississippi.

Meredith graduated from law school in 1968 but never sat for the bar or practiced law. Instead, he performed a series of unrelated jobs over the years, such as tree farmer, nightclub manager, financial adviser, and campaign manager. The University of Cincinnati once hired Meredith to be a guest lecturer, but decided not to renew the contract after several unorthodox—and poorly attended—lectures.

In 1989 Meredith's career took one of its strangest turns, when he took a job as a domestic policy adviser to U.S. Senator from North Carolina Jesse Helms. A staunchly conservative Republican, Helms was a persistent critic of civil rights initiatives who spoke out in favor of South Africa's apartheid government and who openly opposed the Martin Luther King national holiday. Two years later, Meredith went too far even for the most accommodating civil rights leaders when he endorsed the campaign of David Duke, a former Ku Klux Klansman running for governor of Louisiana. At one point, NAACP leader Benjamin Hooks bemoaned that Meredith had "obviously lost his way—if, in fact, he ever had one."

Ever difficult to pin down, Meredith offered various explanations for his counterintuitive maneuvers. At times, he claimed that civil rights members were blinded by their own prejudices against these misunderstood politicians. At other times, he suggested that any actions perceived as contrary to the civil rights movement were motivated more by his Choctaw Indian heritage than his African American heritage. Other times still, he implied that maybe he was cannily trying to keep his friends close and his enemies closer or simply using Helms for unfettered access to Library of Congress archives.

Of his endorsement of Duke, he said, "I would much rather sit at the table with a former Ku Klux Klansman swearing that he would never do anything to my people than to have him in the bush trying to shoot somebody."

One thing is for sure: Meredith was consistently opposed to affirmative action programs. "Our main roadblocks in the '90s," Meredith wrote in *Newsweek* magazine, "are ones that have been created by our own so-called leadership." He believed that programs intended to assist blacks in making social advances did so at the expense of their self-sufficiency.

In 1997 Meredith founded the Meredith Institute to provide young black males with courses designed to teach them how to speak proper English.

"The No. 1 reason" that blacks lag behind socially and politically, Meredith claimed, "is because 99.9 percent speak black English, which is not proper English." The Meredith Institute no longer seems to be an active enterprise, having lost its nonprofit status.

A *Washington Post* reporter in 2002 found Meredith back in Jackson, Mississippi, at the time the proprietor of a hopelessly ill-conceived auto rental and taxi service business. Meredith talked about his life and ambiguous legacy. A month later he would return to the University of Mississippi for the unveiling of a memorial to him on the fortieth anniversary of his crowning achievement, the integration of public education in Mississippi. Meredith attended but did not address the assembled masses. For his money, the proof of the pudding had been tasted earlier in the year, when his son, a graduate of Harvard University, earned a PhD in Business Administration from the University of Mississippi, graduating with highest honors.

Loose Ends

- Having lost his bid to be reelected governor in 1967, Ross Barnett returned to practicing law in Jackson, Mississippi. Many of his clients were African Americans who had difficulty finding legal representation. Lest this be interpreted as a change of heart, Barnett continued to preach the benefits of segregation throughout his life and was known to tell explicitly racist jokes in public. Barnett once pronounced that giving in to desegregation was tantamount to self-destruction. "There is no case in history where the Caucasian race has survived social integration," he claimed. "We will not drink from the cup of genocide." Barnett died on November 7, 1987, at the age of eighty-nine.

- Meredith's attorney in the integration fight of 1961–1962, Constance Baker Motley, went on to become the first African American woman to serve as a federal judge, when Lyndon Johnson appointed her to federal court in New York State. She was also the first African American woman to become Manhattan borough president, to serve as a New York state senator and to argue a case before the U.S. Supreme Court, where she won nine of the ten cases she brought to the nation's highest court. Motley died of congestive heart failure on September 28, 2005.

- John Doar, who worked in the civil rights division of Kennedy's Department of Justice, was one of the government officials who escorted Meredith throughout the violent ordeals of 1962. During the Watergate scandal in 1974, Doar helped write the articles of impeachment presented by the U.S. House Committee on the Judiciary.

Deep Throat Busted

On June 17, 1972, five men were arrested for breaking into an office in the Watergate hotel and office complex in Washington, DC. Junior *Washington Post* reporter Bob Woodward was sent to the courthouse to perform what promised to be a routine bit of reportage. He soon learned he had instead just been dispatched on what would turn out to be the most sensational news scoop of the decade. For, it wasn't just any office—it was the Democratic National Committee headquarters. The burglars weren't run-of-the-mill hoods, either. They were found in possession of lock-picking tools, walkie-talkies, and sophisticated electronic bugging equipment.

Questioned by the judge, one of the defendants identified himself as James McCord, a name that meant nothing to Woodward. But when the judge asked for the defendant's profession, McCord dropped the bombshell.

"CIA," he said.

"Holy shit!" Woodward gasped.

Back at the newspaper, Woodward and fellow reporter Carl Bernstein learned that several of the burglars were former CIA operatives, some with ties to the White House, and at least one on the payroll of the Committee to Re-Elect the President (CREEP). Over the next two years and two months, Woodward and Bernstein would unravel the layers of this political scandal, discovering evidence that the break-in and subsequent coverup were authorized by members of the White House staff. It would change their lives and the lives of political figures at the highest levels of government.

On August 9, 1974, to avoid the ignominy of becoming the first U.S. president successfully impeached by Congress, Richard Nixon instead became the first U.S. president to resign from office.

Woodward and Bernstein wrote the bestselling book *All the President's Men*, which chronicled the tortuous path of their investigation, following leads, many resulting in dead ends, others paying off. They were aided by persistence; dumb luck; and a benevolent secret source, code-named Deep Throat because he refused to go on record. Instead, he provided "deep background"—verification of hunches, cryptic encouragement to follow certain leads—doled out in furtive late-night meetings at an underground parking garage.

In 1976 the book was made into a motion picture starring Robert Redford as Woodward and Dustin Hoffman as Bernstein. Jason Robards won the Academy Award for Best Supporting Actor for his portrayal of crusty *Washington Post* executive editor Ben Bradlee. Hal Holbrook's turn as Deep Throat also created a sensation, as did the famous line, "Follow the money," which was invented by the film's screenwriter, William Goldman, who won the Academy Award for his screenplay.

For the next thirty years, the authors have continued to ply their craft—Woodward more successfully—all the while honoring their pledge to conceal Deep Throat's identity, until his death or until he released them from their oath. It remained the best-kept secret in Washington history—that is, until a 2005 article in *Vanity Fair* magazine spilled the beans. It turned out that Deep Throat was W. Mark Felt, second in charge at the FBI. Felt had been in line to take over when J. Edgar Hoover died on May 2, 1972. But Nixon passed him over, putting an outsider, L. Patrick Gray, in charge. Whether miffed by the snub or, as Felt claimed, offended by Nixon's attempts to use the FBI as the White House's covert political instrument (Hoover's FBI had refused to do Nixon's dirty work), Felt leaked damaging information to Woodward, a reporter with whom he'd become acquainted years earlier.

As long as he remained anonymous, Deep Throat was lionized by people on all points of the political spectrum—especially the left—who decried Nixon's illegal intelligence gathering through so-called black bag operations. As the shadowy figure divorced from contextual reality, Deep Throat seemed like a hero.

The real Deep Throat, Mark Felt, was another matter. At about the same time that *All the President's Men* was hitting movie screens across the country, Felt was in deep legal jeopardy. Under new FBI chief Gray, Felt had orchestrated a series of his own black bag operations, employing the same means that he so deplored in the Nixon White House, but for different ends. At the same time that he was squealing to Woodward, Felt instructed FBI operatives to break into private homes of friends and relatives of suspected members of the Weather Underground Organization, a radical antiwar group implicated in bombings of government buildings. Felt hoped to uncover information that would lead to the whereabouts of Weather Underground fugitives.

In 1976 government investigations spearheaded by the new Democratic administration of Jimmy Carter uncovered the FBI's illegal activities. Felt appeared on CBS's *Face the Nation* to publicly defend the tactics. From the beginning, Felt never denied authorizing the break-ins. In fact, he said he was "proud of what I did." In what must have seemed like a bizarre twist to the two allies in bringing down the corrupt Nixon administration, Woodward and Felt were thrown together once again, but in starkly different circumstances. Woodward and another *Washington Post* reporter went to interview Felt about the allegations. Again, Felt was forthcoming.

"You've got to remember that we were dealing with murderers, terrorists, people who were responsible for mass destruction . . . the key word is violence. They were planning mass destruction. . . . Please emphasize the viciousness of these people. We were dealing with fanatics." Somehow, Felt failed to see the parallels between his actions and Nixon's. The difference he believed was that Nixon broke the law to further his political agenda, whereas Felt did so to protect the safety of U.S. citizens and preserve public order.

The federal grand jury wasn't buying it. On April 10, 1978, Deep Throat was indicted for conspiracy "to injure and oppress citizens of the United States who were relatives and acquaintances of the Weatherman fugitives, in the free exercise and enjoyments of certain rights and privileges secured to them by the Constitution and the laws of the United States of America."

The ironies didn't stop there. At Felt's 1980 trial, Nixon not only testified on behalf of his old nemesis but also contributed money to Felt's defense fund.

What isn't clear is why. A review of subsequently released Nixon White House tapes proves Nixon knew as early as October 9, 1972, that Felt was leaking to reporters and may have been Deep Throat.

"Now why the hell would he do that?" Nixon fumed.

"It's hard to figure," admits Nixon's chief of staff, H. R. Haldeman. "Maybe he's tied to the Kennedy set. . . ."

"Is he a Catholic?" Nixon asked.

"I think he's Jewish," Haldeman guessed (incorrectly).

"Christ! I'm not going to put another Jew in there. Mark Felt is certainly a Jewish name. Well, that could explain it, too."

Whether Nixon let bygones be bygones or was acting in a purely self-serving capacity, on the witness stand he defended Felt's use of dirty tricks to track down homegrown terrorists. Employing the sort of warped logic that helped him justify his own crimes, Nixon testified that as long as it was authorized for a "good cause," an action that "would otherwise be unlawful or illegal becomes legal."

Perhaps it's not surprising that Nixon's testimony failed to sway the jury, and Felt was convicted of a felony on November 6, 1980. Republican President Ronald Reagan pardoned Mark Felt on March 6, 1981. Shortly thereafter, a bottle of champagne was delivered to Mark Felt's house, along with a note saying, "Justice ultimately prevails." It was signed Richard Nixon.

The *Vanity Fair* article disclosing the identity of Deep Throat represents one of the few times Bob Woodward was ever scooped in his successful career. In anticipation of Felt's death, Woodward had long been working on a book about Deep Throat, which he quickly released in the wake of the unveiling. In *The Secret Man: The Story of Watergate's Deep Throat*, published several months later, Woodward offers a tale of regret, sadness, and frustration. He can't help wondering if he took advantage of Felt in some way and hated to see it happening all over again, this time at the hands of Felt's family. Clearly suffering from dementia, the octogenarian agent was now being trotted out before the media by relatives hoping to cash in on the story before Deep Throat's death. Felt died in 2008 at the age of ninety-one.

Woodward's book revealed some other interesting facts about the thirty-year mystery of Deep Throat's identity. Though many tried, nobody successfully deduced who it was. The only people who knew Deep Throat's identity were Woodward, Bernstein, Bradlee, and *Washington Post* publisher Katharine Graham. Bernstein apparently told his then-wife, Hollywood writer-director Nora Ephron, as well as his son, Jacob, who blabbed it to a friend at summer camp. The only other person who found out did so accidentally.

As one of the prosecutors working on the case against Mark Felt, attorney Stanley Pottinger was questioning Mark Felt before the grand jury. During the deposition, Felt made an offhand remark that he spent so much time at the White House that some speculated he was Deep Throat. It was one of Felt's counterintelligence tricks—to throw off suspicion by casually acknowledging it.

At the end of the deposition, Pottinger invited grand jurors to pose their own questions.

"Were you?" one of the jurors asked Felt.

"Was I what?"

"Were you Deep Throat?"

Caught off-guard, Felt stammered, "No."

But Pottinger was convinced that he had inadvertently made a major discovery. There was only one problem. Felt was still under oath. If he was indeed Deep Throat, he could be convicted of lying to a grand jury. Taking pity, Pottinger approached Felt and off the record reminded him of his oath. Offered an opportunity to change his response or request that the irrelevant question and answer be stricken from the record, Felt opted for the latter. Pottinger later confronted Woodward with his theory in a private meeting. Woodward refused to confirm the story. Unswayed, Pottinger graciously promised to keep the information under his hat. Presumably, it was enough for him to know the truth about one of the most enduring secrets in American politics.

Loose Ends

- The post-Watergate lives of the Watergate burglars (aka the Plumbers) range from the prosaic to the fantastical. They all served prison time. One became a real estate broker, another a building inspector. James McCord wrote a book about his role in Watergate and also owned a solar energy company in Fort Collins, Colorado. In one of the more creative conspiracy theories about the assassination of John F. Kennedy, Plumber Frank Sturgis was implicated along with E. Howard Hunt, who planned the Watergate break-in with fellow former CIA operative G. Gordon Liddy. Hunt wrote more than fifty novels. Of all the Plumbers, Liddy served the longest prison term (four and a half years) before President Jimmy Carter commuted his sentence in 1977. Liddy also made the most money, subsequently became a bestselling author, actor, college lecturer, and conservative radio host. The only one of the Plumbers to receive a pardon, thanks again to President Reagan, was Eugenio Martinez.

- Several of the key members in Nixon's cabinet found God during or after their prison terms. Jeb Magruder was ordained a Presbyterian minister in the 1980s. In 1988 the mayor of Columbus, Ohio, named Magruder to a commission on values and ethics. Since then Magruder has been arrested three times, on charges of disorderly conduct, drunk driving, and reckless operation of a vehicle. Former special counsel to Nixon, Charles Colson, who once advocated beating antiwar protesters and firebombing the Brookings Institute, founded a nonprofit organization called Prison Fellowship, which provides spiritual sustenance to prisoners and works for prison reform. President George W. Bush presented Colson with the Presidential Citizens Medal in 2008. After his release from prison, former White House chief of staff Bob Haldeman pursued a variety of business interests. His real estate holdings included eight Sizzler franchise restaurants in Florida. He died in 1993 at age sixty-seven.

- On September 8, 1974, Nixon's replacement in the Oval Office, President Gerald Ford, granted "a full, free, and absolute pardon unto Richard Nixon for all offenses against the United States which he, Richard Nixon, has committed or may have committed or taken part in during the period from January 20, 1969, through August 9, 1974." Nixon spent the next twenty years trying to salvage his reputation, writing ten books and earning praise for his involvement in reestablishing foreign relations with China and the Soviet Union. He suffered a stroke and died on April 22, 1994.

- Frank Wills, the Watergate security guard who discovered the break-in and called the police, quit shortly after the scandal received publicity, feeling that he didn't get the due amount of recognition or recompense. Though Wills did play himself in the movie *All the President's Men*, he had difficulty maintaining a job in the years after. Wills was arrested for shoplifting in 1983 and died destitute in 2000.

Further Reading

In this book I've provided you with the end of the stories. For the rest of the stories, check out the sources listed here.

CHAPTER ONE

Columbus

Boyle, David. *Toward the Setting Sun: Columbus, Cabot, Vespucci, and the Race for America*. New York: Walker, 2008.

Dyson, John. *Columbus: For Gold, God, and Glory*. New York: Simon & Schuster, 1991.

Loewen, James W. *Lies My Teacher Told Me: Everything Your American History Textbook Got Wrong*. New York: Touchstone, 2007.

Markham, Clements R., ed. *The Journal of Christopher Columbus (During His First Voyage, 1492–93)*. Cambridge, UK: Cambridge University Press, 2010.

Morison, Samuel Eliot. *The European Discovery of America: The Northern Voyages, AD 500–1600*. New York: Oxford University Press, 1971.

Morison, Samuel Eliot. *The European Discovery of America: The Southern Voyages, AD 1492–1616*. New York: Oxford University Press, 1974.

Hudson

Hunter, Douglas. *Half Moon: Henry Hudson and the Voyage That Redrew the Map of the New World*. New York: Bloomsbury Press, 2009.

Mancall, Peter C. *Fatal Journey: The Final Expedition of Henry Hudson*. New York: Basic Books, 2009.

Cook

Beaglehole, J. C. *The Life of Captain James Cook*. Stanford, CA: Stanford University Press, 1974.

Dugard, Martin. *Farther Than Any Man: The Rise and Fall of Captain James Cook*. New York: Pocket Books, 2001.

Hough, Richard. *The Last Voyage of Captain James Cook*. New York: Morrow, 1979.

Lawlor, Laurie. *Magnificent Voyage: An American Adventurer on Captain James Cook's Final Expedition*. New York: Holiday House, 2002.

Thomas, Nicholas. *Cook: The Extraordinary Voyages of Captain James Cook*. New York: Walker, 2003.

CHAPTER TWO

John Smith and Pocahontas

Barbour, Philip, ed. *The Complete Works of Captain John Smith*. Chapel Hill: University of North Carolina Press, 1986.

Mossiker, Frances. *Pocahontas: The Life and the Legend*. New York: Da Capo Press, 1996.

Price, David A. *Love and Hate in Jamestown: John Smith, Pocahontas, and the Heart of a New Nation*. New York: Knopf, 2003.

First Thanksgiving

Hodgson, Godfrey. *A Great and Godly Adventure: The Pilgrims and the Myth of the First Thanksgiving*. New York: PublicAffairs, 2006.

Philbrick, Nathaniel. *Mayflower: A Story of Courage, Community, and War*. New York: Viking, 2006.

Salem Witch Trials

Francis, Richard. *Judge Sewall's Apology: The Salem Witch Trials and the Forming of an American Conscience*. New York: HarperCollins, 2005.

Hill, Frances. *The Salem Witch Trial Reader*. Cambridge, MA: Da Capo, 2000.

Roach, Marilynne K. *The Salem Witch Trials: A Day-to-Day Chronicle of a Community Under Siege*. New York: Cooper Square Press, 2002.

CHAPTER THREE

Paul Revere

Forbes, Esther. *Paul Revere and the World He Lived In*. New York: Mariner Books, 1999.

Hackett, David Fischer. *Paul Revere's Ride*. New York: Oxford University Press, 1994.

Declaration of Independence

Cappon, Lester J., ed. *The Adams-Jefferson Letters: The Complete Correspondence Between Thomas Jefferson and Abigail and John Adams*. 2 vols. Chapel Hill: University of North Carolina Press, 1959.

Chadwick, Bruce. *I Am Murdered: George Wythe, Thomas Jefferson, and the Killing That Shocked a New Nation*. Hoboken: Wiley, 2009.

Jenkins, Charles Francis. *Button Gwinnett: Signer of the Declaration of Independence*. Garden City and New York: Doubleday, Page & Co., 1926.

Kiernan, Denise, and Joseph D'Agnese. *Signing Their Lives Away: The Fame and Misfortune of the Men Who Signed the Declaration of Independence*. Philadelphia: Quirk Books, 2009.

CHAPTER FOUR

Lewis and Clark

Ambrose, Stephen E. *Undaunted Courage: Meriwether Lewis, Thomas Jefferson, and the Opening of the American West*. New York: Simon & Schuster, 1996.

Brandt, Anthony, ed. *The Journals of Lewis and Clark*. Washington, DC: National Geographic Adventure Classics, 2002.

Jones, Landon Y. *William Clark and the Shaping of the West*. New York: Hill & Wang, 2004.

Morris, Larry E. *The Fate of the Corps: What Became of the Lewis and Clark Explorers after the Expedition*. New Haven, CT: Yale University Press, 2004.

Custer

Barnett, Louise. *Touched by Fire: The Life, Death, and Mythic Afterlife of George Armstrong Custer*. New York: Henry Holt & Co., 1996.

Leckie, Shirley A. *Elizabeth Bacon Custer and the Making of a Myth*. Norman: University of Oklahoma Press, 1993.

Utley, Robert M. *The Lance and the Shield: The Life and Times of Sitting Bull*. New York: Henry Holt & Co., 1993.

Warren, Louis S. *Buffalo Bill's America: William Cody and the Wild West Show*. New York: Knopf, 2005.

CHAPTER FIVE

Edgar Allan Poe

Quinn, Arthur Hobson. *Edgar Allan Poe: A Critical Biography*. Baltimore: The Johns Hopkins University Press, 1998.

Silverman, Kenneth. *Edgar A. Poe: Mournful and Never-Ending Remembrance*. New York: Harper Perennial, 1992.

Nathaniel Hawthorne

Mellow, James R. *Nathaniel Hawthorne in His Times*. Boston: Houghton Mifflin, 1980.

Turner, Arlin. *Nathaniel Hawthorne: A Biography*. New York: Oxford University Press, 1980.

Wineapple, Brenda. *Hawthorne: A Life*. New York: Knopf, 2003.

Herman Melville

Delbanco, Andrew. *Melville: His World and Work*. New York: Knopf, 2005.

Parker, Hershel, ed. *The Recognition of Herman Melville: Selected Criticism since 1846*. Ann Arbor: University of Michigan Press, 1967.

Philbrick, Nathaniel. *In the Heart of the Sea: The Tragedy of the Whaleship Essex*. New York: Viking, 2000.

Robertson-Lorant, Laurie. *Melville: A Biography*. Amherst: University of Massachusetts Press, 1996.

CHAPTER SIX

Harriet Tubman

Larson, Kate Clifford. *Bound for the Promised Land: Harriet Tubman, Portrait of an American Hero*. New York: Ballantine Books, 2004.

Sernett, Milton C. *Harriet Tubman: Myth, Memory, and History*. Durham, NC: Duke University Press, 2007.

John Brown

Renehan, Edward J. Jr. *The Secret Six: The True Tale of the Men Who Conspired with John Brown*. New York: Crown, 1995.

Reynolds, David S. *John Brown, Abolitionist: The Man Who Killed Slavery, Sparked the Civil War, and Seeded Civil Rights*. New York: Knopf, 2005.

Abraham Lincoln

Goodwin, Doris Kearns. *Team of Rivals: The Political Genius of Abraham Lincoln*. New York: Simon & Schuster, 2005.

Swanson, James. *Manhunt: The Twelve-Day Chase for Lincoln's Killer*. New York: Harper Perennial, 2006.

CHAPTER SEVEN

Chicago Fire

Bales, Richard F. *The Great Chicago Fire and the Myth of Mrs. O'Leary's Cow*. Jefferson, NC: McFarland, 2002.

Gess, Denise, and William Lutz. *Firestorm at Peshtigo: A Town, Its People, and the Deadliest Fire in American History*. New York: Holt, 2002.

Sawislak, Karen. *Smoldering City: Chicagoans and the Great Fire, 1871–74*. Chicago: University of Chicago Press, 1995.

Johnstown Flood

Gallagher, Jim. *The Johnstown Flood*. Philadelphia: Chelsea House, 2000.

McCullough, David. *The Johnstown Flood: The Incredible Story behind One of the Most Devastating "Natural" Disasters America Has Ever Known*. New York: Simon & Schuster, 1987.

San Francisco Earthquake and Fire

Fradkin, Philip L. *The Great Earthquake and Firestorms of 1906: How San Francisco Nearly Destroyed Itself*. Berkeley: University of California Press, 2005.

Winchester, Simon. *A Crack in the Edge of the World: America and the Great California Earthquake of 1906*. New York: HarperCollins, 2005.

CHAPTER EIGHT

Billy the Kid and Pat Garrett
Gardner, Mark Lee, *To Hell on a Fast Horse: Billy the Kid, Pat Garrett, and the Epic Chase to Justice in the Old West.* New York: William Morrow, 2010.
Nolan, Frederick, ed. *Pat F. Garrett's The Authentic Life of Billy, The Kid.* Norman: University of Oklahoma Press, 2000.

Gunfight at the O.K. Corral
Guinn, Jeff. *The Last Gunfight: The Real Story of the Shootout at the O.K. Corral—And How It Changed the American West.* New York: Simon & Schuster, 2011.
Marks, Paula Mitchell. *And Die in the West: The Story of the O.K. Corral Gunfight.* Norman: University of Oklahoma Press, 1996.

The James Brothers
Stiles, T. J. *Jesse James: Last Rebel of the Civil War.* New York: Knopf, 2002.
Yeatman, Ted P. *Frank and Jesse James: The Story Behind the Legend.* Nashville: Cumberland House, 2000.

CHAPTER NINE

Samuel B. Morse
Howe, Daniel Walker. *What Hath God Wrought: The Transformation of America, 1815–1848.* New York: Oxford University Press, 2007.
Silverman, Kenneth. *Lightning Man: The Accursed Life of Samuel F. B. Morse.* New York: Knopf, 2003.

Alexander Graham Bell
Mackay, James. *Alexander Graham Bell: A Life.* New York: Wiley, 1997.
Shulman, Seth. *The Telephone Gambit: Chasing Alexander Graham Bell's Secret.* New York: Norton, 2008.

The Wright Brothers
Burton, Walt, and Owen Findsen. *The Wright Brothers Legacy: Orville and Wilbur Wright and Their Aeroplanes.* New York: Abrams, 2003.
Crouch, Tom D., and Peter Jakab. *The Wright Brothers and the Invention of the Aerial Age.* Washington, DC: National Geographic, 2003.

Howard, Fred. *Wilbur and Orville: A Biography of the Wright Brothers*. New York: Knopf, 1987.

CHAPTER TEN

Al Capone
Eig, Jonathan. *Get Capone: The Secret Plot that Captured America's Most Wanted Gangster*. New York: Simon & Schuster, 2010.
Helmer, William J., and Arthur J. Bilek. *The St. Valentine's Day Massacre: The Untold Story of the Gangland Bloodbath That Brought down Al Capone*. Nashville: Cumberland House, 2004.

Eliot Ness
Heimel, Paul W. *Eliot Ness: The Real Story*. Coudersport, PA: Knox Books, 1997.
Nickel, Steven. *Torso: The Story of Eliot Ness and the Search for a Psychopathatic Killer*. Winston-Salem, NC: Blair, 1989.

John Dillinger
Gentry, Curt. *J. Edgar Hoover: The Man and the Secrets*. New York: Norton, 1991.
Purvis, Alston. *The Vendetta: FBI Hero Melvin Purvis's War against Crime, and J. Edgar Hoover's War against Him*. New York: Public Affairs, 2005.

CHAPTER ELEVEN

Jesse Owens
Bachrach, Susan D. *The Nazi Olympics: Berlin 1936*. Boston: Little, Brown, 2000.
Baker, William J. *Jesse Owens: An American Life*. New York: The Free Press, 1986.
Schaap, Jeremy. *Triumph: The Untold Story of Jesse Owens and Hitler's Olympics*. Boston: Houghton Mifflin, 2007.

Lou Gehrig
Eig, Jonathan. *Luckiest Man: The Life and Death of Lou Gehrig*. New York: Simon & Schuster, 2005.
Robinson, Ray. *Iron Horse: Lou Gehrig in His Times*. New York: Norton, 1990.

Jackie Robinson
Long, Michael G., ed. *First Class Citizenship: The Civil Rights Letters of Jackie Robinson*. New York: Times Books, 2007.
Rampersad, Arnold. *Jackie Robinson: A Biography*. New York: Knopf, 1997.

CHAPTER TWELVE

Pearl Harbor
Prange, Gordon. *At Dawn We Slept: The Untold Story of Pearl Harbor*. New York: Penguin, 2001.
Van Der Vat, Dan. *Pearl Harbor: The Day of Infamy—An Illustrated History*. New York: Basic, 2001.

Iwo Jima
Bradley, James. *Flags of Our Fathers*. New York: Bantam Books, 2000.
Buell, Hal. *Uncommon Valor, Common Virtue: Iwo Jima and the Photograph That Captured America*. New York: Berkley Caliber, 2006.

Atomic Bomb
Bird, Kai, and Martin Sherwin. *American Prometheus: The Triumph and Tragedy of J. Robert Oppenheimer*. New York: Vintage Books, 2006.
Weller, George. *First into Nagasaki: The Censored Eyewitness Dispatches on Post-Atomic Japan and Its Prisoners of War*. New York: Crown, 2006.

CHAPTER THIRTEEN

Hollywood Ten
McGilligan, Patrick, and Paul Buhle. *Tender Comrades: A Backstory of the Hollywood Blacklist*. New York: St. Martin's Press, 1997.
Navasky, Victor S. *Naming Names*. New York: Hill & Wang, 2003.

Douglas MacArthur and Harry Truman
Algeo, Matthew. *Harry Truman's Excellent Adventure: The True Story of a Great American Road Trip*. Chicago: Chicago Review Press, 2009.
James, D. Clayton. *The Years of MacArthur*. Vol. 3: *Triumph and Disaster, 1945–1964*. Boston: Houghton Mifflin, 1985.
McCullough, David. *Truman*. New York: Simon & Schuster, 1992.

Perret, Geoffrey. *Old Soldiers Never Die: The Life of Douglas MacArthur.*
Holbrook, MA: Adams Media, 1996.

CHAPTER FOURTEEN

Rosa Parks
Brinkley, Douglas. *Rosa Parks.* New York: Viking, 2000.
Williams, Donnie. *The Thunder of Angels: The Montgomery Bus Boycott and the People Who Broke the Back of Jim Crow.* Chicago: Lawrence Hill Books, 2006.

James Meredith
Doyle, William. *An American Insurrection: The Battle of Oxford, Mississippi, 1962.* New York: Doubleday, 2001.
Lambert, Frank. *The Battle of Ole Miss: Civil Rights v. States' Rights.* New York: Oxford University Press, 2010.

Watergate
Bernstein, Carl, and Bob Woodward. *All the President's Men.* New York: Simon & Schuster, 1974.
Felt, W. Mark. *The FBI Pyramid: From the Inside.* New York: Putnam's Sons, 1979.
Woodward, Bob. *The Secret Man: The Story of Watergate's Deep Throat.* New York: Simon & Schuster, 2005.

Index